Latin American Studies
Volume 4

OIL AND STEEL

PROCESSES OF KARINYA CULTURE CHANGE IN RESPONSE TO INDUSTRIAL DEVELOPMENT

by

KARL H. SCHWERIN

LATIN AMERICAN CENTER

UNIVERSITY OF CALIFORNIA
LOS ANGELES, 1966

Published under the editorship of

JOHANNES WILBERT

Library of Congress Catalog
Card Number: 66-64652

TABLE OF CONTENTS

IV. CONCLUSION

APPENDICES

ILLUSTRATIONS

LIST OF TABLES

LIST OF FIGURES

LIST OF MAPS

PAGE

LIST OF PLATES

PREFACE

THIS STUDY is the result of nearly a year's work in the field, and of many months of historical research and analysis of the data subsequent to the field research. It is a study of culture change, which in and of itself represents nothing extraordinary. There are many existing studies of this subject, and at one level of analysis or another it continues to be of considerable concern to the anthropological discipline. In most cases, however, studies of culture change have focussed on the impact of missionaries, frontier settlements and traders, or transition to a cash-crop economy. Rarely is it possible to investigate the effects of a *direct* confrontation between modern industrial culture (which tends to be somewhat cosmopolitan), and a conservative indigenous culture. [The monograph by NASH (1958) on the Guatemalan community of Cantel represents one of the few exceptions]. However, this is precisely the situation which we discovered among the Karinya. We were further favored in this study by the discovery that different communities of Karinya are at different stages in the process of culture change, and that the response to the contact with industrialization has also varied from one community to another.

It is all too easy to lay the blame for particular changes in native culture, particularly where they have been deleterious, to governmental mis-administration, or to wilful exploitation on the part of large business or industrial enterprises. We found this to be far too great an oversimplification in this case. The causes of change are complex. For the most part industrial influences are secondary and mediated through other factors which are also impinging on Karinya culture. This is not to imply that the industrial companies are wholly free of any responsibility. Lieuwen (1954) has shown in his study of the petroleum companies in Venezuela that there has been a great deal of duplicity in their activities. We found no evidence of company improprieties in the course of this study, but this was beyond the scope of our concern. We were in the field to study culture change, not to ferret out scandal, prosecute wrongdoing, or seek for reform. If this study can point the way to reform, then that is a welcome bonus, but it is not the principal concern of this research.

I wish to express my profound debt to Dr. Pedro Carrasco and to Dr. Ralph Beals. Dr. Carrasco has given me innumerable insights into the formal analysis of socio-cultural phenomena as well as much counsel and guidance through the latter part of my graduate career. Dr. Beals first stimulated my interest both in problems of acculturation and culture change, and in the Latin American area. It was also he who made arrangements with the Fundación La Salle for an exchange of research and teaching personnel with the Department of Anthropology at U.C.L.A.

The Cordell Hull Foundation provided the grant which made the field work possible. The personnel of the Fundación La Salle de Ciencias Naturales in Caracas were extremely helpful in making arrangements ahead of time and in steering us through official channels. Dr. Johannes Wilbert of their staff was of particular assistance in this regard, as well as helping to familiarize us with what was known of Karinya culture, and suggesting some important topics which might repay more intensive investigation. Mr. George Hall, of the Creole Foundation, was also helpful in making many of the necessary arrangements.

The Mene Grande Oil Co. most graciously placed their guest quarters at our disposal while we were working in Cachama. My thanks also to numerous members of the M.G.O. staff, Dr. and Mrs. Tulio Briceño, Sr. Pedro Felipe Rojas, Mr. John Howland, Mrs. Bernard Vertrees, and numerous others. Their constant interest in our work and desire to assist in innumerable small ways made our stay in that area more pleasant, as well as aiding in the material conduct of our research.

Ana de Gómez, former teacher in Tabaro and Cachama, provided useful information on education in those two communities. She never failed to offer the hospitality of her home when we visited her. While we were in Mamo our only certain line of communications was an ad hoc courier service beginning with Sr. Mario Pietrantoni of the M.G.O. Co. in San Tomé, through Sra. de Gómez, then resident in Soledad, to Sr. José Esteban, the *monguero* from Mamo. All three graciously and willingly cooperated so that we could maintain contact outside that community in spite of the lack of regular postal service.

Toward the end of our stay in Venezuela, we searched for useful historical information in several different archives. The director of the Oficina Principal de Registros in Barcelona, and the staff of the Archivo General de la Nación in Caracas were most courteous and helpful in assisting us in finding and analyzing pertinent documents.

I am most grateful to Margaret Weinrod and John Beardsley for their efforts in preparing the manuscript in final form.

My greatest debt of gratitude is to my wife, who has been faithful companion, invaluable assistant, and helpful critic, both in the field and in the analysis and ordering of the research data after our return. Without her aid, much of this work could never have been accomplished.

Finally, I cannot neglect my extreme debt to the people of Cachama and Mamo. They endured our presence and our prying questions, not only willingly, but often they contributed additional information and insights which they believed might be helpful to us. We left behind not just informants, but sincere friends. May this work be a credit to their traditions, to their present dignity, and to their hopes for the future.

Any omissions among these acknowledgements are strictly unintentional. I am equally grateful to all who contributed in one way or another to our research even though their names might not appear above. Nonetheless, full responsibility for the analysis and interpretations which appear in this study must lie with me.

Costs of publication were defrayed in part by funds from the International and Comparative Studies Grant of the Ford Foundation to the University of California, Los Angeles. The printing of the Plates was made possible through a contribution from the Documentation Funds of the Venezuelan Indian Project of the University of California, Los Angeles. This assistance is gratefully acknowledged.

K. H. S.
Albuquerque, N. M.

I

INTRODUCTION

CHAPTER I

INTRODUCTION

THE KARINYA are a semi-peasant group of Indians who inhabit the Mesas Orientales of northeastern Venezuela. Historical records verify the fact that they have been in that area for several centuries. While there has long been contact with Western culture, first through Spanish missionaries and colonists, and later through Venezuelan peasant *criollos,* intercultural contacts were neither massive nor intensive until the last thirty years. Rapid development of the petroleum industry in that area, with a large influx of North Americans as well as Venezuelans from all parts of the country, has had a profound impact on the local way of life, both for Indians and local criollos.[1] Presence of the oil industry in this area, and later discovery of rich iron ore deposits south of the Orinoco have encouraged the Venezuelan government to attempt further development of the region, and a small but growing industrial-commercial complex is arising between Ciudad Bolívar and the confluence of the Caroní and Orinoco rivers some 65 miles downstream. This too has had a significant effect on local rural life. This study will outline some of the specific factors which have contributed to recent culture change among the Karinya, with an analysis of their impact to date, as well as an attempt to predict some possible future developments.

[1]Criollo is the term used most frequently in Venezuela to designate a native citizen of the country. It has biological, cultural, and social significance. Biologically it refers to a person of mixed racial background — usually predominantly European, but with some Indian ancestry as well. The criollo may also incorporate varying proportions of African ancestry, from nil to a person of predominantly African features. In a cultural sense "criollo" is roughly equivalent to the English "folk," although it is not a generic term, but strictly limited in use to the national context. "Cultura criolla" is Venezuelan folk culture, the culture of the country people, strongly colored by the Llanero (cowboy) traditions. Likewise, there are frequent references to "comida criolla," "música criolla," etc. Socially, "criollo" refers to country people, peasants, llaneros, etc., but it has been extended to mean any person of Venezuelan origin in order to distinguish them from the numerous foreign immigrants. In this last sense it may even be heard in an urban context, though it is doubtful it would ever be applied to the Venezuelan upper classes.

THE SETTING

GEOGRAPHICALLY northeastern Venezuela is a part of the extensive Llanos region which is bounded by the Guaviare and Orinoco rivers on the south, while the Venezuelan Andes and its eastern outliers, the Cordillera del Caribe and the Macizo Oriental, bound the Llanos to the west and north. On the east they are terminated by the extensive delta of the Orinoco river.

Most of the Llanos are rather low-lying, poorly drained, and plagued by an abundance of rain during the wet season, while "desert-like conditions" prevail during the dry season (LEEDS 1961: 14). The Mesas Orientales, or eastern part of the Llanos, differs from the rest of the plains in several respects. This area is characterized by a low plateau which extends from the foot of the Macizo Oriental to within 17-50 kilometers (10-30 miles) of the Orinoco. The elevation of this plateau is from 100-300 meters (330-990 feet) above sea level.[2] Some changes in elevation are rather abrupt, steep cliffs marking the descent from one level to another, strongly impressing the idea of a tableland. Numerous streams and rivers also rise on this plateau, and they have eroded deeply into its surface. More often the divisions created by these deep river valleys have led the local inhabitants to distinguish the tablelands between, identifying each one as a separate mesa. Among the larger ones are, from north to south, the Mesa de Urica, the Mesa de Guanipa, and the Mesa Morichal Largo, though there are many others.

The mean annual temperature in the area of the Mesas is 26° C. (79° F.) with a range from 15° C. (59° F.) at the beginning of the dry season in December or January, to a high of approximately 38° C. (100° F.) near the end of the dry season in April or May. However, all but the very hottest weather is mediated by the almost constant trade winds which sweep across the Llanos from the Atlantic Ocean on the east.

It is these winds which carry moist air in from the Atlantic that provide most of the precipitation during the rainy season from May through September, then tapering off gradually through November or early December. Mean annual precipitation ranges from a low of 800 mm. (31.5 inches) in the eastern part of the Mesas and along their southern edge, to a high approaching 1.500 mm. (59 inches) at

[2] This and most of the following geographic information is taken from VILA (1953: 50-108).

Pariaguán, in the central western part of the Mesas. Considering the area as a whole, the mean is probably closest to 1.200 mm (47 inches).

Even though there is almost no rain from January through April, the region of the Mesas never suffers from the "desert-like conditions" of the western Llanos. Almost all the streams which arise here flow the year around, even though there may be marked fluctuations in the level of the waters. This means that it is possible to cultivate the river bottoms throughout the year, as the bottom lands remain permanently moist. It is not possible, however, to do the same on the mesa lands, since these may lie fifty to one hundred feet above the stream beds. Consequently the mesa soils become quite dry during the period between rains, and cannot be cultivated during that season.

Another factor discourages the cultivation of mesa lands, and that is the composition of the soils themselves. Mesa soils are sandy or gravelly and are underlain by ferruginous lateritic rock and clay. A custom of longstanding on the Llanos is that of burning off the grass during the dry season. This destroys the dry, dead grass without killing the roots, and stimulates the emergence of tender new growth, much more desirable for pasturing livestock. It may very well be that this was also practised aboriginally in order to attract deer into the open. But burning the grass cover also destroys humus, breaks down the topsoil, increases the leaching of nutrient materials, and promotes erosion. Soils on the Mesas tend to be low in acidity, in organic matter, and in nutrient minerals.

Phytogeographically the Mesas are not true grassy plains, but rather tropical savannas. More or less dense groves of scrubby trees [the most common are the curata, *Curatella americana* L.; the manteco, *Byrsonima crassifolia* (L.) Rich.; and the alcornoque, *Bowdichia virgilioides* H.B.K.] are interspersed with expanses of grassland. Along the streams are the famous morichales, gallery forests composed almost entirely of dense stands of moriche palm (*Mauritia flexuosa* L.). A sort of gallery forest also follows the margins of the Orinoco. At some places it is non-existent, but in others where the Orinoco overflows its banks and floods wide areas to the north (the Guiana shield effectively prevents very much flooding to the south) there may be a band of mixed tropical-gallery-thorn forest vegetation as much as ten or more miles in width. Along the northwestern edge of the Mesas, beginning roughly at a line running from Pariaguán to Urica, is the denser thorn-forest type of vegetation, which extends westward through the Unare river basin and along the northern half of the central Llanos. This region is of no particular importance here, since none of the contemporary Karinya inhabit it, nor does it seem to have been much occupied by them in the past. Only Aragua de Barcelona, Santa Ana, and Pariaguán (see Map 1) are known to have been located within the margins of the thorn forest, and no Indians are known to be living in any of these towns today.

CULTURAL RELATIONSHIPS

"KARINYA" IS THE most appropriate name for the Indian group with which this study is concerned. It approximates their own name for themselves, and is the term preferred by most recent anthropological investigators. However, this term was not in use before the present century, "Carib" having been the commonest designation in earlier times. This precedent will be followed here, "Carib" being used in a historical context, while "Karinya" will refer to the contemporary situation.

The native language of the Karinya belongs to the Cariban linguistic family. It is closely related to that spoken by the Barama River Caribs, and also shows many points of similarity with Galibí.[3] Island Carib, or Callinago, also shows many lexical ties with Karinya, but Taylor (1963: 319) has concluded that Callinago "was essentially Arawakan with even in the *langage des hommes* - only a lexical overlay of Cariban Karina."

One interesting point which arises here is that the word "Carib" which is commonly used to refer to all these tribes, as well as others of this linguistic family, is a misnomer. "Carib" seems to have originated in Columbus' word *caribales* (cannibals) which he adopted from the Taino word for the Callinago. Only the name Galibí is cognate with this term. All the rest derive from the Cariban form for "people, person, human being." "Karinya" is derived from the singular form *karíʔnya* — man, person (pl. *karíʔnyako* — people, human beings),[4]

[3] Karinya vocabularies have been published by TAVERA ACOSTA (1907: 108-19, "Caribe"); FEBRES CORDERO (1946); and CRUXENT (1951). The vocabulary and grammar have been studied by ALVARADO (1919) and GOEJE (1909).

[4] For the pronunciation of Karinya terms, see "Note on Karinya Orthography" in the appendix.

which appears as *Cariña* in most anthropological accounts written in Spanish. Popularly, however, they are still referred to as *Caribes.*

Likewise, the Barama River "Caribs" use *karinye to* mean man. And the name Callinago is nothing more than another cognate version of this same root morpheme, probably in plural form (see the quotation from Taylor, above).

POPULATION

POPULATION FIGURES for the Karinya are highly inaccurate, some nearly worse than useless. In 1936, 6,085 indigenes (presumably all or most of them Karinya) were reported for the state of Anzoátegui, but in 1941 the number had dropped to a mere 1,200! The 1950 census reported 1,650 Indians for the whole state (Venezuela, 1955:XX-XXI). The 1936 figures seem too high, while more recent censuses appear rather low. In my observation the time, distance and inconvenience involved in personally visiting small, isolated hamlets of Indians often results in their being neglected by census takers. At best there may be a cursory attempt at estimating the population, based mostly on a guess made by some local person.

No pretense is made that my own estimate for the numbers of Karinya to be found in this area at present are precise with the exception of the two communities where a house-to-house census was made. However, it would appear that the Karinya population has begun to grow again during the last decade and a half. This is clearly the case in the two largest communities, which we studied. The population in Mamo has increased over that reported in 1950 by about 21 per cent, while comparison of my totals with the 1950 figures for Cachama indicates an increase of some 28 per cent in that community. Since these are the two largest Karinya communities, I have assumed that growth in the others has been somewhat slower. Consequently, figures for Tabaro, Santa Clara and El Guasey have been increased by 20 per cent over the population reported in 1950. Population estimates for the other communities have been arrived at in various ways.

From personal observation it is clear that San Joaquín de Parire is considerably larger than reported in the official census — my guess is on the order of 200, which may still be low. The figures for Cabeceras del Pao, Botalón, and Marchanero are based on the number of heads of families reported to me by informants (multiplied by a factor of six, slightly less than the average family size in both Cachama and Mamo). Rumor has it that Bocas del Pao has not grown, and may even have become extinct. The same figure reported for 1950 has been used here. The estimate for Tapaquire and Caño Chiquito was supplied by Hno. Daniel de Barandiarán, missionary of Santa María del Erebato, a Maquiritare community on the upper Caura. Figures marked "?" are strictly guess estimates. All informants agree that these are existent Karinya communities, but I was unable to obtain any estimate as to their size, and it proved to be impossible to visit them while we were in the field.

TABLE I

KARINYA POPULATION CA. 1962

Community	*Population*
San Joaquín de Parire	200
Cachama	696
Barbonero	45
Chive	35
Others	60
Cabeceras del Pao (Agua Fría)	230
Tabaro	333
Bocas del Pao	47
Santa Clara	216
El Guasey (Uverito)	60
Botalón	12
Mamo	381
Marchanero (estimate)	57
La Providencia	89
Isla Grande	100?
Palmarito	150?
Mayagua	150?
Tapaquire - Caño Chiquito	700
Camurica	120?
Caño Escobal	60?
TOTAL	3,728

In addition to those who live in the communities listed above, there are numerous individual families scattered throughout the eastern Llanos, and several families of Mameños (estimated to number about 100 individuals) are known to have emigrated to some of the local towns. These should be included in any really comprehensive calculation.

Another large complement of Indians might de added from Tácata (Santa Rosa). One individual who was visiting Cachama from that community estimated a total of 500 people live in Tácata, with 300 persons sharing in the payments made to them by the oil companies. During a brief visit which was made to that community we were informed by the assistant governor that everyone over 18 participated in these payments. An estimate based on the adult/children ratio in Cachama and Mamo would give a total population in the neighborhood of 700 for Tácata. However, there is some question whether this is truly a Karinya community. While in the field I was aware that there is a minimum of contact between Tácata and the nearest unquestionably Karinya communities. Nor were any instances encountered where Cachamans or Mameños claimed to have kinsmen in Tácata, athough kin ties were reported with individuals in almost all the other neighboring indigenous groups. Since returning from the field, I have found Caulín reports (1958: 462) that Santa Rosa and environs originally consisted of a mission and *reducción* of Chaima and Warau Indians. There is no reason to believe that there has been any change in ethnic makeup since the establishment of the original community, and for this reason Tácata has not been included in the tabulation above.

HISTORY[5]

ALTHOUGH THE coast of Venezuela was among the earliest discoveries of European explorers (it was visited by Columbus on his third voyage in 1498) there is no *specific* mention of Caribs or Cannibal tribes in this region for nearly a century. Nonetheless, there are hints in the reports of both Columbus and Vespucci that cannibal tribes did indeed inhabit the interior plains lying between the Orinoco and the coastal mountains. Not until the expeditions of Berrio and Raleigh,

[5]The material which follows is a very abbreviated summary. A more comprehensive study of the indigenous history of this region has been initiated.

near the end of the 16th century (cf. RALEIGH 1928) is there unequivocal mention of the Caribs, at least some of which must have been direct ancestors of the modern Karinya. Berrio was accompanied on his voyage down the Orinoco by two canoes of Caribs who were on a kidnapping expedition. Raleigh reports on the location of several Carib groups (1928: 35, 57). The *Canibals* of *Guanipa* had a large village a short distance from the mouth of the Guanipa river, and were also said to live along the river Guarapiche. Another tribe of *Canibals* was reported to occupy the whole area between the Rio Cari and the Rio Limo, tributaries on the left side of the lower Orinoco. Their principal town was known as *Acamacari* and was an important trade center. However, Raleigh did not list these Canibals among the four principal nations of the plains, which suggests that they were recent arrivals in the area.

Early relations between Caribs and the Spanish were far from pacific. Spanish lust after wealth and slaves led to many atrocities, which stimulated Indian hostilities in return. The Caribs were effective warriors and successfully prevented Spanish penetration of the plains for better than 200 years after the first settlements were founded on the coast.

They were, however, encouraged in such hostilities by the Dutch who had developed a lucrative trade with them in certain desirable commodities, particularly slaves. In order to protect their commercial interests the Dutch provided weapons, and sometimes even joined their Indian allies in organizing forays against the common Spanish enemy. The French also were active, although their relations with the Caribs were not very extensive until the 17th century. But they, too, encouraged hostility against the Spanish.

As was the case in many other parts of the Spanish colonies, it was the unarmed missionary who eventually succeeded in penetrating the plains and pacifying the hostile Caribs. The first mission on the plains was that of San Mateo, founded in 1715 with Cumanagotos and Chaimas. No Caribs were settled until the founding of San Buenaventura in 1723. There were no further Carib missions until the founding of San Joaquín de Parire in 1736. In spite of frequent threats from a hostile group on the neighboring Mesa de Guanipa, San Joaquín de Parire flourished. Unquestionably, these hostile neighbors were the ancestors of the modern Indians of Cachama. During the next twenty years the missionary fathers extended their influence as far as the Orinoco, founding missions in numerous localities on the plains. In spite of continued Dutch agitation, mission influence on the plains was sufficiently strong by 1755 that further conversions could be attempted across the Orinoco, where mission towns were founded at Muitaco, Tapaquire, and other places.

The successful missionization and pacification of the plains Caribs only opened them to exploitation by Spanish colonists and the injustices of local Spanish authorities. In an attempt to control such exploitation by clarifying the legal rights of the Indians, the Royal Audience of Santo Domingo sent out a commission to survey both Indian and Spanish lands in the provinces of Cumaná and Barcelona (most of which are included in the modern Venezuelan states of Sucre, Monagas, and Anzoátegui). This commission, under the leadership of Don Luis de Chávez y Mendoza, spent three years, 1782-84, in these provinces, surveying lands, recording titles, settling disputes, and making recommendations for the betterment of each community (see PEREZ RAMIREZ 1946). These surveys are of prime importance today, since the claims of most surviving Karinya communities to the lands which they presently occupy are based on the royal grants which originated at that time.

Indigenous life in the 19th century is more poorly documented than during the colonial period, but indications are it was a difficult and disruptive century, a period of wars and progressive loss of community lands. All memory of the War for Independence has been lost, even though the forces of Bolívar were active on the plains, and Bolívar spent three or four years in Angostura (now Ciudad Bolívar) building up his troops before the final successful campaign against the Spanish. Nonetheless, it is probable that some of the events of the War for Independence are reflected in the legends associated with other wars which are still remembered by the modern Karinya.

The Five Years War (1859-63) is said to have been particularly hard on the people in this region. Hunger and deprivation were rampant, and many hid in the woods to avoid the hostilities. At the same time the Karinya also appear to have played a part in this war, for memories survive in several communities of Indian "generals" who had fought in the Five Years War (see ALVARADO 1956: 418). The later War of the Blues is also recalled by some of the older people as having been a difficult period.

More serious and far-reaching in its ultimate effects on the Karinya was the gradual attrition of their land holdings. Various techniques were employed by the rural neo-Venezuelan landholders to alienate Indian lands, from claims through squatter's rights, to purchase, and expropriation to settle "unpaid debts." One of the most amazing of these schemes was that carried out over a period of years against the Indigenous Community of Tabaro, in which their lands were reduced from an original extension of six square leagues to something like one-half square league (Soledad 1911a, 1911b, 1911c; also see ALVARADO 1956: 418).

Unfortunately, official policy tended to encourage alienation of Indian lands, since there were repeated attempts to bring communal ownership to an end, dividing community property among the individual heads of families (LAWS of 1821, 1836, 1904, among others; see ARMELLADA 1954). Often the expense of so dividing communal lands would be met through sale of a part of the property, thereby reducing the amount received by each individual.

Interest in appropriating Indian lands was further stimulated in this century by the discovery of oil in western Venezuela and rumors that similar wealth might be found in the eastern Llanos. As early as 1920 oil concessions had been taken out by Venezuelan Landowners in every state of the republic. In the early 1930's the Gulf Oil Co. acquired extensive drilling rights in Anzoátegui, and their discovery well Oficina Nº 1 was drilled there in 1933. It appears that the loss of one of the four leagues of community land owned by the Indians of Cachama was more or less directly associated with the advent of the oil industry in that region. By 1947 MGO (Mene Grande Oil Co., a subsidiary of Gulf) was drilling on Cachama's lands, and it was not long before they were followed by the drilling crews of Socony (Socony-Mobil Oil Co.). Subsequently wells were sunk on the lands at Tácata, and in the late 1950's at San Joaquín de Parire. To date no wells have been drilled on the lands held by other Karinya communities. In fact, the area of oil production does not extend more than about 25 kilometers (15 miles) south of El Tigre. Thus none of the more southerly communities are likely to be influenced directly by these developments.

Along with the rise of the petroleum industry there was a massive influx of "camp-followers." Some came seeking work and, being unsuccessful, merely stayed on; but many more came to live off the wages of the oil workers and the needs of the companies by offering a variety of goods and services.

With explosive rapidity the once isolated eastern plains entered the 20th century. Where once there had been sandy trails, now there were telephone lines, oil pipelines, and paved higways with considerable traffic criss-crossing the Llanos. Where there had been the scattered huts of farmers, urban complexes of up to 50,000 inhabitants sprang up almost overnight. Modern machinery and constructions were to be seen on every hand. The burgeoning local commerce offered a variety of goods which had been inconceivable a few years before. And, of course, there were those who saw an opportunity to get ahead in easier ways by taking advantage of the poor and uneducated. Uneducated landholders who suddenly began to receive right-of-way payments from the oil companies were particularly attractive to "lawyers" and "business managers" who offered to "protect" them from unscrupulous exploitation by the oil companies.

THE STUDY

THESE CONDITIONS offered a prime opportunity to study the impact on an indigenous tradition when it is faced with rapid and massive modernization, a question of critical importance in our rapidly changing modern world. It was also thought that one of the more southerly Karinya communities, which remain relatively isolated, would offer a significant contrast, as well as establishing a baseline of sorts from which current changes in the oil field communities could be evaluated.

The need for such a study of the Karinya became evident through correspondence and discussion with members of the Fundación La Salle de Ciencias Naturales in Caracas. In spite of their relative accessibility the Karinya were poorly known. Modern scientific reports have been based on brief and often superficial investigations.[6] The basic ethnographic reference for this continent, the *Handbook of South American Indians,* does not even mention them (though their location is shown on maps in both volumes III and IV). Consequently it was desirable to study this group before all trace of the traditional culture had disappeared.

[6] Although limited in scope, some useful data on the contemporary Karinya may be found in ALVARADO (1956, first published in 1915); DUPOUY (1953); FLEURY CUELLO (1953); ORAMAS (1949); and WILBERT (1957).

These several objectives were given formal status through a grant from the Cordell Hull Foundation. Arrangements were made for quarters at the industrial community of San Tomé, which is conveniently located to several of the Karinya communities. My wife and I arrived there near the end of September 1961.

An initial impression that Cachama would be the most fruitful community for study of the impact of the oil industry, both direct and indirect, was borne out by early field investigation, and this community was settled on for one of the two which would be studied intensively.

The first couple of weeks in Cachama were spent in explaining our project in general terms to the community governor, in getting acquainted with the nature of the community, and in a search for useful informants. After the initial contact, a proposal to census the whole community was presented to the governor who appointed his lieutenant as an assistant and guide to facilitate our work.

The census proved to be of inestimable value. Not only did it provide us with statistical information, but of far greater importance, when used in conjuction with a map which I had prepared of the locations of houses, it permitted us to identify and locate every individual member of the community. Since the census asked for names of parents, and included other questions about relatives, a rough genealogical outline soon emerged for the whole community. Again, when census results were used in conjunction with the map, observed spatial relationships proved to be very revealing.[7]

In addition, the necessity of visiting every house enabled us to make our presence known, to give a rough idea of our purpose in being there, and the fact of our being accompanied by an official of the community often served to validate our questions and activities. Several valuable informants were also identified as a result of the census investigation.

Before we had completed the census, however, it became clear that factionalism and conflict were rife in the community. In order not to identify ourselves too closely with a particular side, we decided it might be best to complete the census of certain neighborhoods on our own.

Although we attempted to make a complete record of all cultural

[7] For a copy of the census form, see Appendix B.

information which came to light, our investigation concentrated on the areas of agriculture, economic activities, kinship and family organization, political organization, and value orientations. Aspects such as folklore, the life cycle, and religion were necessarily dealt with less intensively. The Karinya are not very prone to storytelling, and much religion and curing are esoteric activities, carefully concealed from outsiders, in part because of official disapproval and legal sanctions against the *curiosos*[8] or folk curers. Most of the data were obtained through the techniques of free association in conversation and participant observation. Participant observation proved particularly invaluable for bringing out points completely neglected in the course of conversation. If the informant assumes that "Everyone knows that," then he often ignores details, even when prodded, which may be significant for complete understanding on the part of an alien investigator who does *not* know *that*. Finally, for certain topics such as kinship and family organization, and values attitudes, the quickest and surest way to obtain the essential information was through intensive and pointed interviews. Particularly for these purposes it was necessary to employ informants with whom we could work satisfactorily, and also in the case of the values interview, we desired individuals representative of several sectors of the population. Here again, a familiarity with the whole community, which had been obtained by means of the house to house census, served us in very good stead.

By the middle of November we felt that we had learned enough about Cachama that a brief survey of other communities would suffice to identify one which had undergone less culture change, and which, therefore, might provide a significant contrast. Accordingly, we visited Tácata —more acculturated; Mapiricure (San Joaquín de Parire) — less acculturated, but generally very similar to Cachama which it abuts on the southeast; Agua Fría (Cabeceras del Pao) — a very disoriented and apathetic group; and Chive, which proved to be a cluster of five households, economically dependent on local landowners and linked socially to Cachama. Tabaro proved to be very difficult of access. When we finally reached it on our second attempt it was late in the day, and our guide had to return that same afternoon. It was possible to spend no more than a couple of hours there, and we consequently failed to get a very adequate picture of conditions in this community.

[8]Though *curandero* is the usual term for such folk curers in Latin American countries, *curioso* is the one commonly used in eastern Venezuela.

In December we visited what we thought would be a very isolated community, Mamo, located some eighty kilometers east of Soledad in the far southeast corner of the state of Anzoátegui. This time we were able to spend three days visiting Mamo and two of its subsidiary settlements on the Orinoco. To our surprise this appeared by far the most acculturated of the Karinya communities which we had visited. Though they lacked some of the material symbols of modernization such as aluminum roofing, and bicycles, the attitudes and world-view of the Mameños was clearly oriented to modern urban and industrial conditions, and strikingly distinct from what we had heretofore encountered in our survey of other communities. Mamo proved to be the only community which is directly and significantly participant in the urban-industrial economy, with something like a dozen of the young men being employed in the industrial plants which were recently established near the confluence of the Orinoco and Caroní rivers. What was most striking of all was that these Indians seemed to have effected a healthy adaptation to these extensive changes. The community appeared to be well-integrated, and there was evidence of pride in and loyalty to the community and its indigenous heritage. Even though so distinct from other Karinya communities, Mamo yet did not give the impression of just another criollo community. It appeared to be unique. Clearly, here was a great opportunity, two communities of presumably the same original culture had reacted in very different fashion when faced with modern industrial culture. It seemed highly desirable to investigate the reasons for these differences. Perhaps, if we could determine how Mamo had succeeded in changing so profoundly with an apparent minimum of stress, the insights could be useful in future instances of planned culture change. Therefore, we decided to return to Mamo as soon as possible for a longer period of study.

Back in Cachama we pursued the topics already initiated, and spent the holiday season there from Christmas to Candelaria, the week of the 2nd of February. The attitude of the Cachamans, one of disorganization and inactivity through most of this "holiday period" also proved instructive in underscoring the picture which we had already formulated concerning the general character of the community.

After the celebration of Candelaria in Cachama, we returned to Mamo where we were royally received. Almost everyone did their best to be helpful and informative. Within the first three weeks we were able to conclude a census of Mamo, four dependent settlements, and one which appears to have become effectively independent of the mother community. The census proved to have the same value for us here that it had had in Cachama. Similar topics were investigated in this community, and in addition more extensive data on Karinya folklore and religion came to light, partly through the discovery that my most useful informant was also an excellent story-teller.

Aboriginal culture did indeed prove to have been profoundly altered in this community, although it remains distinct from that of the ordinary criollo. Our impression of a strongly integrated community was also borne out by more intensive investigation. On one point, however, our initial impression had been wrong. These changes had not come about without stress. Rather the Mameños had survived the stress and reached a point where reintegration was possible along new lines.

The research in Mamo proceeded so well, that shortly after the Holy Week celebrations we were able to leave for further checking of details in Cachama. However, the poor and sandfilled tracks which we had been driving on for three months proved to be too much for our Volkswagen on the trip out from Mamo. The motor was torn up by sand, and we lost nearly ten days getting our gear back to San Tomé, replacing the motor, and taking care of other necessary details.

During May and part of June we filled in a variety of gaps in our information by working with informants in Cachama. We caught up on further developments in local political activity, and were able to observe certain other traditional activities which had not come to our attention before.

During this final period in the field it was also possible to spend some time in local archives in Cantaura and Soledad searching for documentary material which could fill in legal and historical perspectives. We were further able to spend two or three days in Barcelona where some useful documents dating from the 18th and 19th centuries were located. Unfortunately the time at hand was hardly long enough to carry out a complete search of these archives, and other sources, such as court records, had to be wholly neglected. Nonetheless, even this brief search proved to be most useful, so much so, that we extended the archival search to the Archivo Nacional in Caracas. There we spent two further weeks, just prior to leaving Venezuela, and again succeeded in locating some very useful material. We hope to be able to return in the future for more extensive research on the archival and documentary materials of Venezuela which bear on the indigenous history of the Caribs, or Karinya.

THE FIELD INVESTIGATION itself concentrated primarily on identifying current changes in culture and the factors underlying such changes. We found that to a considerable extent Cachama and Mamo represent a continuum of culture change, the former being more retarded, the latter more advanced along this continuum of change. To the extent that this is an accurate representation, Cachama can be used as a baseline from which to plot the changes which have taken place in Mamo. Nonetheless, this still leaves us without a baseline for Cachama. Even though there has obviously been much less change within the latter group, it is clear that there has been some. The paucity of earlier studies on the Karinya makes it difficult to establish the extent of such change. In spite of this, an attempt has been made to "reconstruct" a probable picture of Karinya culture, as it must have been during the 19th century. This reconstruction is based on hints from historical sources, internal evidence from the field data, and recollections by informants.

Economic activities. The Carib have long depended upon horticulture as their principal means of subsistence. Techniques of cultivation are derived from those which are common throughout the Tropical Forest area, but certain significant modifications of the basic techniques were necessary before it was possible for food producers to permanently occupy the Venezuelan Llanos in any numbers. For the ancestors of the Karinya the most important was that of learning to drain the moriche swamps which follow the courses of most of the rivers in this area. This was undertaken by the men, and along with the initial clearing of a field, was presumably the only male connection with agriculture.

Most of the agricultural labor must have been left to the women, along with their duties in the household and in caring for the children. The importance of agriculture in the 19th century is indicated by the fact that the Karinya had some thirty varieties of manioc in addition to sugar cane and a variety of other crops. Steel tools had by this time replaced the older stone and wooden implements (ALVARADO 1956: 401-02).

Male neglect of the fields was not due to any particular ideological prohibition, but rather because of a commitment to a variety of other activities. Almost from the time of first contact the Caribs were renowned as traders and feared as nearly invincible warriors. In both capacities the men traveled extensively and were absent from the village for long periods of time. Under these conditions it was only natural that cultivation should fall to the lot of the women, since the men would often be unavailable for the performance of a particular task when the time came for it to be done. Even in the 19th century Karinya men seem to have been involved in the frequent revolutions and civil wars which plagued the Venezuelan nation. Petty trade seems to have continued as another factor encouraging frequent absences from the home community. It is doubtful that their participation in agriculture increased significantly before sometime around the turn of the century.

When the men were at home they seem to have engaged mostly in hunting and fishing in order to provide these necessary supplements to the diet, since they long resisted using the flesh of domestic animals as food (RUIZ BLANCO 1892: 51). By this century the Karinya no longer entertained such compunctions (ALVARADO 1956: 402), but game and fish nonetheless have remained more important in the overall diet.

The Dutch first introduced firearms to the Carib, and by the 19th century they were widely used both in hunting and in warfare. In spite of widespread trade contacts, most craft needs were produced locally. Pottery, basketry, hammocks of moriche or curagua fiber, *rallos* for grating manioc, and wooden mortars were all products of local craftsmanship (ALVARADO 1956: 402). Weaving, however, must have been forgotten by this time, since cloth and glass beads were major items of trade. Carib men had long been famous for their characteristic dark blue (azul turquí) kilts, but the demand for cloth increased markedly when the women adopted the ample and all-concealing *bata* some time in the latter half of the 19th century, in addition to the customary loincloth.

Family and Kinship. There is no reason to doubt that Karinya kinship has long been of the bifurcate merging type with Iroquois cousin terms. This is the most frequent kinship structure which is found among the Cariban-speaking tribes of South America. It is also probable that sister's children were equated with cross-cousins, with marriage being permissible, or even preferential, with these relatives. In spite of this apparently unilineal organization, it is quite likely that descent was recognized bilaterally, as this also appears to be a peculiarity of the Cariban tribes (Murdock 1960: 7-8).

Marriage occurred at an early age, roughly coinciding with the onset of puberty. The marriage received public sanction through a ceremony in which the couple underwent an ordeal where they were rolled together in a hammock filled with stinging wasps and ants. Residence presumably was preferentially matrilocal. Nonetheless, the husband was treated with respect and deference, and outwardly at least, had unquestioned authority over his wife and children. Chiefs, however, probably kept their married sons near them (as was the practise among the Callinago, TAYLOR 1946: 181).

The ancestors of the modern Karinya lived in large round communal houses which were divided into a number of separate apartments, "in which each family is lodged and ordinarily all those that inhabit one house are relatives" (RUIZ BLANCO 1892: 51). This description makes it clear that such house groups were kin groups as well as residential groups, but unfortunately it is also sufficiently vague to make it impossible to determine their exact nature. Most likely they represented matrilocal extended families, or even matrilineages,[9] although the sons of *important men* (war chiefs, shamans, etc.) were probably permitted, or even encouraged, to observe patrilocal residence following marriage. When in-marrying spouses were included, such house groups could be characterized as compromise kin groups or clans, in this case, matrilocal clans. (It is possible one would be more accurate in describing residence as ambilocal, but I prefer to characterize it as indicated, since in any case matrilocality was predominant).

By the 1800's the Karinya seem to have given up the communal house and were living in small rectangular houses limited to one or two nuclear families. Nonetheless, the kin group which formerly occupied the communal house seems to have been maintained through residential proximity. Even though they now occupied separate structures, those who formerly lived together within the communal house continued to construct their houses near each other in the same neighborhood.

[9] MURDOCK has called this type of organization "quasiunilineal" and more recently (1960: 8) has designated both patrilineal and matrilineal forms the "Carib type." He points out (1960: 7), for example, that the Sinhalese are essentially bilateral in descent *in spite of* "patrilocal and patrilineal tendencies in the organization of the extended family." In like manner the strong matrilocal and matrilineal bias of the Karinya does not preclude descent from being bilateral. In spite of lineage groupings there is nothing at all that one could identify as a sib or other large, corporate unilineal descent group.

We can expect that there was restraint in relations between parents-in-law and children-in-law, particularly when they were resident in the same neighborhood. Other than parents, kinsmen with whom one was not in continual contact tended to become unimportant, and might even be forgotten. The Carib seem never to have been very interested in their ancestors. A widespread inability even to name grandparents seems to be a characteristic of long standing (ALVARADO 1956: 410). Lineages consequently were very shallow and only weakly integrated according to the hereditary principle. At the same time there must have been other, stronger factors binding the household or neighborhood together. The basic unit which undertook expeditions for trade or warfare was probably composed of the men belonging to the same neighborhood (and formerly the same communal household). The women who were left at home undoubtedly worked together in both the house and the fields, not only for company, but to provide a little more protection for each other.

Discipline of children was lax or non-existent. Certain it is that corporal punishment was never employed. At the same time certain culturally valued attitudes were inculcated from an early age. Chief among these was an attitude of respect for one's elders. Beyond this, few demands were made on small children, and boys in fact, probably had no real responsibilities until they were old enough to hunt, to marry, and to travel away from home. Most likely relative sexual freedom was allowed to boys. On the other hand, girls assumed their responsibilities in their own nuclear family and within the neighborhood at an earlier age, perhaps at six or seven. They were more restricted in their freedom and independence. Virginity at marriage was perhaps not an essential attribute, but an undefiled bride was probably more desirable than an experienced one.

Organization of the community. Unfortunately it is not at all clear whether a village in earlier times consisted of just one communal dwelling, or if several such structures were to be found clustered together in each community. Thus the real strength of the chief or cacique is a matter of debate. However, there is no indication that the cacique ever had influence or authority over more than the local settlement in which he was resident. The Spaniards probably attributed too much authority to the cacique, for it is likely that he only held a position of prestige and influence, rather than one of unquestioned authority. To achieve this position a candidate was forced to undergo a series of ordeals, similar to those imposed on the bridal couple.

Was there a War Chief, who held somewhat greater authority in time of war? Such existed among the Callinago. Several modern Karinya communities have traditions of a local "general" who participated in some of the 19th century Venezuelan wars, and later held the — position of cacique in their communities. Were they granted this rank by Venezuelan authorities as a reward for their services in the wars, or does this represent a traditional procedure for obtaining a position of authority in the community? Evidence from other *Cariban* tribes argues against the latter interpretation. In support of the former view is the fact that sometime during the 19th century (or perhaps even earlier) a complex official structure was imposed on each Karinya community by the Venezuelan authorities. Six or more officials were elected annually, while individual men were assessed for labor in public works (ALVARADO 1956: 417, 402).

The exact relationship of the cacique to the elected officers is not entirely clear, but it would seem that he usually occupied a permanent position in the community. Accordingly he was a more influential figure than those who were elected each year.

Rather than being an authoritative figure, however, his major function was as focus of community sentiment and activity. It was he who initiated group labor *(cayapa)* in clearing new fields or erecting a new house, and it is also possible that he served as the leader in war. The cacique further had an economic function as a redistributive center. Goods and produce were given to him as gifts, and they were used by him to feed the labor on cayapa, or to enhance the festivities on the occasion of a community celebration.

The cacique also served as a central figure through whom communication with outsiders could be channeled. This particular function seems not to have been a part of the aboriginal conception of this role, but rather something which was imposed by European preconceptions about the role of leaders in any society. Thus Europeans wished to deal with the cacique only, whom they viewed as representative of the whole community. The cacique probably found an advantage in this relationship, since trade would tend to be channeled through him. He would find it to his advantage to learn Spanish, and this in turn strengthened his influence with his own tribesmen since almost all dealings with outsiders would then be under his control.

Even so, there seems always to have been a sort of council of elders, who exercised a strong modifying influence on the cacique. They may or may not have been identical to the corps of elective officers. Perhaps they were men who had not undergone the rigors of becoming a cacique, but who nonetheless occupied positions of prestige and influence due to their age and achievements. Finally, there was the shaman, who was also a powerful individual, due to his association with the supernatural. At least in some instances shaman and cacique appear to have been the same person, and in these cases they may have held a rather more formidable position in Carib society, since prestige and influence would be combined with the possibility of employing a certain amount of coercive power through the shaman's control of the supernatural.

Interpersonal relations within the group were calm and smooth, with little or no expression of hostility or aggression between individuals. It is doubtful that a Carib ever raised his voice in speaking to a fellow tribesman. At least, such conditions would be consistent with the great savagery and ferocity with which the Carib pursued war in the past—even to the extent of consuming some of their victims, which was done in the manner of taking a war trophy (RUIZ BLANCO 1892: 51). MURPHY (1960: 130-31) has pointed out a correlation of this type was characteristic of the headhunting Mundurucú, and although headhunting has disappeared today, interpersonal relations still tend to be pacific.

Religion. It is evident that the missionaries were quite succesful in catholicizing the Venezuelan Caribs. Most Karinya festivities conformed to the Roman Catholic ceremonial calendar, with the Day of the Dead, Holy Week, and the fiesta of the local patron saint being most important (ALVARADO 1956: 405). Most of the children were baptised in the church (ALVARADO 1956: 410), while Karinya folklore has been strongly influenced with Christian motifs. This did not mean, however, the disappearance of traditional beliefs and practises. The shaman was still important in supernatural curing, while the ancient god or gods, *Yoroxkan* continued to be recognized. Abuse and neglect of the Indians on the part of the priests during the latter decades of the 19th century probably served to reinforce the importance of the traditional religion and thus enabled it to survive side by side with a diluted and much modified concept of Christianity.[10]

[10]The Karinya remain nominal Catholics today. For several reasons religion will not be treated in the discussion below. There is limited contact with the Catholic priesthood. Many Catholic rituals and ceremonies have become highly secularized. Because of official disapproval, few Karinya are willing to discuss traditional religious ideas and curing practises in any depth. Consequently our field data is weakest in this area.

Values. This is the most difficult aspect of the aboriginal culture to reconstruct, since it is based almost entirely on statements of contemporary informants, with only occasional interpolations from known behavior in the past. Actually, we can expect that restraint and lack of hostility in interpersonal relations was a strong value surviving from an earlier and more warlike period. Closely related to this was the value demanding respect for one's fellow tribesmen, and particularly for parents, elders, and caciques. Respect for one's mother should be combined with a close emotional attachment. One was not expected to be so close to his father. But relations with parents-in-law were always expected to be formal and restrained, perhaps to the point of patterned avoidance.

It is also to be expected that the principal functions of the cacique within the community, as focus and organizer of most communal activities, perhaps even as representative of the community in dealing with outsiders, would similarly be supported by strong values which demanded this sort of behavior from him.

II

CACHAMA

CACHAMA

THE INDIGENOUS Community of Cachama is located along the Río Cachama and the Caño Tascabaña, and possesses communal title to most of the land lying between these two streams which are both tributary to the Río Guanipa.

There is no record of when Cachama was settled, though in 1779 CAULIN (1958: 461) reported that a group of hostile Caribs was occupying that area when the mission of San Joaquín de Parire was founded in 1736. Carib families may have been living there for a number of generations prior to this date, since it would lie along the natural overland route between the important Carib town of El Cari (Acamacari) and the "Canibal" town at the mouth of the Guanipa.

Later on additional settlers are known to have come from Chamariapa (now Cantaura), Cabeceras del Pao, Areo, and other Karinya settlements.

In 1783 the Indians of Chamariapa and Cachama obtained title to the lands along the Río Cachama through the survey conducted by a royal commission under Don Luis de Chávez y Mendoza (see PEREZ RAMIREZ 1946,[1] Cantaura 1904).

In recent years a paved highway was built from Barcelona and Puerto La Cruz on the coast to Soledad, opposite Ciudad Bolívar on the Orinoco. This highway passes along one edge of Cachama and provides ready access to El Tigre, "Tigrito," Cantaura, and other towns in the region.

At the present time most of the Cachamans are living on the three square leagues of land for which the tribe still retains title. In addition there are dependent groups living nearby at Las Potocas and Sombrerito (see Map II) and more distantly in Chive. Other small groups of Cachamans are known to be living "temporarily" at Los Conucos, Diezmero, and Güire, all located in the area north of the Río Guanipa and east of

[1]Though I have seen this source, it is unfortunately not available to me at the present time.

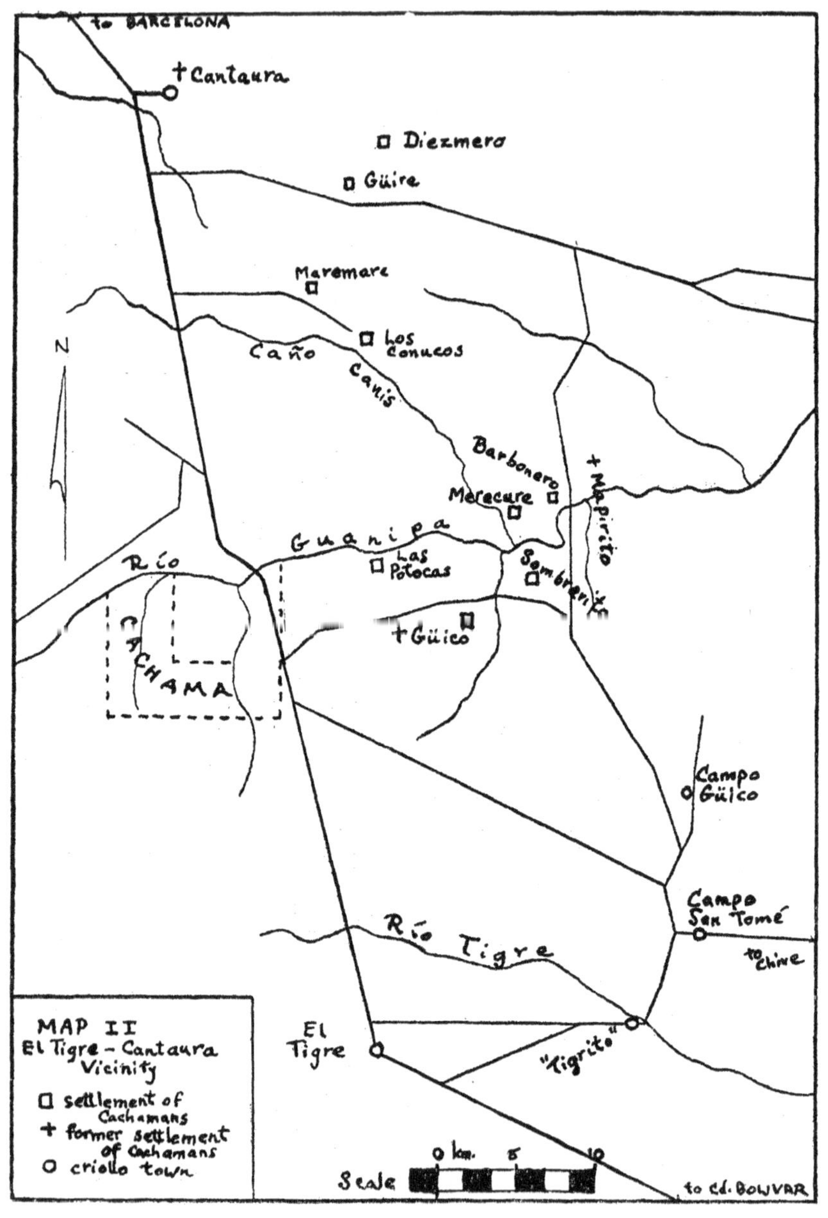
to BARCELONA
+Cantaura
Diezmero
Güire
Maremare
Los Conucos
Caño Canis
Barbonero
+Mapirito
Merecure
Guanipa
Las Potocas
Sombrerito
Río
CACHAMA
+Güico
Campo Güico
Campo San Tomé
to Chive
Río Tigre
El Tigre
"Tigrito"
MAP II
El Tigre - Cantaura Vicinity
settlement of Cachamans
+ former settlement of Cachamans
o criollo town
Scale
0 km. 5 10
to Cd. BOLIVAR

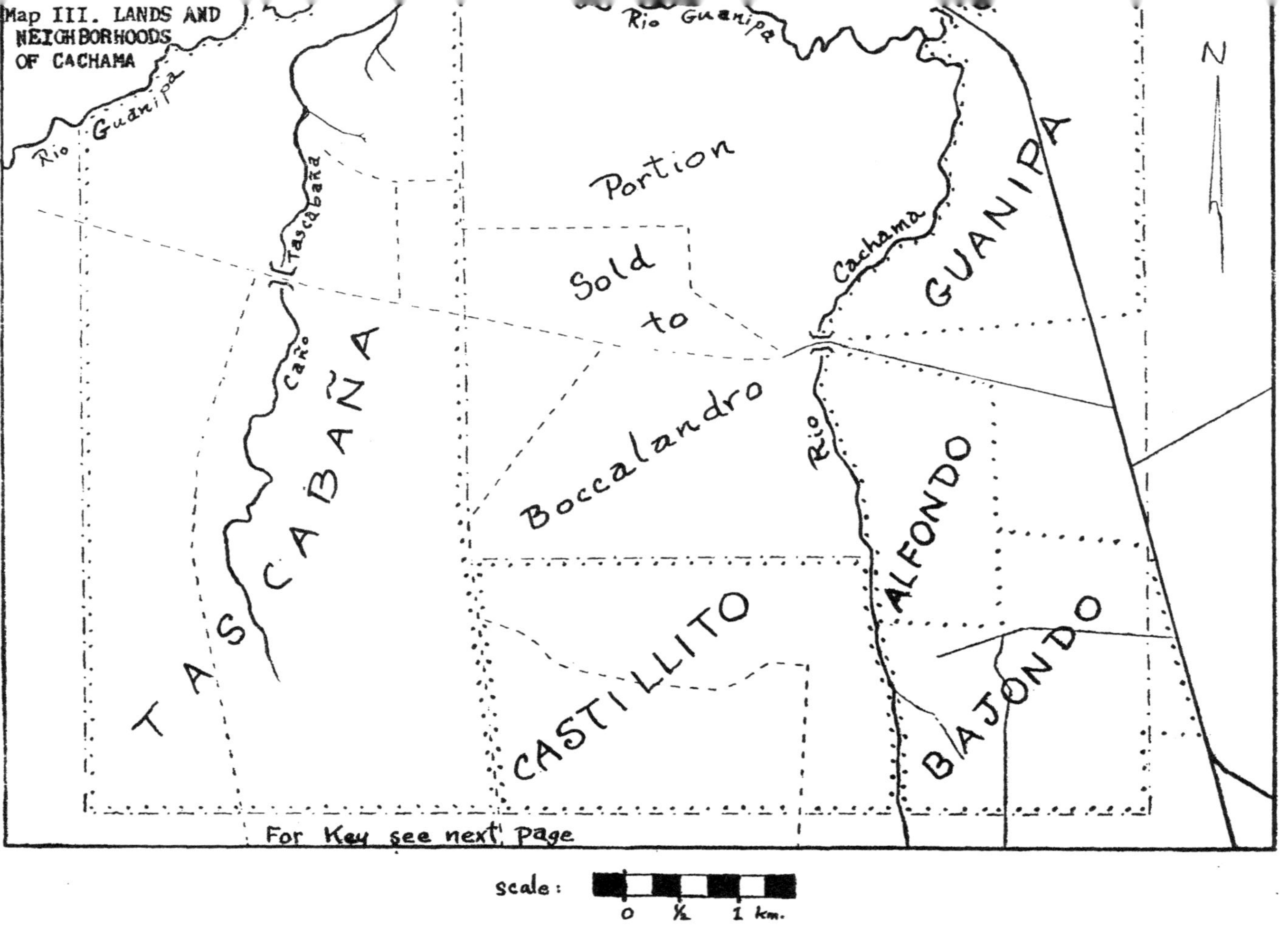

Map III. LANDS AND NEIGHBORHOODS OF CACHAMA

KEY TO MAP III.

Boundaries of Tribal Lands —·—
Neighborhood Boundaries . . . . . .
Paved Roads ———
Truck Trail - - - - -

Cantaura. One group, which lives just north of the Río Guanipa at Barbonero is considered for all intents and purposes to have become independent of Cachama.

In addition to these contemporary settlements, tradition has it that in the past there were sizable groups of Cachamans living in Güico and Mapirito. The former at least appears to have rivalled in size the settlement in Cachama proper. Today most of the settlements off tribal lands are small, and they all appear to be in a process of decline, with the possible exception of Las Potocas.

Within Cachama itself, the inhabitants of the community are widely dispersed over the tribal lands. Small clusters of houses tend to be widely separated from each other, often being completely out of sight. This has led to the delineation of various *neighborhoods* within the community. The most populous of these are Guanipa and Bajondo (Bajo Hondo) located along the highway, and Tascabaña which stretches along the lower course of Caño Tascabaña (though there are cultivated fields along its entire length). The last named neighborhood is separated from the others by the tract of land which was sold to a criollo. Two smaller neighborhoods are found in Alfondo and Castillito. Reference to Map III will indicate that neighborhood boundaries do not always follow the boundaries of tribal property. Numerous inhabitants of Bajondo have erected houses off tribal land in order to be adjacent to the highway. One area (locally known as "Boca") separating Guanipa from Alfondo and Bajondo is effectively free of neighborhood affiliations, for reasons which will be discussed in Chapter IV.

Table II shows the distribution of population in this community.

Table II

CACHAMA: POPULATION BY NEIGHBORHOODS

	Male	*Female*	*Sub-Total*
GUANIPA			
Adults	46	46	92
Children	63	47	110
BAJONDO			
Adults	27	28	55
Children	30	34	64
ALFONDO			
Adults	17	19	36
Children	20	17	37
CASTILLITO			
Adults	14	14	28
Children	16	20	36
TASCABAÑA			
Adults	40	38	78
Children	55	50	105
LAS POTOCAS (Incl. Chimire, Cerro Negro, Sombrerito)			
Adults	13	15	28
Children	12	15	27
TOTAL			
Adults	157	160	317
Children	195	184	379
			696

Chapter 2

ECONOMIC CHANGES

WITH RAPID development of the petroleum industry in eastern Venezuela and the concomitant influx of population there have been inevitable repercussions on the economy of Cachama. The established patterns have been somewhat disrupted, but only in a few instances are there indications that new patterns are beginning to emerge. For the most part, there have been no radical changes in subsistance.

Hunting and fishing are of little importance today. Even though almost everyone engages in some fishing, the local streams are devoid of anything but a few fingerlings (*sardinetas*). The blame for this condition is variously cast on the oil companies, and on "those people from Chive" (Cachamans whose ancestors reputedly arrived in Cachama during the past few decades). By and large the latter attribution seems most correct. For a number of years (I have no idea how long) people of the community have been making extensive use of barbasco (fish poison) to fish in the local streams. In October-November 1961 and again in January-February 1962 every instance of the use of barbasco which came to my attention was recorded. My notes show that it was used a little oftener than once every fortnight. Presumably such over-exploitation has contributed to a decline in fishing resources.

It would be inaccurate to say that this is directly correlated with industrial influences in the region, but it does seem to be related to the generally improvident attitude which one frequently encounters in Cachama. This attitude was non-existent in former times, at least where fishing is concerned, for María Medina reports that barbasco used to be reserved for the period immediately preceding Holy Week, when large quantities of supplies are accumulated to tide the family through this ritual period.

Hunting is pursued even less frequently than fishing. Game is quite scarce around Cachama, and only a few men hunt regularly. An occasional bird, such as a parrot or dove; or more rarely, an armadillo, are about all that ever reward the hunter's efforts. Most of the meat and fish consumed today are bought. Canned sardines and fresh ocean fish, brought from Puerto La Cruz for sale in El Tigre, are especially popular.

Agriculture continues to be the principal base of subsistence for the community. With but few exceptions, the traditional crops are planted, and the traditional techniques of cultivation are employed. The most striking change is the one that is taking place in the pattern of land use, and this in turn is *beginning* to effect a change in crops, and techniques of cultivation as well.

As late as the second and third decades of this century the Karinya seem to have been much more dispersed throughout eastern Venezuela than they are today. Admittedly their numbers were in decline, and through various means much of the land which they occupied was alienated from them. But there seems never to have been any great deterrent to clearing a field and squatting on unoccupied land. "*Now* they are all fenced. No one can put his *conucos* there."

With the recent development of the oil industry in this region land has a new value, property boundaries have greater importance, and legal title to a piece of real estate is of more concern. Since titles are often clouded in this region anyway, property-owners tend to discourage any intrusion on the land which might call their claims into question. But this is probably less than half of the picture. There are still many lands in the area where an enterprising farmer *could* clear himself a field without too much difficulty. Considerable expanses of public domain *(terrenos baldíos)* are to be found scattered throughout the region, and a few Karinya families are known to be exploiting such lands.

In spite of the fact that such public lands could be claimed and worked, there is an increasing tendency to cluster on the lands where legal possession remains in the hands of a Karinya community. Such centripetal movements have especially focused on Cachama, since that community has been alone in receiving right-of-way *(servidumbre)* payments from the oil companies (in exchange for rights to use the land surface) since 1947.[1] San Joaquín de Parire, the second Karinya community to enter a contract with the oil companies to permit exploration and development on their lands, only concluded their agreement in the

[1]Under Venezuelan law all sub-surface mineral rights are property of the nation. Royalties which accrue through the extraction of such minerals are paid directly to the national government. The land-owner is not left completely out of the picture, however, for he must agree to grant the oil companies right to enter his property and make use of the land surface.

late 1950's. In Cachama the practise in recent years has been to distribute such company payments among all adult members of the community.[2] Although the actual sum received by each individual ranges between Bs. 15 and Bs. 30, the total received by the community amounts to several thousand bolívares per year. This pattern of receipt and distribution of considerable sums of right-of-way moneys has acted as a powerful attraction for anyone who could show a valid claim to membership in the community.

It is not the quantity of money which accrues from these company payments which is attractive. The total sum received by any individual in the course of a year could be made up by a week's hard work at day labor. Rather it is the lure of something for nothing, combined with the vision of the great quantity of money paid by the companies *to the community as a whole.* Families who once lived away from community lands have returned to establish residence there and they are wary of leaving for fear they will lose their rights to participate in these distributions.

Those few families who still live some 75 kilometers away in Chive also have a house in Cachama, and they alternate residence between the two places, an obvious attempt to take advantage of the available opportunities in both places. On the other hand, residents in the nearby hamlet of Barbonero, which is off the tribal lands, have but minimal interaction with the Cachamans proper, and they do not share in these right-of-way payments. The Cachamans feel that they are no longer a part of the community. One commonly hears it said that "They have been living over there for two generations and do not really belong here now. They have lost their rights in Cachama."

The residents of other settlements which are located off tribal lands mostly fall somewhere between these two extremes. They do not now share in the company payments, but they could reactivate their rights were they to return to Cachama. Undoubtedly, continued absence from the community for another generation or so would completely alienate any claim which they might now have.

However, the most important point here is that all such settlements off community lands have been in existence for many years. No new settlements of this kind have been founded in the last 15 years and some have been abandoned by the Indians. The young men are not moving out of the community in search of new land to cultivate or other new opportunities. Rather the tendency is to return to Cachama and to stay fairly

[2]For a discussion of the disputes which have surrounded disposition of such payments, see Chap. 4, Cachama as A Community.

close to it in terms both of spatial proximity and of maintaining strong kinship ties.

These centripetal tendencies, combined with a growth of population in recent years, has resulted in increased pressure on the land. All the available river bottom land which is suitable for cultivation is currently being farmed. There is no place where a young man can clear a new *conuco* for himself along the rivers.

As a result some people are beginning to cultivate the drier and less fertile savanna lands which are from 80-100 feet above the level of the river bottoms. These lands are much more extensive, being characteristic of the mesa surface through which the relatively deep river valleys have been cut. But they also place numerous disadvantages in the way of the simple cultivator. In the first place the soil is sandy and relatively porous, and therefore does not hold moisture well. Some crops will grow there satisfactorily during the wet season, but during the dry season most of the savanna plants either dry up or go into a dormant state. In the second place, most of the savanna is an unbroken expanse of coarse grass which is much more difficult to work. The usual practise is to burn off this grass during the dry season, even when there is no intention of working the soil. There is little doubt that this custom has contributed to the third disadvantage of the savanna soils, their lower fertility. Tests of soil samples taken in Cachama show the savanna soils to be low in organic matter, as well as in phosphorous and potassium. In contrast, river bottom soils usually show a high proportion of these components (Servicio Shell, personal communication). Nonetheless, the Cachamans are of the opinion that continued cultivation will *increase* the fertility of these soils, since they firmly believe that this is what happens in their river-bottom *conucos.* (It is certainly possible that the proportion of organic matter would increase if cultivated savanna land were protected from burning.)

Even if this last difficulty is ignored, it takes some labor and capital to cultivate the savanna successfully. Several men have succeeded in cultivating goodsized garden plots by utilizing techniques similar to those employed in the bottom lands. But the production from these plots is nothing more than a supplement to the subsistence diet. If one intends to plant a medium-sized field on the savanna it is necessary to use a plow to break the sod. Satisfactory draft animals are lacking, plows are expensive, and tractors even more so. There is a tractor in Tascabaña neighborhood, but its use is limited due to community factionalism and the high rate of several bolívares (as much as 20) per *hour* charged by its owner. Consequently, only those who are politically aligned with the Tascabaña faction, or those who are relatively wealthy, as are the curiosos, have been successful in cultivating the savanna land. Those men who are wealthy enough to afford use of the tractor can thus enhance their economic standing, thereby becoming almost the only ones who can afford to open new lands. Those who are young, or poor, or who lack land for other reasons are virtually prevented from obtaining much subsistence by cultivation of their own fields.

Along with the introduction of new techniques on savanna lands, such as mechanized plow cultivation, there have also been several new crops (or a new emphasis on old crops), although manioc probably remains most important even in these fields. One of the agricultural banks has encouraged the planting of an annual cotton in this region, and although several Cachama farmers had tried it, none of them had yet undertaken to cultivate it on a large scale. There were several experiments with sesame, and Martín Abaduca had successfully cultivated peanuts as a cash crop.[3] The most common and most successful crop in these savanna fields is the common bush bean *(Ph. vulgaris)*. This would appear to be a new emphasis on a traditional crop which is not very well suited to the moist conditions of river bottom cultivation. Certain individuals harvested sufficient quantities of beans that they could be sold as a cash crop.

There has been no comparable intensification in animal husbandry. If anything, the number of domestic animals has declined. For example, Miguel Tamanaico says that he and his father used to have a number of pigs, cattle and chickens. Now his father has no livestock at all, and Miguel has no cattle and only a couple of hogs. Likewise the older people can remember when there were oxen in the community, used in pulling carts. There are no oxen today, and hardly anyone really owns a burro, though there are a number of feral ones in the vicinity. Only three people actually own any cattle or horses in Cachama, and all these reside in Tascabaña and belong to that faction.

While it is true that few people actually plant a cash crop, the bottom lands are highly productive, and almost everyone with a *conuco* there has an occasional surplus which can be readily converted into cash. The activity of the oil companies has attracted many new inhabitants to eastern Venezuela, even though many of them have no direct connection with the industry. Several new urban centers have come into being, and the rapid increase in the non-agricultural population has created a demand for

[3]Although peanuts are an ancient cultigen in South America, the Cachamans claim they are a relatively new crop for them. Nowhere did we find them to be common in eastern Venezuela.

foodstuffs. Anytime a Cachaman has a few extra yams, bananas, taro, or sweet manioc he can easily dispose of them with a merchant in Cantaura or El Tigre, or even "Tigrito." Only during mango season is the surplus of *this* fruit so great that the market threatens to be glutted.

When he is interested in making more than just a few quick bolívares, the Cachaman can put his whole family to work for a couple of days processing the roots of the bitter manioc and baking the pulp into huge round *tortas,* or cakes of manioc bread. A *cuento* (20) of these cakes can be sold in the towns for about Bs. 25.

The demand is so great, however, that one need not go to town to dispose of his surplus. There are numerous itinerant merchants *(mongueros)* who circulate through the rural areas in trucks, soliciting foodstuffs from the fields and offering cash or other items in exchange. While they will do business with anyone, they seem to prefer dealing with the larger farmers. Since the curiosos control more land than is necessary for their own subsistence, they do considerable business with the mongueros, and in this case it would almost be legitimate to speak of true cash-cropping of bananas, yams, sweet manioc, etc. Both cash-cropping and cultivation of savanna lands remain in an incipient state, but they may represent the beginning of important new patterns.

The Cachamans have also discovered a ready market for their production of hammocks since the recent influx of urban-centered population. All rural people and almost all the urban lower class sleep in hammocks. The commonest type of hammock in eastern Venezuela is woven from a soft, smooth fiber extracted from the immature leaves of the moriche palm *(Mauritia flexuosa).* The Karinya have been weaving this kind of hammock for centuries, and since there is an ample supply of raw materials in the river bottoms, the weaving of hammocks for sale has developed into a fairly important household industry in Cachama. Hammock weaving does not bring in a great deal of income. The larger, finer and better woven hammocks *(aguja* and *cairel)* bring more money (about Bs. 20), but they also take considerably longer to make. The smallest and simplest type *(tripas por medio)* only brings about Bs. 7-8 per hammock, but a skillful weaver can turn one out in about a third of the time necessary for the finer hammocks, which makes this a quick source for small amounts of cash. Hammocks are woven the year 'round, but the craft was pursued with striking intensity during the month preceding the Fiesta de la Virgen de Candelaria, held in Cantaura during the week of February 2. A quick return was necessary to bolster resources depleted during the inactivity of the Christmas season. At other times of the year hammock weaving seems to be responsive to individual needs. In any case the principal reason for weaving hammocks is to provide a quick and ready source of cash, rather than because it provides any significant increase in family income.

Hammock weaving is the only craft which has any significant place in the local economy. Basketry is still pursued by a few men and it may represent some subsidiary income for them. For the most part, however, basketry appears to be dying out, even though there is continued demand for the items produced (such as the manioc press, sifters, and carrying baskets). These things can be bought in the towns, and it may be more convenient to get them there (since they do not have to be ordered ahead), but they are also more expensive in the towns than are those obtained in the village.

Pottery is more nearly a dead art than basketry. The influx of iron, glass, and especially enamel ware (some of it from Hong Kong) has made the slow and laborious process of making pottery vessels impractical and completely uneconomical. Only pottery jugs survive today due to their obvious superiority as containers for drinking water. Being porous they keep the water much cooler and more palatable than when it is kept in other types of containers. Were such pottery water jugs readily available in the towns also, it is likely that the local craft would disappear completely.

With the intensive activity of the oil companies in the area, one would expect that some few of the Indians would be employed, at least occasionally, in a job which was industry related — even if it were only "pico y palo," unskilled labor on a pick and shovel crew. However, this is not the case. Jesús Rodríguez is the only person encountered in Cachama who ever worked for the oil companies. He was employed as a laborer for a few months during 1940-41. It is probably significant that he had no connection with Cachama at the time. Jesús only returned to the Indian community about 1956 when he revived his claim to a share of community lands after his prospects elsewhere evaporated.

The present scarcity of land and the lack of capital with which to open new land is most acute among the younger men, aged 16-30. The situation would be more critical than it is were it not for the fact that generalized economic expansion in the whole of eastern Venezuela has opened up several alternative areas of employment. None of these are very lucrative, but they can provide an adequate substitute for the production of subsistence foodstuffs, and they have also made it possible for more people to remain physically attached to Cachama. Such alternative economic activities have thus tended to reinforce the centripetal tendencies discussed above.

Aside from company payments the only more or less direct economic effect of the oil industry for Cachama has been the creation of a demand for gravel. Much of the savanna land is stony, with ridges and mounds of gravel scattered about on its surface. Gravel is used extensively in construction, road-building and other projects. While some enterprising criollos have set themselves up as mongueros, others have obtained a dumptruck *(volteo)* and make their living hauling gravel. This has provided another new economic opportunity for the Cachamans. Any time one of the younger men needs extra money he need only screen out a load of gravel, flag down one of the dumptrucks as it cruises along the main highway, and shovel in his load. An enterprising individual can make Bs. 10 or more per day by screening and loading gravel. The system seems to work pretty well. No one has to work in the gravel every day, only when he needs to. But every day there are always a few individuals who want to sell a few loads. On those rare occasions when the driver of the dumptruck finds himself without an adequate number of gravel loaders, he can usually find one or two young fellows who are willing to fill his needs for the day.

An interesting pattern of reciprocity has grown up around this exploitation of gravel. In exchange for a constant supply of this material, the dumptruck drivers allow the Cachamans, both men and women, to hitch a ride with them at any time. This system is often used for getting to the towns without cost.

The increase in demand for foodstuffs in the region of oil exploitation has not only created a market for the production of Cachama, but it has also greatly expanded the market for their labor. Numerous individuals hire themselves out for day labor working in the conucos of criollos. The greatest demand for such labor appears to be in the more heavily wooded area around Cantaura, but there is some call for day labor by the wealthier individuals in Cachama such as the curiosos. Although the younger men are most commonly employed in day labor, it is worthy of note that older men also hire themselves out for this kind of work. It requires no more commitment than working in the gravel, and presumably is less strenuous than the latter. Even women sometimes have an opportunity for employment comparable to day labor. Once when a criollo was harvesting a whole field of manioc he hired Crucita

Maita for five days to process the tubers and bake them into manioc cakes.

Occasionally an opportunity arises for employment as unskilled labor over a period of time. In these cases a "contract" is entered into in which the individual agrees to exchange his labor for wages for a specified period of time. "Contract employment" is invariably sufficiently distant from Cachama that one is unable to travel to and from the place of employment every day. Miguel Martínez spent a month near Ciudad Bolívar working in gravel. Julián Maita and Teofanio Carreño both spent several months somewhere to the south along the Río Cari tending a criollo farmer's livestock. In the cases just cited the wife and children accompanied these men during the time they were employed on contract, and this seems to be a general pattern. Yet in every case of "contract employment" the families were absent from Cachama no more than a few months. In some cases the contract was only temporary, but in others such as those of Julián Maita and Teofanio Carreño no such reason was involved. Rather their return seemed to be due to the usual centripetal tendencies: a desire to avoid breaking one's ties with the community.

Many businesses and a number of small industries have grown up in the neighboring towns, especially El Tigre. The Cachamans might profit by taking advantage of employment opportunities offered in these enterprises, but almost no one has been sufficiently motivated even to investigate the possibilities. Near the end of our stay in Cachama Francisco Aray, one of the most progressive and enterprising individuals in the community, secured a position at a brick plant near El Tigre and through him two or three other younger men also obtained employment there. These were described as permanent positions. If so, this would represent the first step toward dependence on non-subsistence activities as the principal source of individual and family income. Francisco's employment may or may not mark the beginning of a trend, but even if it does, it will be many years before outside employment replaces subsistence farming as the principal economic activity.

Communication with the towns is greatly facilitated by the institution of *por puesto* (jitney) service. "Puesto" cars travel all the main highways of Venezuela at frequent intervals and provide an important means of transportation between all sizable towns. One important side effect, arising from such ease of movement, has been a marked increase in business for the Karinya curioso or shaman. They treat many more criollo patients than Indian, even though apparently higher fees are charged the former. There seems to be a general attitude in Venezuela that the more distant the folk curer, the more efficacious are his treatments. Thus with the present easy transportation the criollos flock to the Karinya shaman, while the local people rarely make use of his services. One might think that such criollo patients would be an important channel for acculturative influences, but this does not seem to be the case. In the first place there is a minimum of contact with Karinya other than the shaman. In the second place these patients are in a necessarily subordinate position. Only in Tascabaña did we ever observe new ideas being introduced, and in this case the innovations were being consciously controlled by the local people. Pedrito Tamanaico, cacique of Tascabaña, had discovered that a couple of patients from the coast knew how to weave fishing nets. He immediately put them to work teaching the young men how to do it.

Through employment for wages such as day labor and work in the gravel, a few entrepreneurs have been able to put enough money aside to set up small stores. The local term, *kiosco,* is most descriptive of their size. There were four such enterprises in Cachama at the time we were there, although one was rented out by its curioso owner to a criollo. The inventory in these stores is never great, but one can count on finding two or three kinds of soft drinks, canned fish, bread, matches, salt, macaroni and candles. White rum, which is never in evidence, is probably handled as an under-the-counter item in all the stores. Other items, luxuries such as oil, coffee, yarn and patent medicines are sometimes available there, too. The stores also handle small quantities of produce from local conucos. Almost always a raceme of bananas and a little braided *cogollo,* moriche fiber used in making twine and hammocks, will be found hanging from the ceilings. Credit is allowed, profits are not great, and sometimes the store owner is unable to buy all the stock he would like. Still the stores appear to be worth the while of their owners. None of the existing stores ceased to operate, although no new stores opened for business during the period of nine months when we were able to observe them. The most successful store seemed to be that of Francisco Aray. As stated above, he is a progressive individual, and also extremely hard-working. One of the motivations for seeking work at the brick plant in El Tigre may have been an overextension of credit in his store. The store itself appeared to be somewhat better stocked as soon as Francisco began to bring home weekly wages.

The growth of towns in the area of Cachama, a general increase in commercial activity, and the economic changes discussed above have all contributed to a number of superficial cultural changes, mostly in the realm of material culture. Many items, formerly unavailable, are now readily available in the towns. In addition, there have also been some minor changes in taste. Probably the two items most desired in Cachama are a bicycle and a "zinc" (really aluminum) roof. Bicycles have certain obvious advantages. They definitely increase one's mobility, even though it is still a good bicycle ride to the towns. Furthermore, bicycles can go almost anywhere within the community that one can go on foot, although extensive travel away from the roads might be difficult. In spite of a good deal of wear and tear on tires, almost anyone can afford a bicycle if he sets his mind to it. Their cost runs from Bs. 100 to Bs. 200.

The *techos de zinc* have less obvious advantages to the average Cachaman. They are hot, noisy, and are frequently ripped off by the continually stiff breezes which blow across the Mesas. True, they are free of the dangerous vermin which often infest the thatch roof, but I doubt that the average Karinya considers such vermin more than a minor nuisance. Some people do maintain it is easier to buy one or two dozen aluminum sheets and put them on their roof, than it is to collect 2000-3000 moriche fronds and lay them on one by one. But primarily such metal roofs seem to serve as a status symbol. They are indicative of one's state of being "civilized" and educated. Although metal roofs probably cost no more than Bs. 100-200, they do proclaim to the community that one has that much money to spend.

A contrary trend is the progressive loss of a traditional status symbol — the colorful "typical" Karinya costume. Today there is an increasing tendency to replace it with criollo attire. The younger people would probably have done so under any circumstances since they tend to be ashamed of their Indian background and consciously attempt to conceal it, particularly when they are visiting the towns. On the other hand, most of the older people who have changed their style of dress would not have given up the traditional dress so readily had it not been for the general inflationary conditions of Venezuela. It is much more expensive to buy good quality yard goods with which to make the traditional dress. Even after one has the materials it takes a week of steady hand sewing to put the dress together. (A few people have hand-crank sewing machines, but they are unsatisfactory for a really fine job on the traditional costume.) Most of the women have discovered that it is much cheaper to buy ready-made house dresses, than to hand-sew their own traditional costume. Even those that have clung to the traditional cut have been forced to resort to cheap prints, since they can no longer afford the heavy cloth and solid colors which are not only customary, but much more attractive. In the case of the costume, economic factors seem to have played as large a role in promoting change, as did status considerations.

A number of other goods, available in the towns, have also proven to be cheaper, more satisfactory, or more convenient than local items. As mentioned above, enamel and iron cooking ware and eating utensils have for the most part replaced pottery dishes. The former are less fragile and also easier to obtain when needed. Pottery is only available during the dry season, and then only when the potter feels motivated to work, a distinctly inconvenient situation. Kerosene is used in limited amounts, mostly to provide weak illumination inside the house at night. Hardly anyone cooks regularly with kerosene, though it may be resorted to in an emergency.

Again, contact with the towns has provided a slightly more varied diet. One can get both canned fish and fresh ocean fish. Soft drinks and macaroni have both become important parts of the diet. On the other hand, such typical criollo foodstuffs as *papelón* (raw cane sugar), Quaker Oats and coffee are rarely bought, presumably because of their expense. Powdered milk is unheard of in Cachama (though it is a common purchase in Mamo).

The "something-for-nothing" attitude, mentioned above as one factor in the centripetal tendencies keeping people resident on tribal land, is also evident in relations with outsiders. The Cachaman figures it never hurts to ask for something, he just might get it. Thus an outsider will be asked for almost every small item he possesses, even to the clothing which he is wearing! While this is probably a Karinya attitude of long standing, the development of the oil industry in the area has only contributed to making it worthwhile. The relatively well-paid oil workers think nothing of giving small items away, particularly if they belong to the company anyway. Furthermore, several service organizations composed of company employees have undertaken such "charitable" activities as distributing toys at Christmastime and providing clothing for children enrolled in school. Even the schoolhouse in Guanipa neighborhood was constructed by the Rotary Club of El Tigre. Needless to say, this only encourages the "something-for-nothing" attitude in relations with outsiders. In fact, some individuals have been known to demand even more upon receipt of their share of such gifts. The general tendency toward improvidence is clearly expressed in the attitude of the Cachamans toward this largesse. In most cases these gifts are ruined or destroyed within a couple of weeks. But then what does it matter? It cost nothing, and more will be forthcoming at the next distribution. A token payment for such "gifts" would probably suffice to develop quite a different attitude toward their acquisition and use.

Contact with the towns has introduced at least one completely new culture complex. This is the celebration of the Christmas holidays (Las Pascuas). The Cachamans say of Christmas, "This isn't one of our fiestas. It is celebrated in the towns." Yet for a period of about two weeks, work in Cachama comes to a virtual standstill. Families wander about the community, visiting their kinsmen. The men do considerable drinking, playing of the cuatro, and singing. From the way this holiday season is celebrated it is evident that Christmas truly is not one of the traditional Karinya fiestas. There is little point to the so-called celebration, except that no one does any work. Also the widespread Venezuelan custom of "pidiendo aguinaldos" has been adopted. This is based on the premise that it is better to receive than to give, and is wholly consistent with the mendicant attitude just discussed. The Cachamans miss no opportunity of asking every outsider for a "Christmas gift." However, even they seem to be aware that there is little point to the holiday, because they appear to grow quite tired of the general inactivity by the end of the period on January 6, the Day of the Kings. In fact many seem bored with the whole affair before New Years. Although this new custom involves a fairly complex set of behavior patterns, it is apparent from the manner in which the Cachamans celebrate it that it has not become a very integral part of their culture. The observance of the Christmas holidays could be abandoned any time without causing much disturbance in the rest of the local culture.

It is clear that numerous changes in economic activities have been introduced to the Cachamans, but thus far their impact has been no more than superficial. Certain opportunities, such as day and contract labor, have provided some people with more spending money. But in spite of an indubitable increase in cash income, there has been no radical increase in *actual* income. Employment for wages has merely substituted a cash income for the subsistence one would formerly have obtained from the soil. Most of the men earning wages are doing so because they lack fields of their own. There is a direct correlation between growing scarcity of certain local goods (fish, basketry, etc.) and increased purchase of such items (canned sardines, basketry) which are usually more expensive in the towns. Most increases in income have been met by increased expenses (purchases of foodstuffs, transportation to the towns, cultivation of savanna lands). Practically the only evidence for an increase in standard of living is to be found in the frequent ownership of bicycles and "zinc" roofs. It has already been indicated how little this actually represents.

However, even though changes to date have been mostly superficial, a great many more economic choices are available to the average person. The way is open for profound and extensive changes to take place in a relatively short period of time, were the Cachamans to take advantage of their present opportunities. It would seem that failure to do so thus far is due to a continuing feeling of unfamiliarity and uncertainty with respect to the changes taking place around them. If and when they develop more self-confidence in the industrial and commercial world which has descended upon them, we may expect a greater adaptation to the new economic activities and a greater participation in available opportunities. From a strictly economic point of view the effect undoubtedly will be one of rapid assimilation into criollo culture. But for the present, it is mostly a matter of feeling one's way slowly before one can run the course rapidly.

Chapter 3

FAMILY

Kinship System

KARINYA KINSHIP is basically bifurcate merging, with Iroquois cousin terms. The system is presented diagrammatically in Figures I (male speaking), II (female speaking) and III (conjugal terms, male speaking). Where there are both address and reference terms for an individual, the former appears on the upper line, while the latter is indented one space on the lower line. If the lower term is not indented, this indicates that it is an alternate address term rather than being used for reference. Where one alternative is preferred over another, the subsidiary term is enclosed in parentheses. Obsolete terms are enclosed in brackets, as e.g., [pipi]. In those cases where a root morpheme can be identified, only the root is given here. The first person singular posessive prefix *a-* is usually attached to the following roots: *-nokti, -dümwü, -xsano;* and sometimes to *boxpi* (as *abóxpuli*) as well as to other forms.

Overlying the basic simplicity of the system are a number of complicating factors. The +2 generation fits the bifurcate merging pattern with the exception of FaMoBr. We obtained no indication from our informants that this individual was to be classed in any other way than as *tam., támuru.* On the other hand, this is consistent with the terminology in the −2 generation (SiSoSo = *pwari,* "grandchild"). On the +1 generation the slight modification of terms referring to FaBr and MoSi is in no way variant from a bifurcate merging pattern. With reference to the MoSi we were repeatedly informed, "No ve que uno siempre tiene dos madres?" And a similar, though less intense, attitude obtains with the FaBr.

The modifying term *akonyo* is said to mean "companion," he who accompanies. The most frequent explanation of the term was, "Siempre

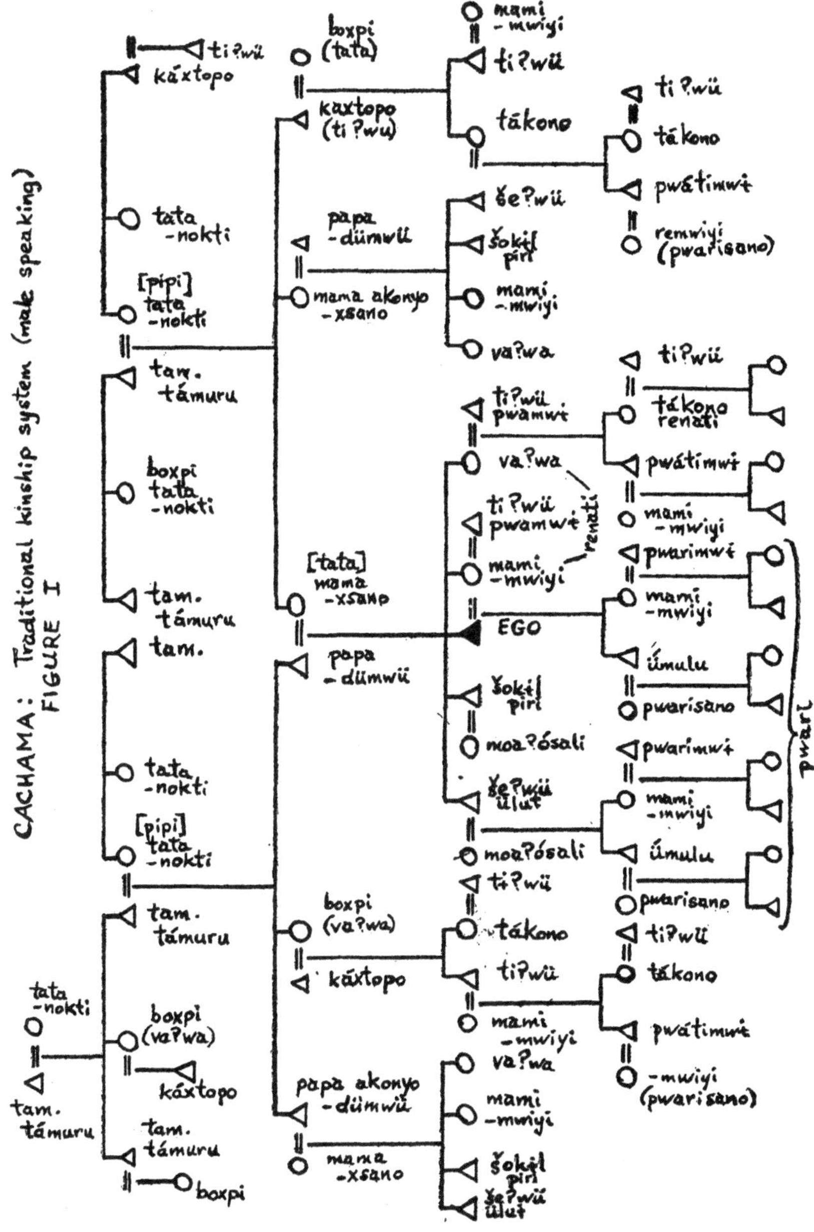

CACHAMA: Traditional kinship system (male speaking)
FIGURE I

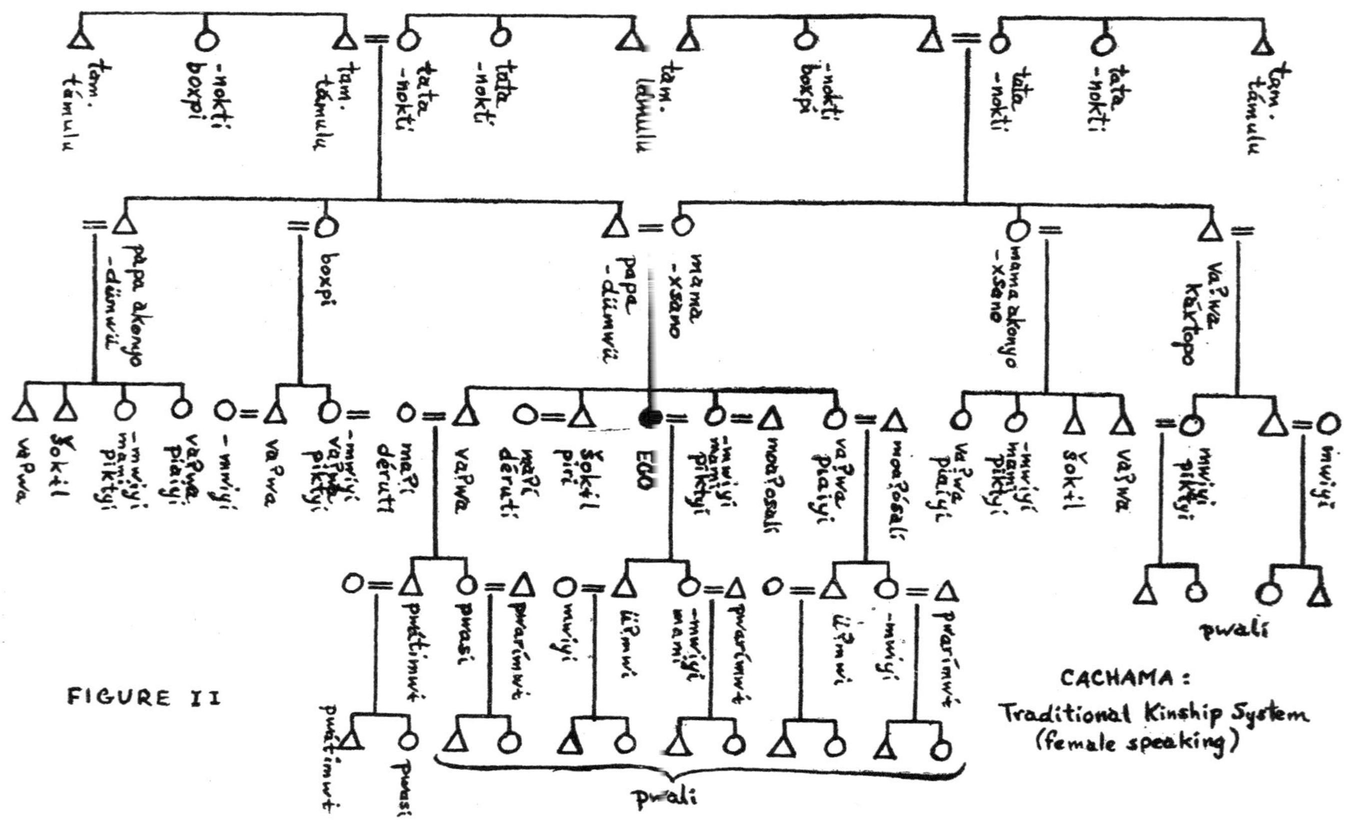

CACHAMA: Traditional Kinship System (female speaking)

FIGURE II

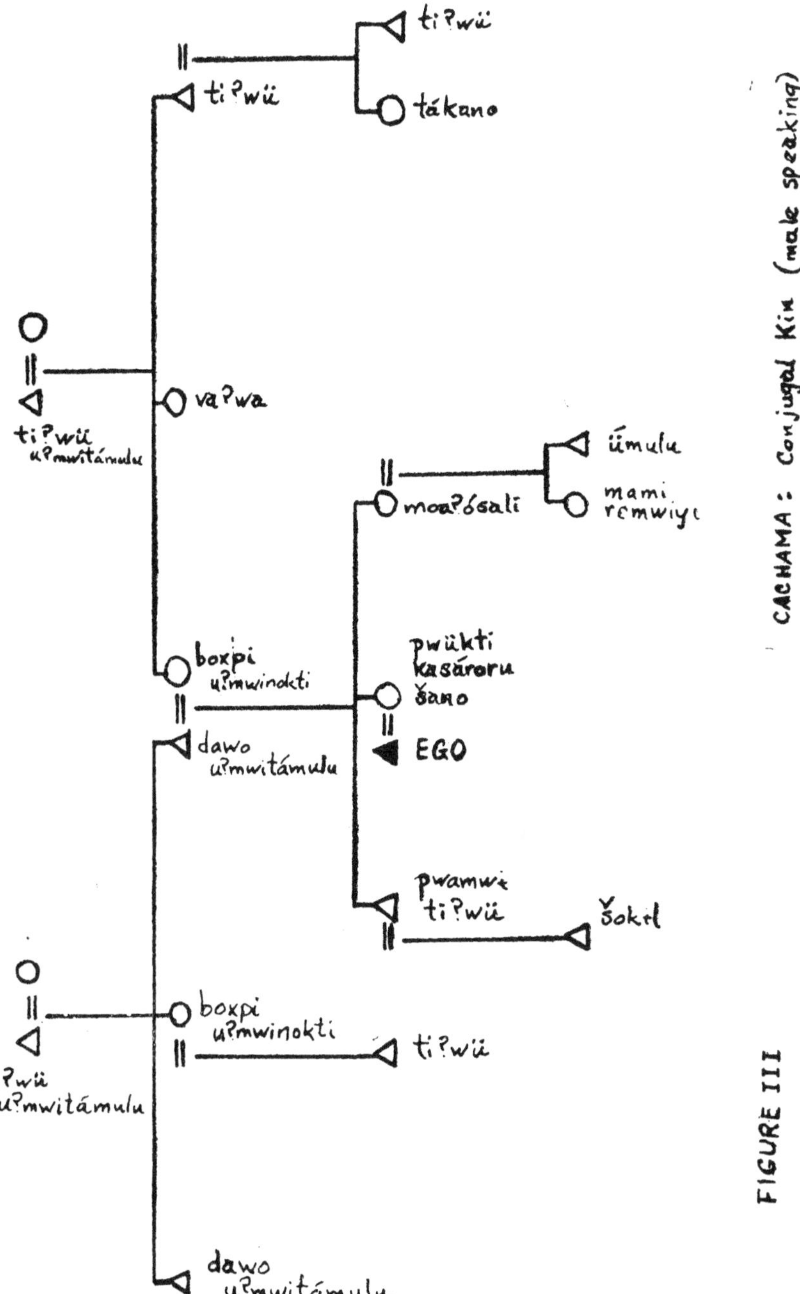

CACHAMA: Conjugal Kin (male speaking)

FIGURE III

van junto los dos." That is, Fa *(papa)* and FaBr *(papa akonyo)*, Mo *(mama)* and MoSi *(mama akonyo)* are always equated and in fact the same reference term is applied to both members within each pair.

Ego's generation is characterized by Iroquois cousin terminology, with cross cousins distinguished from parallel cousins, and the latter considered classificatory siblings. Sex and relative age are distinguished among all siblings, but there are address and reference terms only for the ElBr. YoSi is equated with Da and the term shokïl[1] which applies to YoBr is also extended to refer to a number of other junior kinsmen.

Only those terms which are distinct in the female-speaking terminology are diagrammed in Figure II. Because of spatial limitations the illustration of kinsmen in Figure I has been abbreviated on the −1 and −2 generations. However, the pattern should be sufficiently clear from the diagram. Offspring of parallel cousins are equivalent to those of siblings. Likewise the offspring of both maternal and paternal cross cousins are equivalent. Viewed alone, the −1 generation presents a simple system of bifurcate merging, but closer examination shows that SiCh are equated with cross cousins and cross cousins' children.

This pattern of crossing generations runs all through the kinship system of Cachama and can cause considerable confusion in any attempt at analysis. Theoretically SiDaCh should also be equated with SiCh, but all informants were very vague on these kinsmen and gave conflicting data, although the tendency was to consider them as *pwari,* or grandchildren. At an earlier time these probably were distinguished from grandchildren and equated with SiCh. Perhaps SiSoCh were also, but the indications are even less clear for this assumption.

What I have described above will be referred to hereafter as the "traditional kinship system." Change in Karinya kinship has come about in response to various forces. Probably the earliest change was the introduction and extension of terms which cross generational lines. Admittedly the traditional system which is described above is an idealized picture. More than likely generational crossing was inherent in the development of what I have called the traditional system. Forms such as *boxpi, vaʔwa, pwátimwï,* and *tákono* appear to be older terms which were formerly more limited, but were gradually extended to other kinsmen, often across generational lines.

[1]Although this did not appear to be distinct in any way from other kin terms in Cachama, informants in Mamo claim that it is not a kin term at all, but merely an affectionate nickname for any small boy.

Some of the observable changes seem best explained by internal drift. Thus *tata,* which originally applied to Mo, became attached to grandmother (MoMo, FaMo) as well and replaced *pipi,* the former term. Perhaps this was stimulated by the adoption of the Spanish term *mama* to address the mother. Certainly existence of the latter term accelerated breakdown in the association of *tata* with the mother. This process is repeating itself today, for the alternative terms "papa viejo" and "mama vieja" are commonly applied to all *tam.* and *tata* respectively as address terms.

Likewise *mami, (mamicha, mamanchi)* seems to have arisen spontaneously as an alternative term for all classificatory YoSi and Da. It remains as an alternative, however, and has not succeeded in replacing the older *mwiyi, remwiyi.*

More significant for our purposes are those changes which have come about in response to external forces. Increasing contact with Venezuelan criollos has made the ability to speak Spanish highly useful, if not absolutely necessary. In translating Karinya terms into Spanish many individuals also modify the denotation. Thus we were many times told that "*Boxpi* quiere decir tía," in which the informant clearly linked MoSi with FaSi.

Extension of the term *ti?wü* also seems due to criollo influence. In eastern Venezuela "compadre" is used as an address term to ingratiate oneself with acquaintances. "Cuñado" is likewise used broadly to mean "kinsman." The Cachamans use "compadre" when speaking with a criollo (and it is a matter of note that the compadrazgo is relatively unimportant among the Karinya), and apparently followed the criollo pattern further by adapting a Karinya term to be used in a manner paralleling the Venezuelan usage of "cuñado." Presumably *ti?wü* originally referred only to the cross cousins MoBrSo and FaSiSo. With cross-cousin marriage, however, this individual would also be the WiBr and thus a "cuñado" or brother-in-law. From there it was a natural extension to apply the term to all classificatory brothers-in-law, or the husbands of those women designated as *renati.*

On the other hand, use of criollo terms in Ego's generation has not conflicted with a general trend for the Karinya terms to change from Iroquois to Hawaiian types for cousins. A classificatory sibling, or parallel cousin, may be referred to as *hermano,* or *primo hermano,* whereas a cross cousin is referred to as *primo,* or *primo hermano.* In this way primo→primo hermano→hermano.

As a result the distinction between cross and parallel cousins has become less and the tendency has been increasingly to consider them all as equivalent to classificatory siblings, especially as this is consistent with the Cachamans' understanding of Spanish kinship terminology. As a matter of fact, the only significant distinction between the two sets of cousins today is that of residence.

Many of my informants denied the propriety of marrying a cousin, but there is some evidence that this was a permissible or even preferential form of marriage in the past (cf. GILLIN 1936: 95). One older woman asserted that this is a "very good" form of marriage, and she quoted a proverb — One eats his cousin's flesh in the first stew (La carne de la prima se come en el primer sancocho). — which suggests that intercourse with the cousin is not only permissible, but expected. Certainly in the traditional community interpersonal relations were so structured that the cousin was one of the few individuals with whom a young man could have sufficient intimacy that intercourse would have been possible. Furthermore, those attitudes rejecting cousin marriage seem to have their basis in Roman Catholic doctrine and criollo values. This union is described as a "sin," the sort of practise characteristic of animals rather people *(gente)*. This latter is a critical point among the Karinya, who wish to be considered *civilizado* and *gente* rather than *bruto* (stupid, uncultured). Usually they are eager to assume superficial innovations and practises which will mark them as being "civilized" even though there may be little or no fundamental change. For this reason I rather suspect the repeated assertion that one does not marry his cousin. As will be shown in detail below, actual practise also belies this.

In recent years numerous disputes have caused political and social disharmony to become so acute (see Chapter IV) that Cachama no longer functions as a community. The clan is the largest kin-type unit which remains functional to any great extent, but even on this level it has become so involved in political matters that there is little concern with other aspects of individual and group life. This, combined with increasing independence of the individual, has made it possible not only to marry more widely than formerly, but also more narrowly.

Broadening of marriage patterns has tended to broaden kin terms in every generation, leading to a generational type of terminology. This trend is almost complete on the +2 and −2 generations. On the other hand, as noted above, the attempt to adapt Spanish terminology to

Karinya kinship patterns has tended to favor lineal terms on the +1 generation. Only the −1 generation appears to have remained stable thus far. However, it seems likely that, consistent with the Hawaiian terminology of Ego's generation, the −1 generation will eventually become generational as well.

MARRIAGE

IN THE GREAT majority of cases marriages are consummated with non-relatives, or at least with kin so distant that, while some common ancestry may be recognized, their exact relationship is confused or unknown. From the structure of Cachaman kinship we might expect that cross-cousin marriage would be permissible, if not preferred. In actual fact, out of 126 current unions[2] there are only two with actual first cross cousins, both FaSiDa. There are two with classificatory maternal cross cousins, one of these could also be classified as a "SiDa," in addition to three more unions consummated with classificatory SiDa. This makes a total of seven unions with those kinswomen classified as *tákono.* Surprisingly enough these are outweighed by unions with parallel relatives of which there are five with first parallel cousins, one with a kinswoman who is both a classificatory "MoSi' and "FaSi," one with a classificatory "Si," one with a BrDa, and two with classificatory "BrDa," making a total of ten such unions. It is interesting that six of these occur in Guanipa neighborhood, occupied by the Maita clan, which is reputed to be a recent arrival diverging from traditional marriage practises, but two more have occurred in Tascabaña neighborhood, the stronghold of the Tamanaico and Machuca clans, which pride themselves on being the original settlers.

Girls may be married as young as eleven, or perhaps even younger (see Table III). María Medina reported that her husband's parents had asked for her at the age of nine, although her parents preferred to wait until she was "a formed woman" of thirteen. Since many Cachamans do not know their own age and many guesses had to be made in taking a census, the data may lack precision but the picture they provide is essen-

[2] "Conjugal union" is used freely here to describe the marital relationship since the great majority of couples are linked only in consensual union *(unión libre).*

TABLE III

CACHAMA: AGE AT *FIRST* CONJUGAL UNION

Present Age	11	12	13	14	15	16	17	18	19	20	21	22	23	24	25	26+	Total	Mean	Mode	Range
Men																				
10-19**				1	1 (4)*	(3)	4 (4)	1 (2)	(2)								7 (15)	16-17	17	14-19+
20-29		1	1	2	2	8	5	5	5	14 (1)	4 (1)	5 (2)	4		(1)		56 (5)	18.7	20	12-23
30-39		1	3	1	4	3	1	1		1	2	1		2	3	4	27	19.4	15	12-26+
40-49							1	1	2	2				1	1	3	11	21.8	—	17-26+
50+			2				2					1	1	2	1	3	12	21.3	—	13-26+
	TOTAL																113 (20)	—	—	12-26
Women																				
10-19**	1	3	5	10	11 (3)	6 (4)	9 (1)	1 (1)									46 (9)	15	15	11-18+
20-29	7	4	8	5	8	3	2	4	2		1						44	14.3	13/15	11-21
30-39	4	5	6	1	1	6		2	1	1		1	1?				29	14.8	13/16	11-22
40-49			1	1	3	1	3		4							1?	14	16.1	19	13-24
50+	1			3						2				1?			7	16.7	14	11-24
	TOTAL																140 (9)	—	—	11-24

* Figures in parentheses refer to unmarried individuals.
** Unmarried youths younger than 15 are not included.

tially correct. The modal age of marriage for women is about fifteen, while the mean appears to have dropped from 16 twenty-five years ago to less than 15 today. Men consistently marry at a somewhat later age, the mode being about 17. Again the mean has dropped from 21 twenty-five years ago to about 19 today. A drop in the age of marriage for men may indicate greater insecurity today than formerly. The only possible reason for the (apparent) lowered age of marriage for women is an increasing demand caused by the tendency for men to marry younger. Conjugal unions in Cachama are surprisingly stable, 76 per cent of the women and 69 per cent of the men having contracted no more than one (see Table IV). Those who live to be fifty or more seem certain to have two or more conjugal unions. Most interesting, however, is the increased number of both men and women who have had more than one union in the 30-39 age range. These are people who married some twenty years ago, just at the time that the oil companies began exploration and development in that area. The first right-of-way contract between Cachama and the companies was signed in 1947, fourteen years prior to our census. Forty-six per cent of the men in this category have had more than one conjugal union, as opposed to only 25 per cent in the 40-49 age bracket. Among the women 47 per cent who are between thirty and thirty-nine have had more than one conjugal union, while among those 40-49 the percentage is only 31. This seems a clear indication of the disruption caused by incursion of the oil companies in this area. The next younger age group (20-29) has not had sufficient time to form more than one conjugal union in most cases, or it may be that they have effected a somewhat better adaptation to the radical changes which have occurred all around them. This group is also notable for the increased number of unions with criollos as compared to other age brackets (see Table IV). Among women older than 29 a total of seven in all age brackets have had criollo unions. Among those 20-29 there are six, one of which has had unions with two different criollos. The number among the men is lesser, but even there three who are between 20 and 29 have *criolla* mates, whereas only four older than 29 have criolla unions. No permanent unions have been consummated with criollos by individuals younger than 20, although one youth and two girls have had passing affairs with them — in the latter two cases these were sufficient to produce children. Undoubtedly this has come about primarily becuase there are more criollos in the area, although criollo men are also attractive to some of the more acculturated Cachaman

TABLE IV

CACHAMA: *NUMBER* OF CONJUGAL UNIONS

Present Age	MEN 1	2	3	4	5	6	With criollos	WOMEN 1	2	3	4	5	6	With criollos
10-19	6	1					x	38	2					xx
20-29	50	5					3	38	6					7
30-39	14	12					2	16	11	2			1	3
40-49	8	3	1				1	9	2	2				1
50+	1	10	2		2		1	2	6					2
TOTAL	79	31	3	0	2	0	7	103	27	4	0	0	1	13

Each *x* represents an unstable affair.

TABLE V

CACHAMA: RESIDENCE *

			Matri-	*Uxori-*	*Patri-*	*Viri-*	*Sorori-*	*Fratri-*	*Filia-*	*Filio-*	*Neo-*	*Other*
-local	Male	50+		6(1)				1		1	10	
		30-49		24					1		15(1)	
		-29	24	39(1)	5		1					4
	Female	50+				4			1	1	2	
		30-49				24(1)					5	
		-29	24		3	30(2)		2			1	3
	Child.	-14	357		8							5
-vicinal	Male	50+						1				
		30-49	1		3		1					1
		-29	2		10		3	1				
	Female	50+					1					
		30-49	7		3		6	1				
		-29	25		3		3					1

(Numbers in parentheses refer to criollos).

* The classification of residence utilized here is based on FISCHER (1958).

girls becuase the former have more money to spend than most Cachaman men.

Even before unions with criollos became common, influences from the latter had begun a certain amount of cultural distortion and structural breakdown with respect to patterns of marriage and family formation. The traditional marriage ceremony of the Karinya involved an ordeal with wasps and ants. Later this was replaced to a large extent by the *compromiso,* where there was a formal agreement between the *parents* of the young couple. Neither of these types of marriage was recognized as legal by Venezuelan law, and doubtless they were deprecated by both civil and religious authorities. Legal marriage, however, is expensive and few Cachamans have the means to undertake either formal marriage ceremonies or the celebrations which are expected to accompany them. Six couples reported having been married through the civil ceremony, and only one claimed to have been united by both civil and religious observances.

Official and popular refusal to recognize traditional Karinya methods of consummating a marriage has made the consensual union the most common basis for new families of procreation and, eventually, new households. This being the case, individual wishes and romantic attractions have replaced parental desires and marriage arrangements as the basis for conjugal unions. It may be that this has also made the conjugal union less stable today than in the past, although it is difficult to verify this point.

THE HOUSEHOLD

I CONSIDER A household as comprising all those persons who share a common residence, and presumably share in production and distribution of food among its occupants, in care and maintenance of the residence, in child care and discipline, and the like. Within the matrilineal extended family a young married couple occasionally functions independently, but this is exceptional. Only in the infrequent instances of a sibling joint family (five cases) is it probable that there is a tendency toward independence of the individual segments based on the conjugal tie. The majority of households (69 out of 109) contain but a single nuclear family. Nonetheless, the household in Cachama is cyclical in character. This is shown by the fact that seventeen households are made up of a matrilineal extended family: usually a conjugal pair, their unmarried offspring, and one or more married children (usually a daughter) with their spouse(s) and offspring (usually no more than one). Four polygynous families also fit into this pattern; seven conjugal dyads and two maternal dyads[3] are in no way inconsistent with it. The full circle is completed outside the household. Usually a separate residence is constructed by a young married couple at or soon after the birth of their first child, but most frequently this residence is in the immediate vicinity of the wife's mother's house.

The census material illustrates these patterns very nicely. Out of 143 women 24 are matrilocal,[4] and all of them are under thirty years of age (see Table V). Twenty-five women under thirty are still matri-vicinal even though they occupy a residence separate from that of their mother. As a women becomes older matri-centered residence fades out; only seven women between 30 and 49 are matri-vicinal. Presumably this is because her own mother dies, while she in turn becomes the focus for her own daughters' residential behavior.

The fact cannot be overlooked that even more women are virilocal than are matrilocal and matri-vicinal. Fifty-four women under 50 are virilocal (as opposed to 56 who are matri-centered). In part this represents a continuation of household cycle, where the couple has been living together for a number of years and feels self-sufficient enough that the husband moves out to set up his own neo-local household essentially independent of kin ties. When a couple's daughters begin to marry and bring their new husbands home for the initial period of marriage the cycle is complete. In part, however, the relatively large number of virilocal women, especially those under thirty, seems to represent a weakening of the traditional matrilineally biased extended family, and perhaps even of the clan (but see discussion below, pp. 80-83).

---

[3]These dyads are "incomplete families" consisting of only husband and wife (conjugal dyad), mother and children (maternal dyad), or father and children (paternal dyad).

[4]In the analysis of residential patterns I have followed FISCHER (1958), where each individual is classified separately according to the immediate person who "sponsors" his presence in the household. Thus in a matrilineal society where the groom moves into the wife's natal household, *his* residence will be *uxori*local, while the bride's will be *matri*local.

Table VI

CACHAMA: FERTILITY & CHILDHOOD MORTALITY

Mothers Present Age	Nº	*Nº pregnancies* *Births*	*Miscarriages*	*Mortality* *Infant* -6 mo.	6 mo.-1 yr.	*Childhood* 1-5 yrs.	6-15 yrs.
50	7	52	2	2	1	3	2
30-49	47 1*	333 5*	10	28	9	7	3
-29	70 1*	220 3*	2	18	5	6	2
Causes of Death (as reported by informants)							
50	diarrhea				1	2	
	fever					1	1
	gastroenteritis			1			
	unknown			1			1
30-49	diarrhea			2	4	1	
	gastroenteritis			3		2	
	fever			3	1	1	2
	grippe			5	1		
	whooping cough			4		1	
	ulcer			2	1		
	tumor			1			
	cold (resfriado)			1			
	accident				1		
	stroke						1
	mozozuelo			1			
	"disipela"			1			
	measles				1		
	mumps					1	
	prenatal injury			1			
	unknown			4		1	
-29	whooping cough			3	1	1	
	mozozuelo			3			
	grippe			3			
	gastroenteritis			1	1	1	1
	fever			3	1		1
	diarrhea			1		1	
	measles					2	
	bronchitis				1		
	smallpox			1			
	unknown			3	1	1	

* Union of criolla and Indian.

Fertility and Health

THERE APPEARS to be no appreciable change in number of children born per mother (see Table VI). The data are complete only for those women under 50, but in the group 30-49, the majority of which are at or near the end of their child-bearing period, the average number of live births is 7.1, while the average number of deaths per mother in children under one year is 0.8. Compare this with an average number of live births of 3.1 among those women under thirty, the majority of whom are in the first half of their child-bearing period. Within this group the average number of deaths per mother in children under one year is 0.4.

While in Cachama my impression was one of improved infant and childhood health, but this is not borne out by the census data. If anything the evidence would indicate that there is a slight increase in infant deaths among the group of younger mothers, even though medical attention and medicines are more available than previously. The difficulty is not that medical attention is available, but the conditions under which it is available. Obtaining medical aid means making a trip to one of the nearby towns, waiting a half day or more, often having to stand the whole time, for only brief attention from an overworked doctor or nurse. In severe cases a child may be removed from his mother and hospitalized, the mother and other kin being restricted to seeing the child only during visiting hours. The end result is that medical attention is rarely sought for the ill as the conditions under which it may be obtained are extremely distasteful to most Cachamans. The actual causes of infant death have not changed appreciably, with the one exception of *mozozuelo (tetanus neonorum),* which has increased in frequency according to the reports of informants. This is surprising, since at least some of the midwives have recently adopted more hygienic techniques in the delivery of infants.

Another factor which undoubtedly contributes to poor health and mortality among children is the generally inadequate diet in Cachama. Meals consist primarily of manioc bread and starchy vegetables raised in the fields. There is insufficient protein in the diet. Few fish are obtained in local streams, game is even more rare. Legumes are eaten irregularly. Milk is unknown. Most of the protein consumed is in the form of canned fish, or occasional purchases of fresh meat or fish, but this does not appear to provide an adequate supply.

As a consequence children are listless and uninterested in their surroundings. I have seen infants of a year or more in age sit quietly in one place for minutes, or even hours, whereas a North American infant of comparable age hardly remains still for a moment. Nor is there much interaction between infants and others, except for mothers and older sisters. They engage in very little active play. Infections of the upper respiratory tract are common and seem to be hard to cure. The same is true of intestinal parasites. In general Cachaman children are lacking in energy, expression of personality seems to be depressed, and they have a rather low resistance to infection.

Functions of the Family

THE HOUSEHOLD is the basic economic unit in Cachama, although the ramage is also of economic importance. Most of the agricultural labor, from clearing and draining the fields to planting and weeding, is undertaken by the men, although women and children do most of the harvesting. There is some reason to believe that in the past, when men devoted themselves much more to war and trade, a greater proportion of the agricultural labor was in the hands of the women, the men being concerned with little more than clearing new fields. Men likewise assume the occasional task of house building which also is heavy labor. It is the woman's duty to prepare the produce of the field, and the task of processing manioc, the principle staple, into edible form is indeed an arduous one. This, combined with the care of house and children leaves time for little else except the manufacture of hammocks.

The dividing line between men's and women's work is not actually so rigid as is indicated here, for there is a good deal of cooperation in many activities. The primary duties of each are as I have described them, but a woman frequently accompanies her husband to the field where she assists him with the lighter labor, such as planting and weeding. In house-building she may assist with plastering of the walls, although the heavy work of erecting the house frame is left wholly to the men. On the other hand a man will help in harvesting the crops, the whole family works together in peeling manioc tubers, pressing the poisonous juice from the grated tubers is frequently relegated to the men, and a man sometimes distributes the baked manioc bread (cassava) in the sun to dry, as fast as his wife turns them off the griddle. The important thing here, however, is that in all such cooperative activities they are defined *primarily* as men's work or as women's work. The opposite sex may assist the individual primarily responsible for their completion, but such duties are so defined that the opposite sex would never, or almost never, undertake them alone. He remains auxiliary to their proper performance.

As children become older they relieve their parents of numerous familial tasks. Girls in particular take over much of the responsibility for cooking and keeping house. Women with a couple of adolescent daughters are often able to enjoy a good deal of leisure.

Women are also attaining a new economic importance, though for the most part this remains within the context of the family. For example, the woman is indispensable in processing manioc tubers into cassava bread which can be sold in the towns. Hammocks, which are in such great demand, are mostly woven by women. At least one case where a woman hired herself out for several days "wage labor" came to our attention. In this instance she was processing the manioc of a criollo, which he in turn sold in the towns.

Even children can now make a significant economic contribution. Single young men who have any outside income are expected to turn most or all of it over to their mothers. Petra Aray, a progressive young woman from a progressive family, told of the financial straits her mother faced at the death of her father. Though only nine years old at the time, Petra and her sister were placed with criollo families in Puerto La Cruz. All the money Petra earned for her assistance in domestic tasks was sent to her mother to help pay for food and clothing for her younger siblings. Though it is unlikely that many Cachaman families would go so far as to send their children out of the home for long periods of time, the example of Petra and her sister are indicative of the felt "duty" of children in terms of contributing all income to their parents (especially the mother) until such time as they have achieved the independent status of a "married" adult.

Nonetheless, the economic activities of the average family are still controlled by the male head of the household. No hammocks can be woven for sale unless the man cuts the green leaves of the moriche, from which the fiber is drawn; and only men can string the supporting cords at the two ends of the hammock net. Furthermore, it is the man who handles all errands and the sale of hammocks, cassava and other produce in the towns. A woman may accompany her husband on such trips, but she would never undertake to sell such items herself. Often, in fact, a woman will refuse to sell them at home in the absence of her husband.

On the other hand, it is possible in Cachama for a strongwilled female to assert herself with a good deal of success. Indeed, those women who have been most influenced by modern developments have greater independence of action than those which are more tradition-oriented. Nonetheless, women remain subordinate to men. The traditional woman is expected to be submissive, retiring, hard-working, and attentive to the needs of her husband and other members of the family. She is *not* supposed to be friendly or even communicative with strangers, be they criollo or Indian. Children may even hide on the approach of strangers. Adult women will usually receive a stranger in their dooryard, but remain highly uncommunicative as to their husband's where-abouts, their own name, or any other detailed information. In conducting a census I found it extremely difficult to obtain any information when the man of the house was absent. As one woman explained, "Women are ignorant. They don't understand about these things. A woman might commit (her family) to something without realizing it. When her husband came home and found it out, he would be very angry." It's better not to say anything, and strangers should be discouraged in every way possible from any scheme which they might be pursuing. The traditional woman depends on her mate to deal with the world beyond the local community, and sometimes beyond her own clan.

Of course, adult women are rarely or never completely alone in the house. There are always children around. A young woman who lacks children, or whose children are yet small, is still living in the vicinity of her mother and sisters.

Even today a woman has only infrequent contacts with any individuals beyond those belonging to her own localized clan. Her chances of meeting them during a trip to the towns are as great as those of an encounter on the occasion of a funeral or a town meeting, none of these providing much opportunity for intimate exchange.

Children are closest to their mothers, whom they "love and respect" all their life. Love and respect for the father is said to be mixed a little with fear, but only a little. Patterns of child-rearing and discipline are certainly beginning to change. Traditionally, small children are never disciplined until they reach the age of six or seven. Infants are fondled, and nursed a good deal by their mothers, but they begin to be ignored about the time they start to walk. After they are weaned, which may be anytime between fourteen and twenty-four months, infants are left to the care of older siblings, whose primary duty is to keep them out of the way, and away from harm. It is said that small children "don't know what they're doing," and that discipline is to no avail, since they don't understand it until six or seven anyway. Partly on this account corporal punishment is extremely rare in Cachama. The demands and misdeeds of children are ignored rather than being rewarded or punished. It is possible that this has a good deal to do with childhood personality, since children are less active and extroverted in Cachama than in Mamo or in criollo communities. They never fight nor quarrel. If one is struck by another child, he rarely strikes back. In all fairness, however, I should stress that the differences may be as much due to the differences in diet mentioned above, as to differences in child-training.

This pattern remains characteristic of the majority in Cachama. But there is a small group of better educated individuals oriented to the criollos and the towns, which has quite different ideas about child-rearing. Petra Aray believes children should be spanked when disobedient, and Miguel Martínez added that, "He who doesn't punish his child doesn't love him." These two are both literate and very progressive in outlook. Furthermore, they feel that obtaining an education for their children in the public schools is an express duty incumbent upon the conscientious modern parent. A greater number have not appreciably altered their own practises of child-training, but they do agree that schooling and literacy are desirable for their children. They see a variety of advantages: getting along better in the modern world, getting a good job out of the heat of the sun (usually they are thinking of a clerical position, or that of a taxi-driver), protecting oneself from swindlers and shysters, etc. (Overt affirmations are not always strongly supported by value orientations as will be pointed out in Chapter V). Unfortunately many of those who so firmly emphasize the importance of education are rather lax in enforcing their children's regular attendance at school. In this they express no more firmness than they do in home discipline. There seems to be a direct relationship between degreee of criollo influence, firmness of home discipline, and the actual amount of education attained by one's offspring.

Attendance at school has made it possible for children to be somewhat freer in their activities and doubtless has fostered a slightly greater sense of independence and even responsibility among them. However, girls who live beyond the immediate vicinity of the school rarely attend on days when they would have to walk to school unaccompanied. They are still expected to stay close to home. Even so, girls who have not attended school are much more shy and retiring than are those who have. Boys, of course, have always been much more independent. Even so, the ability to read and write can sometimes make a real difference. Twelve-year old Ramón Celestino has been given a great deal of responsibility in the operation of his parents' little store, since he is literate and they are not. At times he is left home alone to operate the store in his parents absence.

RAMAGES

DUE TO THE PREVAILING matrilineal bias in Cachama I have previously (SCHWERIN 1963, 1964) identified that kin group next larger than the household as a matrilineage. Intensive analysis, however, shows that membership in these groups is optatively ambilateral. Their structure therefore, more nearly approximates that of the ramage (as defined by MURDOCK 1960: 11, also see FIRTH 1957). As social units they are significant both spatially and operationally.

At marriage it is customary for the groom to move to the home of his bride's parents. Here the young couple remains for a year or so, or until the birth of their first child, at which time they construct a separate house *in the vicinity of the wife's mother's house* (hence use of the suffix "-vicinal," as in matri-vicinal, sorori-vicinal, etc., where residence in proximity to another kinsman appears to be functionally significant, see CARRASCO 1963). This practise indicates a minimum of change from the ancient custom of inhabiting a large communal house. My guess is that in former times a daughter would usually move with her spouse to a separate apartment in the communal house at the time of their marriage. Disappearance of the communal house meant that movement of the daughter and her husband is delayed for a time, but when it does occur, the pair continues to reside in the immediate vicinity of the wife's mother and sisters.

The resultant cluster of households comprising three generations —a mother and several daughters and their families— is what I have previously referred to as a matrilineage. Sometimes, however, it is the sons who remain with or near their family of orientation at marriage, drawing their spouses away from their maternal homes. This occurs with sufficient frequency that the pattern is better described as ambilocal/

ambilineal. This three generation kin group is the one which is functionally active on a day to day basis and which I shall henceforth refer to as a minimal ramage. When in-marrying spouses are included, it is best designated as an extended family.

The minimal ramage composed of María Maita and her offspring offers a particularly clear picture of the predominantly matrilineal basis of residence patterns. The diagram (Fig. IV, cf. also Map III and Fig. VI) presents a schematic picture of the inter-relation between

Figure IV

MINIMAL RAMAGE OF MARIA MAITA

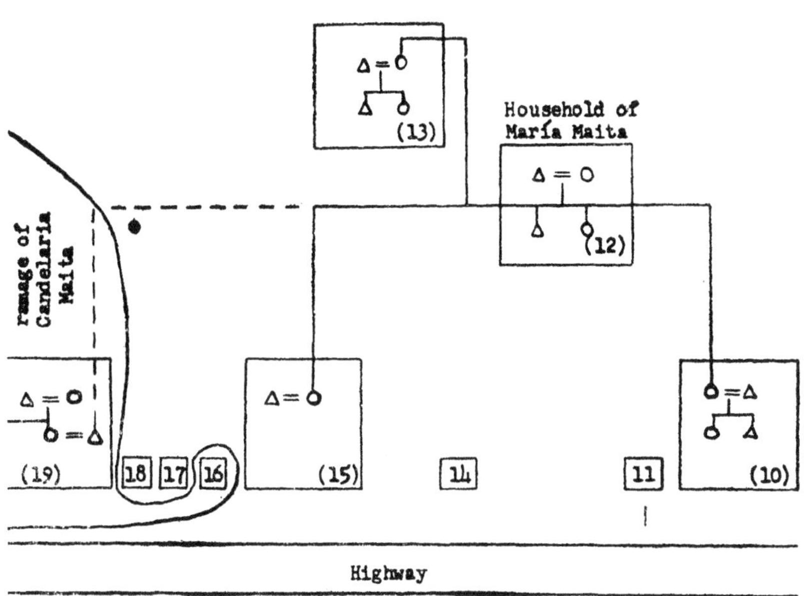

spatial proximity and kin ties among the households which make up the ramage. Three daughters have settled with their husbands in the immediate vicinity of their mother's household, By marrying his MoSiDaDa, her son Gregorio has assured his continued residence nearby. (The empty boxes represent the location of households not directly related to this minimal ramage.) In at least three distinct ramages of Tamanaicos, however, it is the sons who have maintained *patri*-vicinal residence. Various intermediate combinations are to be observed in other ramages. Nonetheless, the prevailing bias continues to be toward matrilineality.

For the most part the new, matrivicinal households never move very far away from their original location as they grow older, even though the mother which served as the original nucleus may have been dead for many years. However, the bonds of kinship which originally linked the "founding mothers" (or occasionally, fathers) of the present ramages continue to be recognized for several generations. Ideally they might be described as based on descent from a common ancestor lying four or more generations back, though in actual practise few people can name such ancestors. They only know that "My mother and her mother were sisters" (which term also includes parallel cousins). There is a tendency for members of such "minor ramages" to live together in the same neighborhood, even though there is some uncertainty as to who the common ancestor was or how many generations back the common link occurred. If we include the spouses who marry into these larger coresident kin groups it is legitimate to speak of an ambilocal clan (cf. MURDOCK 1960: 11). Such entities do not often function as a unit in Cachama, although they may be important in certain contexts. They would also appear to be the largest units recognized by the Cachamans which are based primarily on bonds of kinship.

It is a fact that most members of the minor ramage share a common surname, such as Maita, Aray, or Tamanaico, but this probably lacks any great significance. In my experience the common practise among Indians and criollos alike is for the children of a consensual union to take their mother's surname unless "recognized" by the father. If the parents are legally married, they generally take the father's surname. In Cachama, however, there is no great concern over this question and various other factors may determine which is used. Some informants were even found to use their father's surname on one occasion, their mother's on another.

In later life a conjugal couple will sometimes settle in a house site independently of external kin ties, but this occurs much less frequently than is suggested by the statistics. Out of 109 households, thirty-four are reported based on a neolocal individual. All eight of the neo-local females etiher lack close kinsmen or have located in the vicinity of more distant relatives. Six households are made up of individuals who have no close kin in Cachama (based on three women, three men). Only twelve of the men can be considered one hundred per cent neolocal in residence. For the remainder their choice of residence was clearly influenced in part by the location of other kinsmen. It is striking that no neolocal man is under thirty, and in fact, only three are less than thirty-five. This provides a clear indication that in Cachama one must develop a good deal of maturity and independence before he feels himself free to strike out on his own.

In many instances choice of residence is based primarily on one consideration, such as continuing matrilocality of the wife, but since the clans are agamous, it often means that one can continue to reside in the vicinity of other kinsmen as well. Thus the three sons and one daughter of Candelaria Maita all live near each other in Guanipa neighborhood *(vecindario),* yet two of the sons are classified as uxorilocal since they live with their wives in the vicinity of the wives' mothers (Fig. V, cf. also Map III).

Another example is Rafael Machuca (in Alfondo) who is classified as neolocal. Today he lives at a distance from both his own kinsmen (in Tascabaña) and those of his wife (in Guanipa and San Joaquín de Parire), but he has located his house quite near the site where his wife was reared as a child, and the husband of her foster sister, with whom she is quite close, later built his house in the same neighborhood. Numerous other factors may also affect choice of residence. A man may locate near his matrilineal kinsmen because his wife is criolla or his wife's mother lives in another Karinya community. Sometimes a married son will remain near a widowed mother where he can continue to provide for her. In some cases a particularly dominant father may induce his married sons to settle near him rather than in the vicinity of their wives' mothers. This is particularly frequent among the Tamanaicos and Machucas (principally in Tascabaña and Las Potocas) and has resulted in part from an attempt to maintain political support in the face of divergent factions in other parts of the community.

One might expect external influences to cause a modification in residence patterns, with neolocal residence becoming more common, but to date there is little to suggest such a change. Even Petra Aray and her sisters, who have been much influenced by criollo culture, remain matrivicinal in residence.

The extended family can be viewed as a group based on three dyadic relationships: parent-child (usually Mo-Da) where both members are adult, sibling (usually Si-Si), (together these two compose the minimal ramage), and conjugal (Wi-Hu). This group has functional

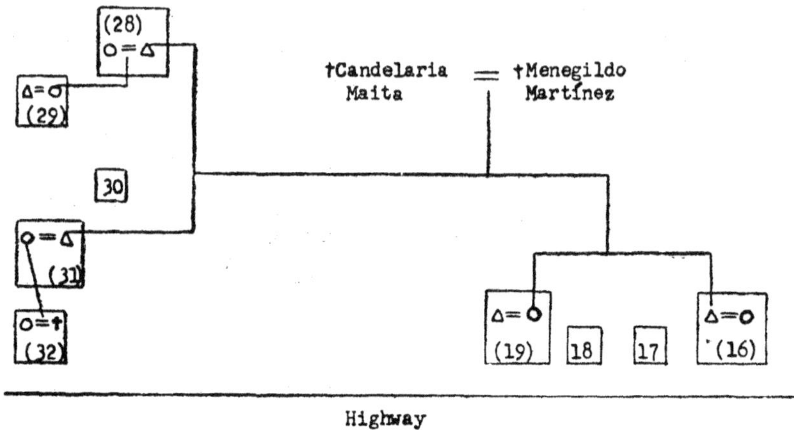

Figure V

reality in that it is the unit which cooperates on a day to day basis. Much of the work undertaken each day is carried on jointly by the men and women of the extended family. They work together in the fields, cooperate in collecting and preparing moriche fiber for the weaving of hammocks, and help each other in many other ways. One of their most important joint activities involves the harvesting of manioc tubers, their preparation for baking into bread, and the final process of baking. Ordinarily this process requires two days, and is one of the few activities which is usually undertaken by the whole group, since nearly everyone is involved at one or another stage of the process. Every member of the extended family — man, woman and child — who is large enough to wield a knife works together at peeling manioc tubers, an activity more unifying of the group than meals, since the men eat separately from the women. As a matter of fact meals are usually prepared separately in each household, although the women and children of each minimal ramage occasionally eat together in the absence of the adult men. Much leisure time is also spent together within the extended family. During the afternoon and evening the daughters and their families gravitate toward the house of the mother where they sit in the dooryard to converse, play and listen to the cuatro, or simply relax.

In-marrying men are clearly expected to labor for their father-in-law on demand, an informal sort of bride service. Patterns of land tenure in Cachama are not clear, but it appears that at least sometimes one can receive agricultural lands from his father-in-law. It *is* certain that the two may work together in draining and clearing new fields along the river bottoms. Gifts of food and other small items may also be exchanged with one's in-laws, as well as being sent back to the husband's own family of orientation. A young man's own father may also give him a plot of farm land before or at the time of marriage, but even this is not a well-established custom, since in the past there has always been sufficient land for one to clear a new plot in a convenient location.

Siblings who reside with different minimal ramages do not appear to work together with any exceptional frequency, although both brothers and sisters may assist each other in other ways. It is difficult to refuse a sibling's request for food, clothing, money or other gifts, and the average Cachaman feels a certain restraint in demanding repayment of such a loan. In the words of María M., "I've given lots of things to Francisco (her brother) without ever being paid. It grieves me (me da pena) to refuse him, and it grieves me to demand payment afterwards." The strength of sibling ties varies from one family to another, but in general they seem to remain strong for many years after the siblings have married. Two of María Medina's brothers live near her although their mother now lives across the Río Guanipa in the indigenous community of San Joaquín de Parire. María has been married for twenty-seven years while her brother Pedro has been married for about twenty-one. When María took ill, the second nearby brother and her husband vowed to give a fiesta if she recovered. Upon her improvement preparations were made for the fiesta on 8 December, the Day of the Immaculate Conception. All who attended the fiesta were members of María's extended family or that of her husband.

Nonetheless, sibling ties seem to be weakening among the younger generation. Exchange of gifts between siblings seems to be less frequent, and even María's own children have drawn the line at cooperative sharing within the extended family. They still exchange gifts of food or trinkets bought in the towns with their parents and mother-in-law, but they reserve all cash income obtained at day labor for their own use. Cash is a new economic resource for the Cachamans and its manner of exploitation is clearly separated from the traditional pattern of sharing economic goods such as produce, fish and game, and wild vegetable products. In a later section I will discuss how the Mameños have adhered to this customary practise in their adaptation to new economic resources.

It is probable that the minimal ramage has replaced an earlier matrilineage, where parallel cousins would have been inappropriate as spouses. This interpretation is supported by the traditional kinship terminology, which equates parallel cousins with siblings. The census revealed nine instances of endogamy within the minimal ramage (i.e., marriage with first cousins, which constitutes six per cent of all unions. The preponderance of parallel cousins in such unions —five cases— may be an indication of a certain amount of recent cultural distortion.) In at least three of these cases some embarrassment was expressed over the fact, although in three others the information was freely volunteered. Marriage with any type of cousin appears to be increasingly disapproved in Cachama, a phenomenon which is certainly related to an increased importance of ramage organization.

Sexual relations with members of one's own minimal ramage are either considered incestuous, or strongly disapproved (as with a grand mother or granddaughter). The one possible exception is the kinswoman designated *tákono* (SiDa, as well as female cross cousins). As indicated above the relationship with these relatives is not too clear, but it seems likely that both intercourse and marriage were permissible with them in the past, and perhaps were even preferential.

In the wife's ramage only women of her generation *(moaʔósali)* are permissible sexual partners, and may be taken as secondary wives if they are still single. (Adultery with *moaʔósali* may, of course, be cause for retribution on the part of the woman's huband).

Although the ramage has probably replaced a former matrilineage, the change is not as profound as it may seem. As pointed out above, there are numerous indications that in spite of a unilineal type of organization the Karinya have long recognized bilateral descent.[5]

Undoubtedly the ramage has come about as a consequence of the many disruptive influences which are impinging on Cachama. In spite

[5]Cf. BEFU (1963: 345-48) for further discussion of this type of organization.

of the rather gross disturbances which continue to be found in many areas of their social structure, particularly on the level of community organization, there is to date little or no evidence of transition toward breakdown in the ramage. It continues to be one of the stronger institutions. Undoubtedly this has come about as the result of an increased tendency toward cognation in the last thirty (or more) years. Such cognatic tendencies have been reinforced by the very factors which have produced breakdown in other spheres — criollo influences, new economic opportunities, political factionalism, and the like. It is possible, however, that certain of these influences may begin to have a distorting effect on the ramage within the next few years.

Criollo influences undoubtedly will increase, though they have been somewhat limited to date. Most present contacts between Indians and criollos are rather structured; as long as they remain so the influence of the latter will continue to be limited. Should such structuring of contacts disappear, it is difficult to predict just what repercussions will appear in Cachaman culture from criollo influences.

The distinctive attitude toward sharing of cash income may very well have a corrosive effect on the minimal ramage unless its utilization is redefined more or less in the manner worked out in Mamo.

It is doubtful that present political factionalism will have much disruptive effect on the ramages, since encouragement of ambilocal residence prevents dissipation of ramage and neighborhood membership. There is a growing tendency to avoid contracting unions across neighborhood, and particularly across factional, boundaries. Such unions will probably be increasingly discouraged, but this will only mean more neighborhood endogamous unions, where the partners can participate to some extent in more than one ramage at a time; and an increase in community exogamy, a process which is already under way in Tascabaña where there are three unions with criollos and eight with individuals from other Karinya communities (principally Santa Clara).

Opportunities for wage labor, on the other hand, might have the effect of reemphasizing the matrilineal nature of the kinship structure, since this work usually requires the man to be away from home a good deal. Nonetheless, where a contract for several weeks or months labor is accepted, a man usually takes his (nuclear) family with him. Should this kind of work become more common, it is possible that a neolocal rule of residence might result.

Clan and Neighborhood

THE TERM "CLAN" is used here to refer to a compromise kin group as defined by Murdock (1949: 68). At the present time neither endogamy nor exogamy appears to be particularly important so far as either neighborhood units or the community of Cachama as a whole is concerned (see Table VII). It is therefore difficult to consider these residential units as demes. In actual structure they most closely resemble the clan, and this is the term which will be used henceforth.

TABLE VII

PERCENTAGES OF ENDOGAMY/EXOGAMY (144 UNIONS) *

	Ramage %	*Clan* %	*Neighbor.* %	*Community* %	*Tribe* %
Endogamous	6	12	33	71.5	92
Exogamous	94	88	63	28.5	8
Undetermined			4		

* The apparent discrepancy with "present number of unions," cited above, is due to the fact that previous unions, as well as those of widowed persons were considered in this tabulation.

Murdock defines the clan as a residential unit of households comprised of individuals of one sex who are related through a unilineal rule of descent, their inmarrying spouses, and their dependents, i.e., a unit based on both kinship and residence. As is indicated above, descent in Cachama is ambilineal and although the minimal ramage tends toward matriliny, in actual fact it often includes siblings of both sexes. When in-marrying spouses are included the result is an "ambilocal clan" (MURDOCK 1960: 11).

A number of related minimal ramages combine in one neighborhood *(vecindario)* to form the consanguineal core of an ambilocal clan. Often, however, more than one such ambilocal clan is to be found in any one neighborhood. Thus Guanipa neighborhood includes both the Guanipa (Maita) and the Rancho Martínez clans. Again, Bajondo neighborhood is occupied mostly by members of the Martínez and Aray clans who live interspersed with each other. However, the Sesenta clan, which is also considered a part of Bajondo neighborhood is based on a core of

Aray siblings who are only distantly related to the other Arays in the neighborhood. Spatially, Sesenta is located at a distance from the other residences in Bajondo, but the half-dozen houses of which it is composed are clustered close together.

Map IV diagrams the structure of the Guanipa (Maita) clan. As can be seen, the majority of the individuals are members of two large minor ramages (based on four generations). The ambilocal pattern of residence as well as the ambilineal nature of ramage membership can easily be discerned by referring to the map and the skeleton genealogy (Fig. VI).

Simón Marcelo Martínez (32) is technically uxorilocal since he is living with a daughter of Francisca Maita. At the same time his mother, the widow Emilia Martínez, resides with him, while her daughter Carmen and *her* spouse reside next door (31). Luisa Carreño (21) is the daughter of Bartola Abaduca and Pedro Carreño, but her mother is dead. Her father, however, now lives with Francisca Maita (8) and Luisa has taken up residence in Guanipa neighborhood,[6] since her father is the nearest living relative. Juan Maita (11) has settled near his half sisters, since his wife is a criolla and she therefore lacks matrilineal kinsmen in the community. It is interesting that Juan has chosen to live near his sisters rather than his father, who is one of the wealthiest men in the community, although in part this is due to the availability of a house in Guanipa neighborhood.

I have already discussed how attachment to one minimal ramage does not necessarily preclude participation in another, particularly where marriage is endogamous within the neighborhood. Reference to Figures IV and V will aid in locating on the map some of the examples mentioned above.

The permissive character of ambilocal residence has been fully exploited in Tascabaña where political and egotistical factors have combined to retain the majority of married children of both sexes in their father's neighborhood (see Map V). Two clans are to be found in Tascabaña neighborhood — Tamanaico and Machuca.

Clan affiliation, however, appears to remain optative nonexclusive.

[6] Not to be confused with the Guanipa clan. The neighborhood *(vecindario)* is a geographical area, and each is clearly distinguished by the Cachamans. The clan is a sociological abstraction which appears to be conceptualized only vaguely by the Cachamans. In general clan and neighborhood are coterminous, but in some cases it is necessary to distinguish between them (see the discussion which follows).

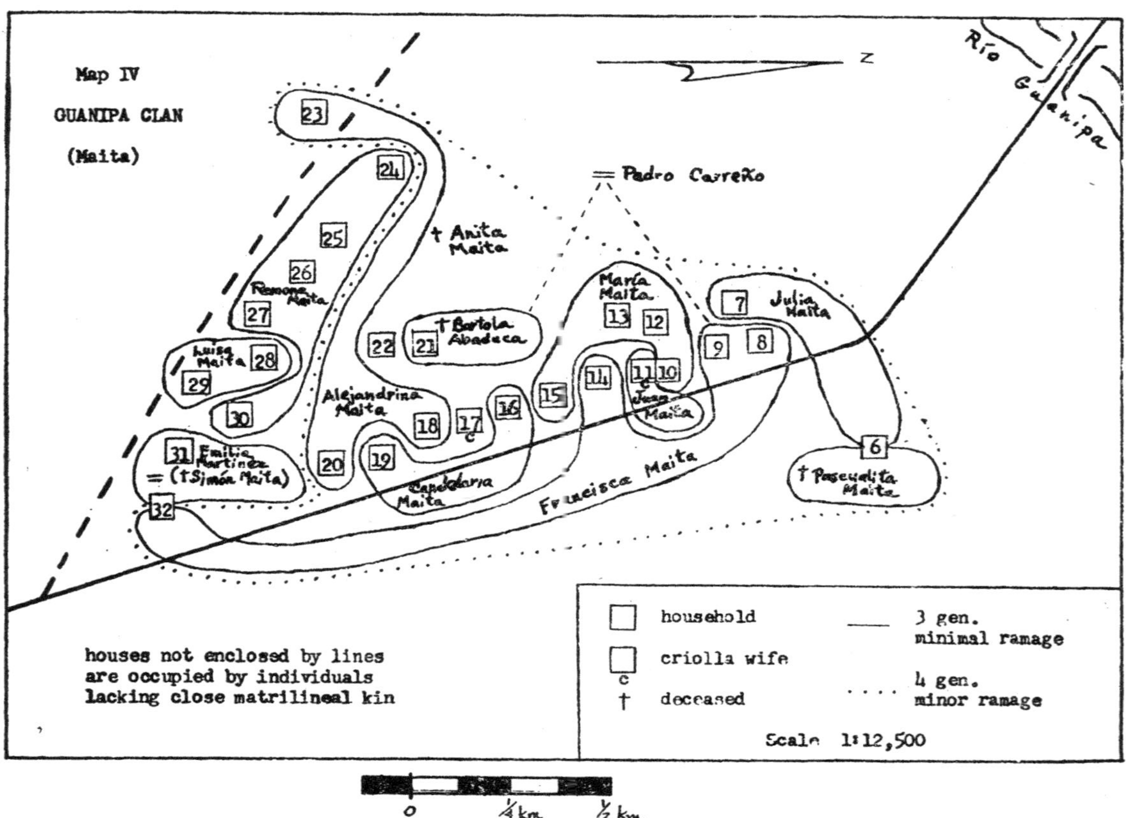
Map IV
GUANIPA CLAN
(Maita)
Río Guanipa
Z
Padro Carreño
† Anita Maita
Ramona Maita
Luisa Maita
† Bartola Abadeca
María Maita
Julia Maita
Alejandrina Maita
Juana Maita
Emilia Martinez
= († Simón Maita)
Candelaria Maita
Francisca Maita
† Pascualita Maita
23
24
25
26
27
28
29
30
31
32
22
21
20
19
18
17
16
15
14
13
12
11
10
9
8
7
6
c
household
criolla wife
deceased
3 gen.
minimal ramage
4 gen.
minor ramage
Scale 1:12,500
houses not enclosed by lines
are occupied by individuals
lacking close matrilineal kin
0
¼ km
½ km

Figure VI

SKELETON GENEALOGY - GUANIPA (MAITA) CLAN

(see Map IV)

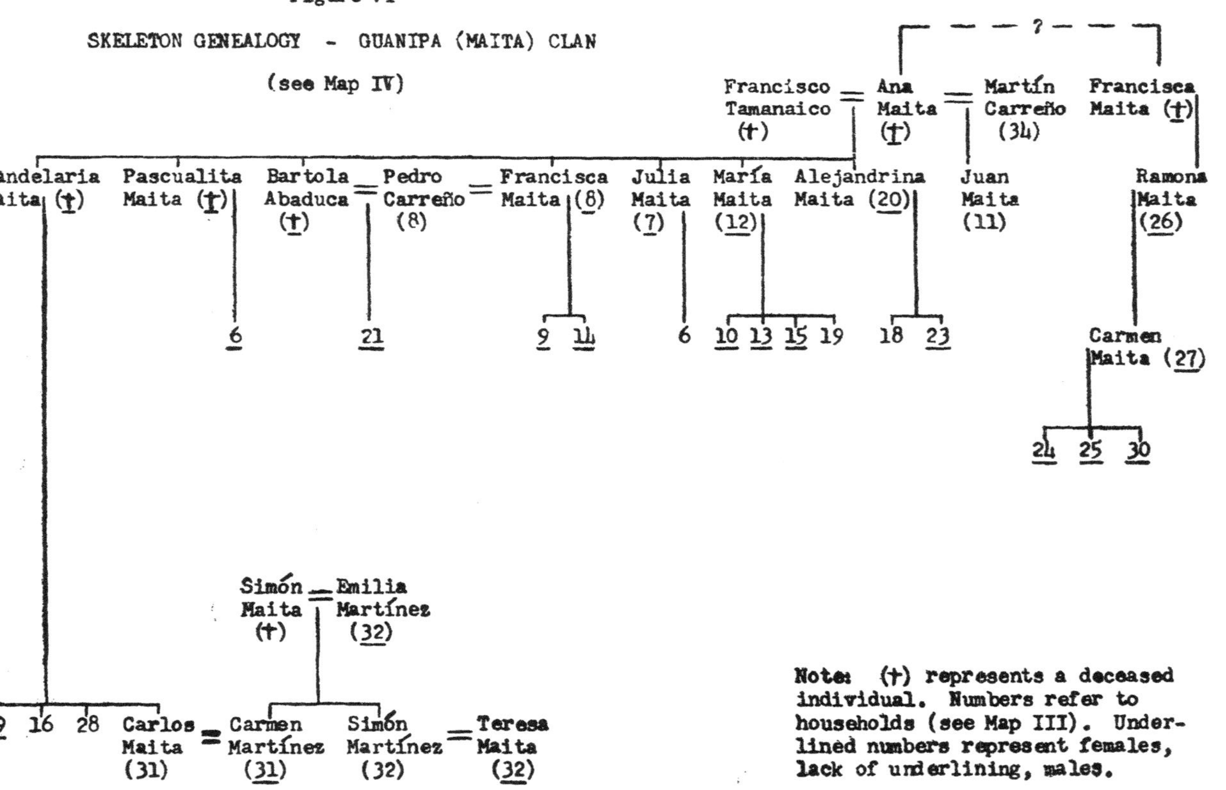

Note: (✝) represents a deceased individual. Numbers refer to households (see Map III). Underlined numbers represent females, lack of underlining, males.

José de la Cruz Tamanaico maintains two residences, one in Tascabaña, the other in Castillito neighborhood. In either place he has patrilineal kinsmen with whom he can affiliate. Undoubtedly the Medina siblings were first drawn to Alfondo neighborhood by their parents' residence there. Now their parents have returned to Mapiricure, but the siblings remain. There is some indication that the Martínezes once lived together in a single clan, but today there are two Martínez clans in rather widely separated neighborhoods (Bajondo and Guanipa). Two or three individuals are definitely known to have changed their residence from one to the other within the past few years.

The Cachamans are only vaguely aware of the clan as a unit but there is evidence that they feel it to be distinct from the neighborhood. Some good examples are to be seen in their clear recognition of Sesenta and Rancho Martínez (structurally clans) as distinct sub-units of Bajondo and Guanipa neighborhoods, respectively. Today the clan is not very important, although it does function as an occasional kin group (as when a private fiesta is held, or sometimes for *cayapas*). It seems probable that the importance of the clan must have been much greater in the past, when it may have been active in ritual as well as economic activities. In the days when warfare was still practised the clan may have been the important unit in small raiding parties, and a basis for organizing warriors on major expeditions.

It is a matter of note that clan boundaries are always contained within neighborhood boundaries. Never does one cut across the other. Today it is the neighborhood, rather than the clan, which is functionally important, even though the boundaries of the two frequently coincide. For example, Sesenta always aligns itself with the rest of Bajondo on any questions of major importance. Neighborhood boundaries mark the limits of familiar, or home territory. Everything beyond the neighborhood is alien, or if not alien, at least unfamiliar. Most visiting between households occurs within neighborhoods. Visits made to kinsmen who live in other neighborhoods are usually limited to special events such as a holiday. But even on the occasion of a major fiesta, such as Día de los Muertos, visiting between neighborhoods remains at a minimum.

Cayapas, or cooperative labor parties, which are convened when there is a great deal of work to do in the fields, almost always draw their personnel from other members of the neighborhood. The only major exception is Tascabaña which attempts to maintain the political allegiance of Castillito by exchanging cooperative labor. Fishing with *bar-*

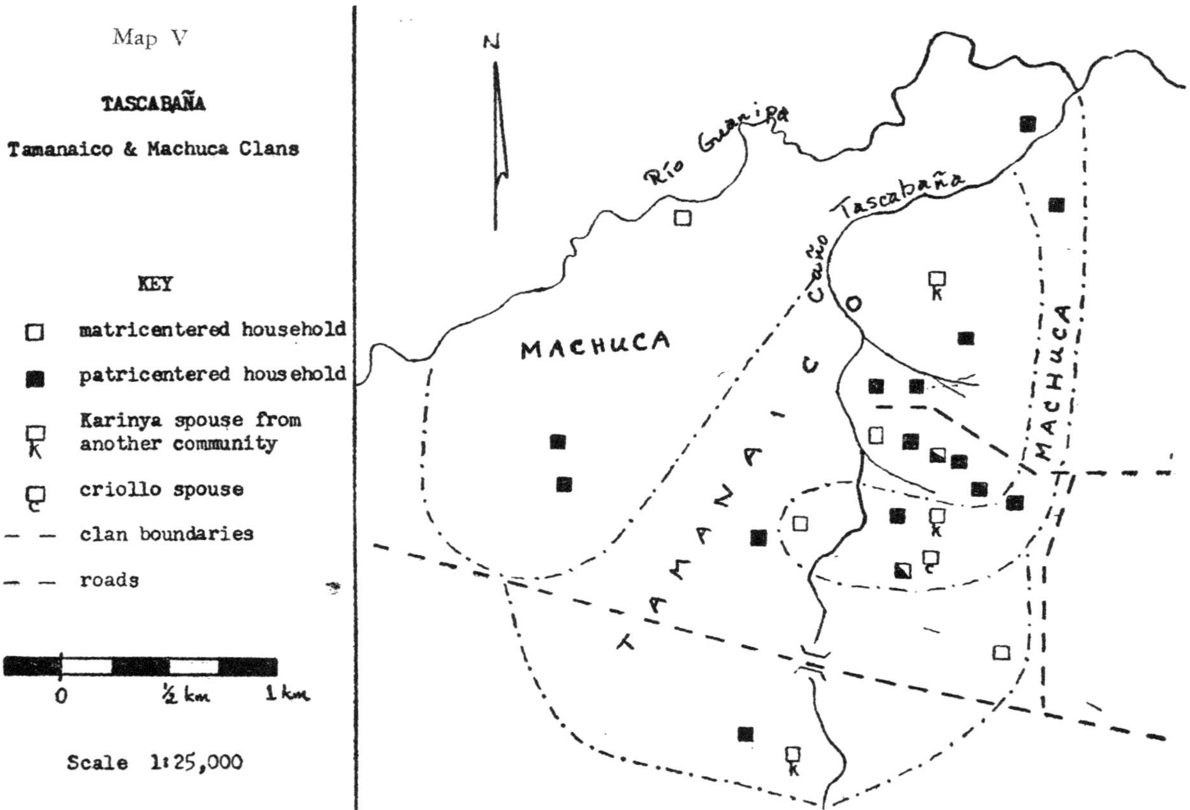
Map V
TASCABAÑA
Tamanaico & Machuca Clans
KEY
matricentered household
patricentered household
Karinya spouse from another community
criollo spouse
clan boundaries
roads
0
½ km
1 km
Scale 1:25,000
N
Río Guanipa
Caño Tascabaña
MACHUCA
TAMANAICO
MACHUCA
K
C

basco (fish poison) is also a neighborhood project. True it is that news of the venture travels rapidly by word of mouth and individuals from other neighborhoods often arrive to take part. But it is the men of a given neighborhood who plan the undertaking, collect and prepare the poison, and go out to the river selected in a body. Fishermen from other neighborhoods might be considered "party crashers" although their presence never seems to provoke active resentment.

An appreciable portion of marriages are neighborhood endogamous (one-third). After all, the majority of social contacts, through visiting and work alike, are with other members of the neighborhood. One is more likely to be attracted to a girl who he sees frequently than one who he rarely or never sees. With the present state of community factionalism, interneighborhood contacts will probably become even less frequent, with an increase in neighborhood endogamy being an expectable consequence.

When we arrived in Cachama there were two major factions which had split over differences of opinion on matters of internal politics. These two factions comprised the neighborhood of Tascabaña on the one hand, with Bajondo, Alfondo and Guanipa on the other, while Castillito attempted to straddle the fence (see Chap. IV). Las Potocas has long constituted a separate, and relatively insignificant political clique. During the course of the study further dissension developed, a new faction was organized, and the whole of Guanipa neighborhood broke away as a separate group. It is most significant that the lines of cleavage between factions closely followed neighborhood boundaries, even though close kin ties are to be found cutting across these boundaries. Residents of the Rancho Martínez clan within Guanipa neighborhood are closely related to the leader of the "Cachama" (Bajondo neighborhood, *et al*) faction, yet they threw their support to the leader of their own Guanipa neighborhood. Not a single instance was encountered in the whole of Cachama where there was an expression of individual or household disagreement with the majority opinion of the neighborhood.

What has happened is that the neighborhood has replaced the community as the major integrative unit. The only sense of belonging to Cachama as a community is the fact of having been born there, or of having one's fields on community territory. But it is the neighborhood which works together on matters of concern — a *cayapa,* fish poisoning, or protecting the felt interests of the neighborhood against the political machinations of other neighborhoods. One may be a Cachaman in name, but his allegiance is to the neighborhood, and he will seek to disparage the opposing neighborhoods in any way possible.

While the community has broken down as a social entity, there is no evidence of a similar process of deterioration within the neighborhood. Not only is the neighborhood strong as a social unit, its strength has increased in recent years as a direct result of political and social factionalism in the community. It is likely that the neighborhood will become an even stronger social unit in the near future, with divisions between neighborhoods becoming sharper as the ties linking them together become weaker and fewer.

Kinship ties, in the form of the ambilocal clan and the minimal ramage provide the basic social organization upon which the neighborhoods rest. In actual fact then, neighborhoods are also kin groups.

It is highly probable that Cachama has always had some form of cognatic structure in the past, but contact with criollos and rapid economic and technological change in recent years have resulted in increased emphasis on a cognatic form of social organization. Evolution in the direction of a ramage organization, rather than toward a bilateral kindred, has undoubtedly been encouraged by the continued importance of extended family groupings. Also consistent with this change is an increasing attitude of disapproval toward any form of cousin marriage, with a very low incidence of such unions. At the same time residence patterns have become increasingly ambilocal. Furthermore, Cachaman kinship terminology is tending toward a generational system (with Hawaiian cousin terms), even though there are some conflicting instances of lineal terms on the +1 generation (cf. MURDOCK 1960: 14). Unless political dissension becomes so acute as to break down Cachaman social institutions completely, we can expect the ramage and neighborhood structures to become more solidly integrated in the future. But as kin groups *clans* have lost much of their significance, and it is doubtful they will ever regain much importance. At the present time there is little to indicate the possibility that ramages, or clans, or neighborhoods can recombine to give functional viability to Cachama as a unified community.

CHAPTER 4

CACHAMA AS A COMMUNITY

POLITICAL ORGANIZATION in Cachama has changed considerably in recent years. Of the half-dozen elective officers reported by Alvarado (1956: 417) only the governor and the *segundo* (or *alguacil*) have survived to the present. Although the comisario is still an important local official, he is always a criollo in the two communities which we studied, and appears to be appointed by the *municipio* or *distrito* government. Of perhaps greater import for the political life of the community is the definitive separation of the hereditary leadership from the office of elected governor. Parallel with this there has been a progresive breakdown of the community with development of extensive factionalism which has served to isolate various segments of the community, making these smaller segments more important as integrative units than the community as a whole. These patterns of breakdown have been encouraged by the intervention of numerous non-Indians whose interests at best have not been wholly directed to Indian welfare. In the present stage of disorganization the future may see nothing but further breakdown, but it is also possible that some sort of equilibrium may be achieved which would prevent further deterioration.

LEADERSHIP

POLITICAL AUTHORITY in Cachama was vested in the hereditary cacique, who was traditionally elected to the office of governor year after year. It is doubtful that the average cacique had much authority in the community, for the most part he probably served only as a focus for the organization of communal activities, such as cultivation of fields, erection of a house, or fish poisoning. To judge from present-day attitudes, he and his house were also the focus for community fiestas and ceremonies. The present-day elected governor is still expected to provide drink, food, and entertainment on holidays, though he seldom does so. The ability to celebrate such festive occasions seems to have been made possible by gifts of food, game, livestock and other items which were presented to the cacique by his followers. Most likely such gifts were spontaneous and irregular (in spite of the assertion by one informant that each man in the community was expected to pay the cacique a bull calf once each year). A leader of this type could suggest, or direct, but was hardly in a position to give orders to his followers.

By combining the office of cacique with that of *pwüle* or shaman the community leader could greatly enhance his authority, for then he could control both supernatural power and temporal prestige. The most recent of the traditional caciques in Cachama were of this type. "El Viejo Yornaldo" Tamanaico, who is reputed to have lived to the venerable age of 112, is still remembered as a powerful *médico* who could cure or kill, and who regularly talked with the "masters" of the streams and the cliffs. His youngest son Pedrito[1] who succeeded him as cacique is also a famous and powerful *médico* or curioso.

"El Viejo Yornaldo" held the position of cacique for many years. Several informants claimed that he had been cacique ever since the Five Years War (1859-63). Sketchy as it is, the evidence suggests that the office could be inherited bilaterally by any of the cacique's male children or grandchildren. Toward the end of Yornaldo's life his youngest son Pedrito assumed the leadership. Pedrito remained as cacique from sometime in the late twenties, until 1941, when he was replaced by his half-sister's son, Francisquito, the daughter's son of "Viejo Yornaldo." It is not certain that Francisquito's succession followed traditional patterns since, according to all informants, he was *elected* to the office by majority vote of the men of the community.[2] Still he is usually identified as the "elder brother" of Pedrito, which would indicate that kinship ties and the traditional patterns were still considered to be important at that time.

Another factor served to enhance the authority of the traditional Karinya cacique. The ordinary Karinya had little contact with his Spa-

[1] For reasons which will become obvious, this and several other personal names which appear below are fictitious.

[2] Although the governor is democratically elected by the community, he must be confirmed in the office by the Prefect of the District.

nish-speaking criollo neighbors. In fact, until recent years few Karinya were even conversant with Spanish. As the officially recognized representative of the community the cacique served as the primary channel of contact between criollo and Indian. Thus he became the principal authority in matters concerning relations with the criollos; and this situation also gave him full control over innovation and culture change within his community.

Pedrito assumed community leadership during the Gómez regime, a time when *caudillismo* was rampant in Venezuela. He appears to have been less sympathetic to the needs of his community than he was to the furtherance of his own interests. After all, there was nothing in the political climate of the day to discourage such an attitude.

Thus, it is claimed that he would take other people's livestock and either butcher it, or sell it outright. The cacique of the neighboring Karinya community of Mapiricure charges that Pedrito once "sold" a child to a North American who took it away with her to the United States. In addition, there are numerous tales of his meddling with the monuments which mark community property lines. The most serious misdeed laid to Pedrito, however, was the sale of one square league of community lands, one-fourth of the total which was owned at that time. This act has been the basis for continuing conflict and dissension in Cachama down to the present. Since this has continued to be a major bone of contention for so many years, it is well to examine the transaction in detail, at least to the extent that it can be reconstructed from the memory of informants and the available records.

For some reason community lands were surveyed in 1928. Perhaps it was due to the Cachamans having lost their copy of the document giving them title to the land. If the crude map dated "Cantaura 9-22-1928," which I have seen in private files near Cachama is the legal record of this survey, the results were highly inaccurate, and probably useless for any legal purpose. Nonetheless, the surveyor demanded payment for his services, and the Indians were unable to meet the fee charged. Someone, most likely the surveyor, suggested that they sell a portion of their land in order to obtain the necessary funds. Two telegrams dated January 1929 (copies of which are also in the private files mentioned above) from governmental offices in the state capital of Barcelona indicate that the Cachamans were investigating the possibility of selling some or all of their lands. Although my informants indicated that there had been an initial resistance to selling any part of the community property, official transfer of ownership was recorded in the District Court at the end of July 1929. Nonetheless, the criollo purchaser appears to have felt insecure in his title to the land, since he had the document of sale officially recorded in the Registro Subalterno of the district in 1934 (Cantaura 1934). The bringing in of the discovery well in the nearby Oficina field the previous year (cf. LIEUWEN 1954: 63) may have been an important factor stimulating this attempt to strengthen his title. The sale contract, however, states that the community had sold "one league of land... in pure, perfect, irrevocable and quitclaim sale" (hemos dado en venta real, pura, perfecta e irrevocable... una legua de terreno... see Appendix C for full text of the document), for which they received the sum of Bs. 2,200. Expenses associated with the sale of the land were to be paid for out of this sum, the remainder to be used for the purchase of wire with which the Cachamans agreed to fence their *conucos* or cultivated fields.

The disparity between legal fact, as recorded in the documents cited, and the nature of the sale as understood by the contemporary Cachamans is rather great. The most common version of the story is that the criollo purchaser offered to pay the expenses of the survey, allowing the community to repay him in kind. But the community decided to sell one league to meet their expenses. They received "100 pesos" (Bs 400) and the criollo purchaser agreed that if the Cachamans ever had need of the land he would return it to them. Pedrito distributed some raw cane sugar, cassava, and a new machete to every man in the community as their share of the proceeds, but it is generally agreed that he pocketed the major part of the profit.

Numerous attempts have been and are being made to "reclaim" the land, but so far without success, and it is to be expected that the Cachamans will continue to be unsuccessful unless there is direct government intervention in the matter.

Eventually, so it is claimed, the Cachamans tired of the machinations of Pedrito. During the unprecedented liberal administration of President López Contreras they petitioned the state government in Barcelona for his removal, which finally came to pass about 1941. His successor was his nephew Francisquito.

Francisquito must have been satisfactory to the community at the time, for he remained in the position of "Gobernador de la Tribu de Cachama" until 1947. However, today most informants express some dissatisfaction with Francisquito's leadership. Most of this dissatisfaction is rather vague: "He must have shared with Pedrito the profits from the sale of community land," "He was taking community money." It is striking that the first right-of-way contract between the Indigenous Community of Cachama and the Mene Grande Oil Co. was concluded at the end of 1946 or the early part of 1947 (CANTAURA 1947), yet before the end of the year Francisquito had been replaced by a new governor. M.G.O. Company records show that on 2 October 1947 Antoñico Tempo, as governor of the community, formally recognized the contract with that company, and in addition received Bs. 1,500 from the company for damages resulting from company exploration and construction on community land.

What had happened? As nearly as it can be reconstructed, the intrusion of company vehicles first for the removal of sand and gravel, then construction of a telephone line across one edge of Cachama, and seismographic exploration had created considerable disturbance within the community. When it became known that Francisquito had signed "a contract" with the company, the immediate conclusion was that he had sold out his fellow tribesmen, just as had his "brother" Pedrito before him. More than likely present expressions of dissatisfaction with Francisquito stem from this period. Due to the suspicion of questionable dealings with the company Francisquito's name has become linked with that of the much more machinating Pedrito. At any rate, Francisquito was summarily removed from office. His removal marked the beginning of open breakdown of the community and increasing disorganization of political control and activity.

This disorganization began with a shift in the nature of the community leader. Up to 1941 his position had been hereditary, and during the Gómez regime even the form of going through an election seems to have been dispensed with. While they appear to have lacked formal coercive authority, those caciques which are remembered by living informants were influential leaders. Between 1941 and 1947 hereditary succession to leadership was gradually replaced by the idea of selecting leaders by majority election alone. As this change occurred there was simultaneous loss of much of the prestige and authority which had been associated with the office. With each new governor new suspicions and new accusations came to the surface. Needless to say partisans of Pedrito the former cacique, as well as supporters of disgruntled former governors lost no opportunity to discredit each succeeding incumbent. Commonest are accusations of underhandedly selling community rights to the oil companies for personal gain, and misappropriation of community moneys received as right-of-way payments from the companies. Consequently the mean term of office served by community governors since 1947 is about two and one-half years.

Most people still exhibit respect toward the governor in face-to-face contact, but hardly more than toward any older man. Actually he has little real authority. Even those families which are not really committed to any particular faction can effectively ignore the governor without fear of serious consequences. In fact, at the present time the governor seems to have very few functions within the community. Rather he serves as a sort of spokesman for the community in their relations with outsiders. He is an identifiable figure which can be approached by company or government officials, missionaries, and visiting anthropologists as the official and legal representative of the community. Often he serves as a channel for community requests for assistance (e.g., a tractor, irrigation, electricity) from the state or federal government, or for receiving and distributing right-of-way payments from the oil companies. In these cases one might argue that he is serving his community, but his service is mostly limited to acting as a channel for communication. One could hardly characterize his role here as being that of an organizer or director. He is nothing more than an intermediary.

FACTIONALISM

FACTIONALISM HAS BEEN a factor in Cachama ever since Pedrito was ousted from the caciqueship. The amount of factionalism appears to have varied through the years, but since the signing of the first oil company contract in 1947 there seem to have been two major alignments, with less significant splinter groups appearing and fading out from time to time.

Pedrito and his partisans have removed themselves to a distance from the other Cachamans. They have their houses and fields along Tascabaña creek, some five kilometers distant from the next nearest neighborhood, along the western edge of community lands. There is considerable ill feeling between Tascabaña on the one hand and the other neighborhoods on the other. On either side there was hardly any hesitancy about openly expressing criticism of the opposite faction, even when we had first arrived there and were almost complete strangers to the community.

There is a minimum of visiting between Tascabaña and the other neighborhoods. Tascabaña never attends community meetings (even their share of the company payments is distributed to them separately. in Cantaura). Conjugal unions between residents of Tascabaña and other Cachama neighborhoods are even less frequent (14.3 per cent) than they are among the other neighborhoods (44.6 per cent). Only recently has there been some increase in contact between these other neighborhoods and Tascabaña. The apparent superiority of the Tascabaña school has led several parents to send their children there regardless of their political feelings.

At the time of our arrival in Cachama the factional groupings stood as follows (see Map III): All neighborhoods east of the Cachama river supported the elected governor. Tascabaña, located to the west along the creek of the same name continued to support Pedrito, the hereditary cacique. Castillito, located on the west side of the Cachama river attempted to straddle the fence, and though their sympathies seemed to be somewhat greater with Pedrito, they were in most instances disregarded by both sides. However, the Tascabaña faction was intelligent enough to see that they could derive an advantage through labor exchange with Castillito, since the fields of the former are far more extensive than those of the latter. Finally, Las Potocas constituted an unimportant splinter group of six families living off tribal lands.

During the time of our study, however, factionalism became more intensive and the splits between factional groups grew deeper. Early in 1962 people in Guanipa neighborhood began to grumble that "This governor isn't doing anything for us. He makes lots of trips —to San Tomé, Anaco, Barcelona— but he never seems to get any of the things he says he will." "He hasn't been near the *gobernación* for more than a month." About this same time the "community" purchased a dilapidated panel truck with a portion of the company payments. The truck was to be used only for "official business," but the young fellow who drove it seemed to be using it a good deal more than was neccesary for strictly "official" purposes. Apparently there was a dispute over who should use the truck for what, and for how long.

The neighborhood of Guanipa agitated for removal of the governor and election of a new one. Unable to develop support in the other neighborhoods, they went ahead and selected their own "community leader." From this point on this neighborhood was as completely alienated from the rest of the community as had been Tascabaña all along.

As was stated in the preceding chapter, it is significant that such splits broke cleanly along neighborhood lines, for in reality the neighborhood constitutes a sort of kin group based on ambilocal clans, and furthermore the majority of interpersonal relations occur within the neighborhood.

This newest faction centered in Guanipa neighborhood was not entirely a spontaneous development. For some years a criollo outsider has been representing himself to the Cachamans as a legal advisor who can help them improve their present conditions, and help in protecting them from exploitation by the oil companies. He claims to have been employed by the national Comisión Indigenista when he first appeared on the scene in 1958. At that time he succeeded in obtaining the signature of the community governor to a document which gave him the power to:

> ...represent us and defend our rights in all the affairs which concern us. In that capacity, our aforesaid proxy is empowered to receive from the Petroleum Companies Socony Mobil Oil Company and Mene Grande Oil Company... the payments corresponding to the damages and injuries provoked by the companies alluded to on the lands of the said Indigenous Community of Cachama, of which we are co-owners. In a word, he is empowered to agree to, to compromise, to waive any point related to the said contracts or issue releases, receipts and in general perform all those acts destined to the greater defense of our rights and interests.[3] (CANTAURA 1958)

Once granted these extensive powers Cachama's criollo "representative" began a fantastic though short-lived career. According to the accounts obtained from various informants he invested a large sum of money received from the companies in foodstuffs, beverages, and clothing, then set up a store in the Gobernación[4] where he offered these things for sale to the Cachamans. Some reports add an electric generator, lights and a jukebox to the equipment in the store as well as a pickup bought for the community, but registered in the name of the

---

[3] "...nos represente y sostenga nuestros derechos en todos los asuntos que nos concernan. En tal virtud, queda facultado nuestro expresado apoderado para reclamar de las Compañías Petroleras Socony Mobil Oil Company y Mene Grande Oil Company... los pagos correspondientes a los daños y perjuicios ocasionados por las aludidas Compañías en los terrenos de la referida Comunidad Yndígena de Cachama, de los cuales somos copropietarios. ...En una palabra, queda facultado para convenir, transigir desistir sobre cualquier punto relacionado con los mencionados contratos, o otorgar finiquitos, recibos y en general, realizar todos aquellos actos destinados a la mayor defensa de nuestros derechos e intereses."

[4] The building where the community documents are kept and "official business" is supposed to be conducted.

"representative." At least one informant claims that he also made use of his position of influence with the governor to obtain the favors of local women. Undoubtedly these accounts are somewhat exaggerated in detail, but they are consistent enough to indicate a solid basis of fact.

It wasn't long, however, before the situation became uncomfortable, and the representative was forced to leave, taking the "community" pickup with him. Just what precipitated his disappearance never became clear, almost everyone had a different version of what had happened. A new governor was elected, and he attempted to continue the store operation. But resentment seems to have been widespread. Business fell off (some informants maintain there was a formal boycott), the store languished and died. A second election was held and another new governor elected. This individual, Francisco Tempo, had not been in office very long when we arrived in Cachama.

Nor was it long before the former "representative" made his reappearance. This time he began by taking the names of all adult Cachamans who claimed that they had not been in accord with the sale of a league of community land in 1934, the avowed purpose being to reclaim that land. He began to accompany the governor on all "official" business trips. There was much talk of dividing community land into individual plots, of obtaining wire to fence it, a tractor to cultivate it and an irrigation system for water. Enthusiasm ran high for awhile. The panel truck was bought "for the community." Then relations between the governor and his "representative" cooled noticeably. The governor claimed that the latter had been taking money from the company payments, and would have nothing more to do with him. At this point Guanipa neighborhood declared its effective independence and brought forward their own favorite as the "legitimate" leader of the community. Soon they were accusing the governor of swindling the community and disappearing with community funds. Certainly the governor had not disappeared, since we talked with him in Cachama several days after these accusations had received national attention ("ANTORCHA" 1962; "EL NACIONAL" 1962).

In reality these developments were nothing more than an expression of underlying resentment. Since the present governor was a resident of Bajondo neighborhood there had been some fear that he might remove the Gobernación to his own neighborhood, or otherwise neglect the more populous Guanipa. Guanipa's leader had been a losing candidate for the governorship in the preceding election. By taking advantage of the situation he stood to gain a certain amount of prestige and authority, at least within Guanipa. If he were lucky he might emerge as governor of all the neighborhoods east of the Cachama river. The criollo representative was closely involved in these machinations, since apparently his relations with Francisco Tempo had lost all utility. Certainly he was not the origin of the feelings of resentment in that neighborhood, but apparently he encouraged them, and took advantage of them, thereby stimulating the appearance of a new faction.

It is doubtful whether this third faction would have developed at just this point without outside intervention. But it is nonetheless equally clear that such a situation was likely to occur sooner or later in Cachama. Widespread apprehension, resentment, and unfounded accusations against successive governors all tend to break the community apart. Simply in terms of population numbers (641 inhabitants, 458 excluding Tascabaña) internal fission was likely to occur. Political authority, which is weak in Cachama, is very similar to that of the typical Tropical Forest tribes in South America. CARNEIRO (1961: 52) has argued convincingly that internal sociocultural stresses in such cultures are increasingly likely to lead to fission as population figures approach 500. The intervention of an outsider in Cachama's politics merely served as a catalyst stimulating an earlier eruption of the inevitable.

Under aboriginal conditions conflict would probably have led to the movement of one or the other factions to some other area and the founding of a new community. The centripetal tendency in Cachama, caused by the lure of right-of-way payments from the oil companies, has prevented such a response and has produced a chronic situation of conflict. Since neither side can successfully escape the opposition, conflict remains strong and factional divisions become ever more firmly entrenched.

This is not the only instance of direct criollo intervention in Cachama.[5] The local people do not understand national politics, they see no direct benefits to be gained from supporting one or another party, and they have no emotional or ideological commitment to any of them.

[5]The great influx of population in the wake of the developing petroleum industry undoubtedly served indirectly to stimulate exploitation of the Indians, and rural criollos as well. LIEUWEN (1954: 52-53) indicates that the majority of camp followers who were unable to obtain employment in the oil industry turned to parasitic occupations "in the local commerce which lived off (the industry)." He might have added that at least some of these camp followers also live off the local population which has benefited from the activity of the companies in one way or another (such as receipt of right-of-way payments, similar to those paid to Cachama).

Most of the Cachamans have gone along in supporting Acción Democrática (A.D.), the majority party, though few could give a good reason except that it is a "politic" thing to do (as is generally true throughout Latin America. One does not openly support a party which is out of power, since he is only inviting official discrimination, and perhaps even direct reprisals.) Undoubtedly such support was assured in Cachama through "campaign promises" of government help with local problems on the part of local A.D. party representatives.

Since Tascabaña had set itself in opposition to the rest of Cachama on local matters, it also set itself in opposition in terms of national politics and favored the party Copei. In exchange for political allegiance the Tascabaña faction succeeded in obtaining its own legal representatives through Copei, and in 1962 they signed an agreement (CANTAURA 1962) granting more extensive powers to these "representatives:"

> in order that. . . they represent us, sustain our rights and defend our interests before whatever Civil, Commercial, Administrative or Judicial authority, or public or private entities, natural or juridical person, and especially, in order that they sustain our rights and exercise our representation before the petroleum Companies. . . (the document goes on to grant these representatives extensive powers to handle and administer all financial transactions relating to any of the above-named entities.)[6]

Although no informant ever indicated such a possibility, in retrospect certain details appear to suggest that Pedrito and his Tascabaña faction may have had in mind a legalization of the split between themselves and the rest of the Cachamans. As the people east of the Cachama river discussed the "imminent" distribution of land parcels among themselves, the Tascabaña faction went ahead making their own plans with their own legal representatives. They were having a separate map of their landholdings drawn up, and it very well may be that this was being done with the end in view of obtaining a separate title. The document cited above is very careful to make no reference to the Indigenous Community of Cachama, yet the language used to refer to the lands in Tascabaña is such as to suggest that the signers of the document did not have exclusive proprietary rights there:

---

[6] ". . .para que. . . nos representen, sostengan nuestros derechos y defiendan nuestros intereses por ante cualesquiera autoridades Civiles, Mercantiles, Administrativas o Judiciales, o entidades públicas o privadas, personas naturales o jurídicas y en especial, para que sostengan nuestros derechos y ejerzan nuestra representación por ante las Compañías petroleras. . . (folio 12).

> . . . likewise our attorneys are authorized to conduct any indemnitory claim which is referred to the lands that are our property or which we possess in the place called "Tascabaña," Mesa of Guanipa, Distrito Freites of Anzoátegui state,. . . (CANTAURA 1962, folio 12)[7]

Naturally the legal aid and moral support afforded the Tascabaña group only served to further widen the split between them and other groups in Cachama.

Toward the end of our stay a rather tragic incident provided another opportunity for the intervention of outsiders in the internal affairs of Cachama. Francisco, one of the young men of Cachama, was struck and killed by an automobile while riding his bicycle along the highway. Temporarily this served to bring some of the dissident groups together. The young man had been living in Tascabaña with Pedrito for several years, but his father lived in Bajondo and supported the elected governor. Furthermore, young Francisco had only recently acquired employment at the brick factory in El Tigre through the brother-in-law of the elected governor. His untimely death was a great blow to everyone and the funeral was attended by scores of people from at least two of the three factions.

On the day following the accident the governor was visited by some men who, according to his account, claimed to be representatives of the U.R.D. party. They argued that the driver of the fatal vehicle was in the wrong and that she would have to pay damages for Francisco's death. They promised to settle the affair in the interests of Cachama (presumably in exchange for political support at the next national election). The governor became quite excited over this prospect, and it was not long before a number of people had become rather heated over the "criminal act" which had caused the death. I was present later in the day when another criollo arrived to discuss the matter with the governor. He assured the latter that justice would be done "This woman has money. The costs of burial are paid by the person (causante) who caused the death, let's say by the criminal." The governor was eager to settle the whole affair right away — 8:00 o'clock Monday morning. "Some people say the Indian isn't worth anything, but now they'll see just how much an Indian's worth!"

---

[7] ". . . asi mismo están facultados nuestros apoderados para tramitar cualquier reclamación indemnizatoria que se refiera a las tierras que son de nuestra propiedad o poseemos en el sitio denominado, "Tascabaña", Mesa de Guanipa, Distrito Freites del Estado Anzoátegui . . .".

Needless to say the matter was not settled immediately, nor had it been settled before we had to leave Cachama some three weeks later. But in the meantime old hostilities had come to the fore again and accusations were already flying that Pedrito intended to appropriate the money paid in settlement by claiming to have been Francisco's stepfather since Francisco had been a small child. Indeed, said some, he had already taken the wages which Francisco had earned at the brick plant, though all agreed that at least a portion of them should have gone to the latter's father.

In every case the intervention of outsiders, be their intentions for good or ill, has resulted either in furthering the process of factionalization, or in deepening the rift which already exists between different segments of the community. Had Cachama been a unified community there would have been little need to listen to any outsider. Had the Cachamans seen such outside interventions as a threat to themselves, they would have united to oppose and reject them. Instead, each group has sought to gain temporary advantage over the opposing factions by "exploiting" the presumably superior position of an outsider who appears to be more powerful (principally because of his superior educational and economic resources) than themselves. It is questionable whether more is gained by using such outsiders to secure advantage against fellow Cachamans, than is lost through the concurrent exploitation of the Indians to the advantage of the outsider.

This is not to imply there is no need for outside help. The Cachamans are insecure and disoriented in their rapidly changing world. They lack the educational background and economic resources with which to defend their interests in such an environment. But rather than uniting and seeking to defend their interests as a community, they have instead sought to protect the interests of one segment in opposition to the others.

The main point to be emphasized here is that Cachama no longer functions as a community. The residents no longer hold any primary loyalties to the community as a whole. The former "we-ness" of being an Indian has been replaced by the much less satisfying "we-ness" of being for or against such and such a faction. At the very least there are three separate "communities" in Cachama, but none of these possess much stability, with the exception of Tascabaña. Even there we find constant additions or deletions of borderline groups, depending upon the winds of expediency. In the following paragraphs I will show that not only is there a lack of community when Cachama is viewed as a whole, but that the functional community is in most cases much smaller even than the factional groupings.

Neighborhoods. The lack of functional community becomes more fully evident in the informal patterns of interpersonal relations. There is very little personal interaction between persons belonging to different neighborhoods. In contrast interaction within each neighborhood is frequent and often intensive.

Such interaction tends to focus at one or two spots within each neighborhood. An outstanding example is the store operated by Francisco Tempo in Bajondo. At almost any hour of the day one or two people may be encountered lounging about the store. In the afternoon when the men have returned from the fields the number may swell to a half dozen or more. Neighborhood women come to the store to buy salt, lard or canned fish, and linger to exchange a little gossip. Even neighborhood children tend to be drawn to the store in order to play with Francisco's children, rather than the latter seeking playmates elsewhere, and this in spite of the fact that the children of Francisco are much more sophisticated and outgoing than the average. In addition the store serves as a sort of meeting place. Young men wait there for the arrival of a gravel truck, people going to town or arriving from there may stop for a while at the store. In addition to the chance to meet other people in the neighborhood, the store is attractive because of the constant activity which is going on there —a Pepsi truck, the bread man, someone looking for the governor, etc.— all stop there, and of course there is always a constant flow of traffic on the highway. But personal and political factors also enter the picture. Less than a quarter mile away Obdulio Tamanaico maintains a store which is much larger, better stocked and physically more attractive than Francisco's. However, Obdulio is a staunch partisan of Pedrito. He only left Tascabaña in order to set up his present enterprise on the highway. Nonetheless, there are always more people around Francisco's store than at Obdulio's.

In Guanipa the activity to be found around the household of Martín the curioso likewise tends to draw his neighbors in that direction. Martín used to maintain a small store, but it had a less important integrative function than the store of Francisco in Bajondo. The same is true of the small store of Pedrito. In the latter case it is more than just the building which attracts people, since there is a cluster of houses arranged around a little square. One of these buildings serves as the school to which members of the Tascabaña faction send their children. In the center of the square is a round "guest house," with walls reaching only half-way to the roof. Here the men of the community can relax, converse, and watch the activities of the neighborhood going on around them. Like Martín, Pedrito is also a curer, and curiosity —a desire to see those people who have come seeking a cure— serves as a further magnet drawing people to this center.

Castillito lacks a center of any kind. There is no focal point in this neighborhood and consequently there is a minimum of communication from one side of the neighborhood to the other, in spite of the fact that rather close ties of kinship link most of the people who live there. Instead they are drawn to the store of Francisco Tempo which they visit whenever they have some excuse for going down to the highway; or to Tascabaña on the occasion of work parties.

The house of Alfonso the curer is rather anomalous since it serves as a center without being strictly tied to a particular neighborhood. Spatially it is located between Guanipa and Bajondo, although it is a sufficient distance from Bajondo that few residents of the latter are drawn to it. But in addition it is strategically located at the point where the Boca road, which connects with Tascabaña and Alfondo, reaches the highway. People from these two neighborhoods generally stop there whenever they have occasion to come to the highway. Thus Alfonso is spatially in a position to mediate between four of the five major neighborhoods, and he appears to be successful in doing so with three. He has succeeded in remaining neutral, even in the face of new and more bitter factionalism. He is a clever man and is greatly respected in Cachama. Extensive kin ties in both Guanipa and Alfondo further serve to ensure good relations on both sides. More than that, however, it would appear that his spatial relationship has served Alfonso in good stead whenever it was advantageous to remain neutral.

Since the majority of informal day-to-day contacts thus tend to occur within each neighborhood, it is likewise understandable that patterns of informal visiting also tend to be restricted to that entity. During the week there is little opportunity to visit outside the clan except for casual meetings at the "neighborhood centers" just discussed. However, one does not generally go to the fields on Sundays, but instead may pay a more formal call on some relative or friend. Once again, the majority of such visits are kept within neighborhood boundaries. Only rarely do they cut across these boundary lines and in such cases the visit is invariably to a kinsman. Ties of friendship alone are almost wholly restricted to the neighborhood. Even they are unusual since most neighborhood residents are kinsmen anyway. As was pointed out above, marriage across neighborhood lines is infrequent, so that there is less cause for paying a formal visit to another neighborhood.

The same patterns hold for cayapas (mutual labor exchange) and fiestas. People from neighborhoods other than one's own are not invited to participate in a cayapa. During fiesta celebrations, which may last several days, it is rare to see residents of one neighborhood participating in the celebrations of another. Such celebrations also tend to focus on the various "neighborhood centers." And in Castillito the lack of such a center may mean that there is no celebration. Lorenzo Tempo prepared a number of *zaranda* tops for his daughter to spin for the traditional Holy Week game of "Breaking the Zaranda." The tops were still whole after Holy Week because "Nobody came to break them."

The essential lack of community in Cachama is most evident perhaps in the breakdown of one of the most basic factors binding a community together — gossip and communication via "the grapevine." Frequently people in Bajondo had no idea what was going on in Guanipa. Alfondo was completely cut off from both. We found ourselves serving as a channel of communication between the various neighborhoods, since we were almost the only individuals who came into frequent contact with representatives of them all. Castillito was always left out, for news seemed to reach it very slowly, whether it was coming from Tascabaña or from across the river. We were in Cachama several weeks before getting to Castillito. When we arrived we had to start all over again, for no one had even heard that we were in Cachama, much less had any idea what we were doing there.

Part way through our stay arrangements were made for a nurse to hold a weekly clinic in Bajondo. The governor assured her that he would notify everyone. Almost no one but those in Bajondo came to the clinic during the two or three months that it operated. Four weeks after it had been started, the widow Martínez, who lives just behind the house where the clinic was held, told us that she knew nothing about the clinic until that very day.

Again, when the North American Association offered to distribute hybrid seed corn in Cachama the governor said he would notify everyone. Since this was after the split between Bajondo and Guanipa, we knew he would not notify Guanipa. We left the word in key houses in each neighborhood, but when the day came, only a couple from Alfondo showed up. The truck had go to Sesenta to notify the people there, and only by chance did a family from Castillito come to Bajondo to sell cassava, and thus learn of the distribution. This lack of grapevine communication which is always so efficient in spreading news, sometimes of importance, is indicative of a real breakdown in all aspects of informal relationships in the community.

It is clearly evident then that the Indigenous Community of Cachama does not represent a true community in any sense of the word. Almost all social interaction is restricted to the neighborhood, and relations between individuals, members of different neighborhoods, are infrequent. When they do occur they tend to be casual, perhaps even impersonal. The neighborhood would appear then, to be the largest socially functional unit in Cachama, not only in day-to-day relations, but also as the basis for factional splits. While the community has disintegrated as a unitary group, the neighborhoods have remained well-integrated. In fact they may be stronger today than they were in years past. At present it would appear that the neighborhoods will continue to be important integrative units in Cachama and that they will serve as major mechanisms facilitating or retarding change.

CHAPTER 5

VALUES

VALUES ARE A BASIC part of culture, for though they are rarely formulated overtly by the individual, they nonetheless provide a focus for the integration of culture; they give it direction and meaning. Since the values system is so basic, comparison of it with the rest of the cultural whole should provide valuable insights into culture change.

At the time we were in the field we were not familiar with any specialized techniques for getting at the value orientations of a given cultural group. Consequently we designed a series of formal questions relating to possessions and material prosperity; nature of the family and the relationships within it; the processes of individual maturation; group organization, types of leadership, and attitudes about leaders; contacts outside the group and attitudes toward change and "progress." In effect our question about the proper type of compadrazgo relationship belongs to this last category. A question about the nature of religion was also useful. A final question, relating to conceptions of art and beauty was for the most part unsatisfactory, since informants had difficulty conceptualizing what was meant by the question. Most of the answers which were finally elicited relate to everyday objects and *activities.*

The questions were presented in a series of formal interviews. Since each interview took considerable time, we selected an individual who appeared to be a "typical" representative of each of a series of categories of sex, age, and conservative versus progressive orientations. A complete series of responses was obtained from the following individuals:

Conservative:

older

Hilario Aray	60 years old, 14 children; philosophical, relatively traditional in outlook.

Mariquita Tamanaico	63 years old, traditional in orientation, but an atypical individual since she is a long-time widow, and therefore self-sufficient and independent. All her children have died, she is raising one surviving grandson. A potter and practising midwife.
younger Miguel Tamanaico	45 years old, 9 children, a very rational attitude toward life, but relatively traditional in orientation.

Progressive:

older Francisco Tempo	32 years old, 5 children, farmer, store owner, progressive orientation.
María Martínez	33, mother of 5, store owner, semi-oriented to criollo values, semi-progressive orientation.
younger Gregorio Tempo	26, father of two, occasional laborer, has no field of his own, hard worker, progressive.
Petra Aray	19, two children, very progressive, has lived with criollo family in the towns, shares numerous criollo values.

It should be pointed out that the sample is not complete for a variety of reasons. None of the older people in Cachama can be considered progressive, while a fair proportion of the younger people tend in that direction.

The one representative of the traditional female was interviewed because she is atypical. Ordinarily older women in Cachama are withdrawn and reticent with strangers, some take a slightly different attitude and are shrewish (the same is also true of many younger women, though to a lesser degree). They would answer to their husbands for any other type of behavior. It is difficult, if not impossible, to draw information out of these women in any sort of interview situation. Because she has no one to answer to, and because she has had to be dependent on herself for so long, Mariquita's response to strangers is more "masculine," i.e., she is outgoing, friendly, and readily communicative. Thus, although she is not a typical representative of her category, she nonetheless was the only possible member of that category who could be readily interviewed. Even though atypical, she is in many respects the most conservative individual in the sample.

Possessions and material prosperity. Almost all informants agree that the most essential articles for the home are dishes, kitchen utensils, and furnishings. The exact items of furniture mentioned vary, although the two oldest informants sepecifically mention hammocks. All the men except landless Gregorio also specify fields. The two youngest and most progressive individuals differ strikingly from the others in their concept of what is essential for the home: beds rather than hammocks, "a fenced yard for animals and plants," a cement floor in the house, doors, and a *kerosene* stove instead of the usual wood-fueled open hearth.

An interesting trend from traditional to progressive is observable in the ways in which various individuals would make use of improved economic circumstances in order to enjoy "luxury" items. The older conservatives would merely increase their consumption of goods. Hilario, for example, would buy more processed foodstuffs — "Pepsi, salt, salmon ("Salmonete" a brand of sardines) to keep in the house."— as well as clothing. If he were wealthy enough he would buy a car or pickup to bring crops in from the field. Even this is more in the nature of increased consumption, since it would make transport faster and easier. A tractor, which would be more directly concerned with production, is less important to him.

Miguel, the younger conservative, and the older progressives all mention increased consumption, but far more important to them is the opportunity to increase production. They would invariably invest in livestock, poultry and diversified crops. Miguel succinctly observed that "A really wealthy man would move to the city." Francisco and his wife María are more interested in continuing to increase their income. María envisions surplus production of manioc cakes which can be sold. With the money from that enterprise one could open a *kiosco* (small store). Profits from the store could then be invested in livestock, a larger and more convenient house, and fruit trees to plant around the house. Fruit from such an orchard would also have cash value both within Cachama and in the nearby towns. In addition to investing in livestock, Francisco would obtain another house *which he could rent.* Surprisingly the younger progressives are less concerned with increasing income, but this may perhaps be because they lack steady income —they both possess neither land nor steady employment. However, in increasing their consumption their goals are very different from those mentioned by the traditionalists. If they did not already possess them, they would buy a kerosene stove and lay a cement floor in the house. Beyond this they would invest in a radio and put pictures up in their house, something which is a distinctively criollo pattern.

The picture which we get here is one of broadening of objectives as one becomes more progressive. An increased standard of living means increased consumption for the older conservatives. The younger conservative and the progressives see the opportunity for greater production equally important to increased consumption. Nonetheless, it would appear that some prospect of achieving increased production, or perhaps the experience of already having done so is necessary before it can be mentally translated into an increase in actual income.

Nature of the family and intrafamilial relations. With respect to proper relations between husband and wife the ideal is remarkably uniform among all categories of persons. Emphasis is placed on a calm quiet attitude in either spouse. Anger and frequent "talking back" are frowned upon. A good husband is industrious and provides for the needs of his wife and children, while the proper wife prepares food, takes care of clothing, keeps house, and tends the children. Although anger is universally disapproved, there is an equally strong value placed on the husband's firmness.

The wife must always be subordinate to her husband, who should correct her if she does wrong. Interestingly enough, only the younger progressives specifically mention the use of corporal punishment in correcting one's wife. Only two of the men mention failure to provide for her because of another woman, and both strongly disapprove of such behavior. Yet Hilario also feels that there is nothing improper "if he can support two women well enough. . .," though he sympathises with the feelings of a woman who refused to live with a second wife. In spite of these comments, there is little overt concern with sexual faithfulness in one's spouse.

In the relationship between parent and child most of the concern is with caring for the needs of the children — food, clothing, shelter, medicines when ill, etc. Parents in Cachama are generally quite permissive, so it is not surprising that the only individuals who evince any concern about the *training* of children are the younger progressives who emphasize discipline, teaching the difference between right and wrong, and in general, ensuring that they are well reared (bien educados).

It is believed in Cachama that small children "don't understand" when they are corrected, and consequently there is marked permissiveness toward children under the age of six or seven. At about that point, however, it is felt that they should assume more responsibility, should begin to assist in their parents' work, and are also old enough to receive punishment for wrongdoing. Even so, scoldings and verbal discipline are much preferred, although recourse may be had to corporal punishment in instances of repeated misbehavior. The only exception to this rather uniform pattern is provided by the younger progressives, who are much more severe. They seem to feel that corporal punishment is called for in most disciplinary contexts.

Boys are allowed more freedom than girls. Usually by the age of six or eight it is thought permissible to allow them to range on their own as far as the next neighborhood. More restrictions are placed on girls and their freedom of movement. It is surprising to find that the progressives are more protective of their children, for three of the four clearly indicate that even boys should not be permitted the freedom to range out of sight of their own home much before puberty.

A boy should respect and obey his parents at least until he takes his own spouse. If anything, the more progressive individuals place greater stress on obedience. They also evince considerable concern about fighting, stressing that such behavior is bad both within and outside the family. Perhaps this attitude results from the progressive's greater familiarity with criollo behavior, where there is considerably more open hostility than among the Karinya.

There is a consistent value that adolescent boys should turn over all earnings to their mother so long as they are living at home. Even after marriage they are expected to look out for their parents and to care for them in time of need. Here is one point where values and behavior are clearly at variance. All the evidence we could obtain indicates that young men employed in the gravel or at day labor retain all their earnings, although they might be somewhat more generous in buying gifts for their mother and sisters.

In general a child should have feelings of respect and love (in that order) for his parents, but the more progressive individuals feel that a modicum of fear for one's parents is also desirable. The ties to one's mother should always be closer and warmer than they are to the father.

Relations between siblings are expected to be characterized by mutual protection and assistance, with elder siblings assuming greater responsibility for the younger, with brothers protecting sisters, and sisters caring for the needs of their brothers.

There is an interesting contrast between the attitudes of men and women concerning the proper behavior of a young man who is searching for a mate. The women all stress that the young fellow should be respectful of the girl, should not be daring or make advances, and should early make his interest in her known to her parents. In contrast the men hardly make mention of such relations. The feminine concern may be indicative of an underlying feeling of insecurity with respect to the opposite sex. In actual fact there is considerable freedom in sexual matters, and it is doubtful whether any of the values expressed above are rigidly adhered to. It is to be expected that in most cases the men are the aggressive individuals, and therefore, even though it is doubtful that the women resist their advances very strenuously, the latter may nonetheless feel themselves to be in a vulnerable and insecure position.

Girls are expected to show more responsibility and industriousness around the home, and at an earlier age, than boys. There should be many more restrictions on their freedom, for both girls and women are considered to be vulnerable when they are alone and unaccompanied. Ideally no girl should ever be permitted to leave the vicinity of her house when unaccompanied by some responsible member of her family. For both sexes there is considerable emphasis on "learning their work," mastering the appropriate roles, before they begin to think seriously about marriage. Here again practise frequently does not correspond to the held value, both because of youthful marriages, and as a result of parental laxity in inculcating all the necessary skills in their offspring.

Although it is difficult to assess actual family integration, there is a rather clear trend toward increase of intrafamilial interaction as we move from conservative to more progressive individuals. Among the conservatives the whole family is together only in the evening when everyone relaxes outside the house and discusses the events of the day. Even meals do not bring the family together, for although they may eat at the same time, men and women always eat apart from each other. Among the progressives more work is undertaken jointly within the family, both around the house and in the fields. Furthermore, everyone in the family may go along to visit at some other house. But only the younger progressives are oriented to share in most of their activities. Among them the whole family might even go together on a trip to one of the towns.

With marriage there necessarily comes a readjustment of relationships, even for the girl, who usually remains living in her mother's house for a time. There is general agreement in the feeling that her primary responsibilities are now to her husband, even though it is recognized that her parents may give her orders and continue to instruct her in her proper duties as a mature woman. All food and and game coming into the household should be shared among the members.

A woman's relations with her in-laws are less intensive. She should respect her in-laws and provide them food when they visit, but there is no pattern of daily food exchange. The conservatives still feel that a woman's behavior toward her father-in-law should exhibit respect and restraint, whereas she deals more easily with her mother-in-law. The progressives on the other hand, show little concern about relations with the father-in-law, but rather there is a suggestion of increased tension between daughter-in-law and mother-in-law.

A young man goes to live in the house of his bride, and consequently his primary relationships are now with his newly acquired conjugal kinsmen. He is subordinate to his father-in-law and must work for the latter whenever requested to do so. He should share his fish and game with all of his in-laws. A former respect relation with the mother-in-law, which is still stressed by the conservatives, has been replaced among the younger progressives by a feeling that a man's father-in-law is more important, and therefore worthy of a special attitude of respect. Again this may be a result of criollo influence.

With removal to his bride's house at marriage the average young man does not have much opportunity to continue interacting with the members of his own family. Nonetheless there is a felt obligation to visit them frequently —at least once a week during the early married period. It is also felt that he should take small gifts to his parents, particularly his mother, during this period. Only one informant mentions that the man should share game and other *food* with his parents, which would suggest either that this practise has disappeared, or, what is more likely, that sharing with the man's parents never became an established pattern, probably because the uxorilocal residence pattern at marriage would tend to discourage such a practise.

By and large, value orientations concerning the nature of the family have undergone but minimal modification so far, only minor distinctions in values are discernible between conservatives and progressives. However, even these minor differences do suggest that a number of trends have begun and that we may expect more extensive modifications to take place in the future.

Individual maturation. Although we obtained rather detailed responses as to the proper sequence of skills which should be learned by both sexes, it is appropriate for this analysis of culture change to consider only the nature of the skills which are thought to be important. For girls the most important training *in every case* is said to be in the various tasks of keeping house, in preparation for their future role as housewives. Some would add sewing as an additional useful skill. Only the younger progressives mention the possibility that girls might learn to read and write, even though a number of the other informants have daughters attending school.

For boys, learning to farm is most important. It is indicative of the limited returns to be gained by hunting and fishing that the former is mentioned by respondents only twice, and the latter not at all. Even for boys, none of the conservatives, and only three of the four progressives, give any indication that learning to read and write should be considered a part of the process of learning. This suggests that the great emphasis placed on formal education by most individuals when they are queried directly is not very deeply rooted, for it does not come to mind as an important part of the individual's preparation for adulthood.

Group organization, leadership, etc. Respect is an essential feature of interpersonal relations, and one which appears to have been highly valued traditionally. There appears to be little differentiation between respondents as regards the individuals who should receive one's respect. Almost everyone agrees that first and foremost one should respect elder persons and one's own parents, the mother perhaps a little more than the father. The cacique or governor should also receive respect, though some informants clearly feel that this continues only so long as he remains in office. Mariquita adds that formerly the *principales*[1] who served as moral advisors and community leaders, also received great respect. The only distinctive value concerning persons that should receive expressions of respect is that of the female progressives. They are less concerned with political figures and tend to be more diffuse in their

---

[1] We were unable to ascertain whether these *principales* were identical to those officials elected annually by the community, an informal body of respected elders, or represented some other type of body not previously reported.

extension of this attitude (friends, hard workers, etc.). They also agreed in including compadres within this category.

Values placed upon the characteristics which are most desirable for leadership are also fairly consistent, although they are expressed more variably. In a roundabout way several of the responses indicate a feeling that a leader should be concerned with his own community or group such that he puts their interests above his own personal or family interests. Thus he should be a man of conscience, pacific, and of good conduct; he should treat all members of the community equally; he should be considerate, helpful, and be able to treat with outsiders. The women place particular emphasis on the criterion of age, stressing elder status as a prerequisite to leadership.

When questioned in more specific terms about the mutual obligations of governor and "citizen" most informants were unable to divorce themselves from reality. This gave them an opportunity to express their feelings about the *current* tension-producing situation and consequently any expression of value ideals was subsidiary. However, Mariquita very nicely sums up the traditional ideal, "Formerly everyone helped the governor with his work, and the governor helped them when they needed help." In general the women seem to view the governor's ideal role in more integrative terms than do the men. They feel that he should handle disputes in the community, maintain order, and advise his people. María Martínez who is also the sister of the current governor, emphasizes that the governor has no prerogative to demand things of his people, nor should he even ask favors of them. This is definitely a change from the old value, and undoubtedly is a result of the frequent accusations that governors have been exploiting the position to their own advantage. Francisco Tempo cautiously advises that one shoud not offer his assistance to the governor until he has actually received aid and assistance from him. Both the most conservative and the most progressive view the principal function of the contemporary governor to be a source of help, you merely ask him for whatever needs you cannot easily satisfy yourself. Here only half of the older pattern of mutual assistance has survived, and, as might be suspected, it is the more selfish half. Actually, there seems to be increasingly great emphasis upon looking out for one's individual interests today. As it was cynically expressed by one progressive informant, the governor comes to the people when he needs money for a trip or some other enterprise. (This is in fact, the practise, although the governor always presents his requests with the plea that these enterprises are in the community interest.)

The responsibilities of the individual toward the group were once centered in the formal labor exchange, where food was contributed by all to the cacique who then redistributed it to those persons participating in a series of such exchanges. The cayapa or labor exchange survives, but has become completely divorced from the cacique today, and most of the food consumed during a cayapa is provided by the person who organizes it.

Generally the feeling is that you should help the governor when your assistance (usually pecuniary) is requested. The progressives also put great stock in community meetings and feel a real obligation to attend when they are called. Perhaps this is because democratic processes —the election of the governor and other community leaders— depends upon such community meetings. The progressives naturally favor such practises more than do the conservatives, not through any philosophical convictions, but because they are identified with education and modernity.

When asked what they thought their governor could and should do for them, most respondents thought that he should provide material aid, such as organizing a cayapa to cultivate their fields, or lending them money. "Anything you can't do yourself he has to do for you." Several people also feel that it is his duty to "advise" his people on matters of concern. The older progressives occupy an interesting position among the respondents. They see the governor serving no other function than seeking assistance for the community from the state and federal governments or from other entities —machinery, an irrigation system, money, etc. Perhaps thus attitude survives from an earlier period when the cacique's principal function was that of mediator between the local community and Spanish colonial society, but in point of fact this *is actually* the primary function of today's governor.

Even though there is a minimum use of national legal forms in cases of dispute in Cachama, the Venezuelan government is so centralized, and there is sufficient bureaucratic domination from the top down, that our respondents found it difficult to conceive of conditions where the community would be totally independent and self-sufficient in legal affairs. Very little ingenuity is displayed in describing possible community adaptations to such a state. Where any centralization of rule is mentioned at all, it would invariably be vested in the governor or *jefe,* who would presumably be elected by popular vote, as he is at present. Two individuals also suggest a popular council which would make the decision in cases of serious dispute. The informants split quite evenly in their emphasis on laws which would relate to desirable versus anti-social behavior. On the desirable side there is emphasis on industry and peaceful relations between people. One should stay out of other people's affairs, avoid insults and malicious gossip. In terms of the answers which were obtained anti-social behavior ranks in seriousness, from high to low, as follows: murder, incest, drunkenness, fighting, rape, insults, theft. The older and more conservative individuals favor much more severe sanctions for antisocial behavior than do the younger and more progressive persons. Perhaps this is because the older people remember a time when internal strife was non-existent and there was great emphasis on smoothness of relations. Today such smoothness of relations is difficult to maintain. The less severe attitude which the younger people take toward anti-social behavior may be due to the fact that they do not connect factionalism and strife with any lack of adequate sanctions against such behavior.

It may be significant that when discussing political organization the women appear to show more accord, and also to be somewhat more conservative than the men. After all, this is one sphere of Karinya culture where women have never been permitted to participate to any significant degree.[2] There is a tendency for the women to be more diffuse in determining which persons are worthy of an attitude of respect, but they are consistent in demanding that age be one of the determinative criteria of leadership. Although they are fully aware of the present ineffectual position of the governor, they tend to view his role as one of a central integrative symbol for the community as a whole.

On the basis of these responses, it would appear that there has already been considerable modification in this sphere of the values system. Consequently both conservatives and progressives are more uniform in their views than we would ordinarily expect. Nonetheless, certain differences in value orientation are discernible between them.

With the rise of factionalism, and a consequent breakdown in community integration at least some of the progressives are beginning to look for bases of individual and familial support which are broader than the traditional kin, neighborhood, and tribal ties. Thus the pro-

[2] All women in Venezuela have had the franchise since it was granted to them in the early 1950's by the Pérez Jiménez regime, which, in fact, made it mandatory for every adult citizen to vote in the national elections.

gressive women are attempting to reinforce the compadrazgo by *stressing* that the proper relation between compadres is one of respect.

The greatest modification in values centers on the role of community leader, formerly a hereditary cacique, and today the elected governor. There appears to be considerable confusion and disagreement about his exact functions in the community, partially I am sure as a result of the different points of view taken by the warring factions.

Change, progress, and contacts with non-Indians. All individuals interviewed claim to view formal education as a very definite means to certain economic and material advantages (but see above). Knowing how to read and write will enable one to get a commercial or clerical job which pays well and avoids the necessity of "working in the sun." Proper schooling will also better enable one to defend his interests and those of the tribe, since (it is assumed) education makes one familiar with legal matters. There is less agreement on the advantages for a girl to become literate. There seems to be a feeling that it is generally a good idea, but that knowing how to read and write would be less useful for her than for a man. Only the younger progressives differ markedly in their attitudes toward education. Education, they feel, makes it possible for one to seek out a professional career, such as a teacher or a doctor. It could be equally useful for girls who might also seek employment in the towns. Petra provided the broadest definition of education, for she added learning to pray and to have respect for authority to the usual reading and writing.

Increased contact with criollos and with the oil companies in recent years has introduced profound changes in the Cachamans' way of life. The conservatives tend to view such changes with misgiving, ranging all the way from Miguel's vague objections about the seductive influence of city evils and vices ("You're apt to throw your money away in the saloons on jukeboxes and beer—even if you have a hungry wife and family at home.") to more specific complaints, such as breakdown of established patterns of cooperation and the rise of factionalism in the community. Among the conservatives only Hilario has very much that is positive to say about the new era. He cites improvements in transportation and communication, which provide better access to doctors and medicines. But the same company-built highway which provides these improvements in transportation also increased the dangers of injury or death through highway accidents. In addition Hilario agrees that these changes have had much to do with the present divisive conditions in the community.

As might be expected, the progressives take a somewhat more positive view of these changes, although they too voice certain complaints about present conditions. Improvements in transportation are mentioned most frequently, and along with this they point to "improvements" (changes) in material goods, particularly foodstuffs and medicines. The progressive women also feel that these changes have provided the possibility of obtaining outside employment and thereby increasing one's earnings. Schools are another benefit of this new era. On the whole change has been mostly for the good, the two most serious complaints about present conditions object to factionalism in the community and an increase in the liquor traffic (promoted by criollo merchants). The progressive men seem to feel that it is too easy today for outsiders to enter the community and make trouble.

In spite of increased contact, relations with criollos remain limited for the most part to more or less structured situations. One of the most frequent occurs in the institution of the compadrazgo, although it remains relatively weak in Cachama. Two forms of the compadrazgo are common. The first is linked with a naming ceremony. Shortly after a child is born a couple is selected to anoint the infant's head with water (thus these individuals are known as *compadres de agua*) and bestow a name on him. Usually this couple volunteers to name the child, and in most instances the volunteers are criollos.

At the Fiesta of Candelaria, held annually in Cantaura on the 2nd of February, infants of a year or less are formally baptised in the Church. Again a criollo, often a complete stranger, generally volunteers to take the child and stand with it in the church as godparent. Although the ceremony of baptism is more formal, it appears to have less significance for the Cachamans, and the identity of the *compadre de bautizo* is rapidly forgotten (provided it was ever actually known). The *compadre de agua,* on the other hand, represents a somewhat more important individual.

The essential weakness of the compadrazgo in Cachama is evident in the fact that criollos are preferred as godparents. The principal reason for this preference is that "Indians don't respect you." They become intoxicated and insult their compadres, they are quick to take offense if the *padrino* doesn't treat his *ahijado* just so. It is highly probable that an economic difference between Indians and criollos, permitting a criollo godparent to give more lavish gifts to his godchild more frequently, is also a factor in this Indian attitude. Four of our seven informants definitely prefer criollo compadres, one feels that either a criollo or Indian would do. Two express a preference for Indian compadres, but the nature of their answers indicates that they prefer an Indian for personal or sentimental reasons, and that they are not unaware that others have had difficulty maintaining a relationship of respect with Indian compadres. The fact that Miguel and Francisco are very specific about whom they would choose as Indian compadres suggests a desire on their part to avoid just such difficulties. Miguel prefers a close kinsman (presumably taking advantage of an already existent relation of respect). Francisco on the other hand, suggests that the ideal Indian compadre should be an older person, one you can respect because of his age, and preferably an unrelated person from the opposite end of town. Thus he would attempt to maintain a relation of respect on the basis of social and spatial distance.

While there is some difference in the attitudes toward criollos as compadres, there does not appear to be any recent change or trend in such attitudes. As a matter of fact, this particular custom has probably changed but little during this century. The only modification may be an increased exploitation of this sanctified relationship on the part of the Indian.

Religion. Our one query about the ideal religious training brought a variety of responses. The women all phrase their answers in terms of learning certain aspects of Catholicism, particularly learning how to pray, but also learning about God and the story of creation. One of the women indicated that formerly they had been taught that failure to observe certain kinds of behavior (such as "Taking care of your mother") would result in your going to the devil.

Hilario also views religious training in terms of instilling discipline and proper behavior in one's children. The men tend, however, to interpret "religious training" to mean learning about curing and the activities of the curiosos. Formal training, however, is limited to actual apprenticeship to a curioso. Most youngsters obtain a rudimentary knowledge of the techniques of curing through the children of curiosos, or by listening to the conversations of adults.

The younger progressives exhibit a greater orientation to formal religion. It was indicated that one should cultivate the worship of a particular saint, and both respondents stress the importance of learning how to pray. Gregorio indicates quite a libertarian attitude when he states that one should put his children "into a religion that pleases them" (que van a querer).

With the exception of Gregorio, the men appear to be more conservative about religion than are the women. It may very well be that the women are somewhat more attracted to Catholicism, since the esoteric knowledge and practises of the curiosos are barred to them. Nonetheless, it is possible to discern the beginning of a trend away from traditional Carib beliefs concerning the supernatural toward the beliefs of more formalized Christian cults. Although formal religious expression is not very important in Cachama today, it could become the basis of further disorganization and factionalism in the community since there are at least a couple of Protestant evangelists who visit the community sporadically, although most of the Cachamans are nominally considered Catholics.

Summary. Recent years have seen the introduction of a variety of new material items at the same time that the Cachamans have found it increasingly possible to enjoy many of these new things. Given this as the existent trend, it is only natural for them to assume that the situation will continue, and they will continue to inhabit a world of expanding opportunities and increased satisfactions.

The progressive's increased concern with his children's behavior may be nothing more than a reflection of his awareness that the world is far more complex, and the individual is faced with a great many more responsibilities in interpersonal relations than was the case one or two generations ago. However, it would appear that this is also a reaction to an increasing threat of familial breakdown. Greater severity in discipline (of both children and the wife) may be an unconscious attempt to maintain family solidarity. Certainly it does not seem to produce better mannered children, for children of families of severe discipline are, if anything, less well behaved than children from permissive families. Again, the feeling that families should do more things together undoubtedly arises from the same fear of breakdown. It is more difficult to ascertain valid reasons for the recent shift in the respect relationship from the parent-in-law of opposite sex to the parent-in-law of same sex.

The area of greatest apparent change in the values system has been that relating to community organization and leadership. While the conservatives appear to yearn for the former era of pacific conditions, the progressives have generally approached present problems with an attitude of replacing former relations and values with new ones, of redefining certain existent social roles and social attitudes so that they might serve as foci for reintegration of the community. So far there is little indication, even among the progressives, that they have had enough. They are not yet ready to throw over the community, to get out and seek the miserable anonymity of existence in the towns or cities. Though the initial reaction to an outsider is to deny one's "Indian-ness" and to stress one's present "civilized" state, the people of Cachama remain Karinya at heart, with a definite commitment to their past traditions.

This is not to say that they cannot and will not change. The traditional way of life has already been profoundly altered, and the progressives in particular are eager to continue to "civilize" themselves. For one reason or another almost everyone considers education to be a good thing, and even though attendance at the school is sporadic and learning is slow, formal education may well prove to be one of the major channels of culture change.

Attitudes about "religion" appear to have begun a process of redefinition, too. With increasing "rationalism" and greater and greater facility of obtaining modern medical assistance, the role and influence of the curioso in the community will diminish. As the curioso disappears many of the traditional beliefs about the supernatural will disappear, or become submerged in generalized folk belief.

Viewing the values system as a whole, however, we can expect that no major changes will occur here without prior reorganization in those areas of social structure and cultural behavior to which the values refer.

III

MAMO

MAMO

THE INDIGENOUS Community of Mamo is located in the southeast corner of the state of Anzoátegui, on the southern edge of the Mesa de Uracoa. Although named for Laguna Mamo, the largest body of water in the area, the town itself lies some five kilometers (three miles) distant from the lake.

As with Cachama, there is no record of when the town was settled. A Warau mission founded near Laguna Mamo in 1735 was destroyed that same year by a force of Caribs (CAULIN 1958: 470-71). Presumably the Karinya settlement was established there sometime after 1783, since there is no record that the commission under Don Luis de Chávez y Mendoza ever surveyed lands in that area. By 1841, however, Mamo was the *cabecera* of the local parish, and according to local tradition, the ancestors of the present inhabitants had been living there some time when the Five Years War broke out in 1859. Most likely the first Karinya settlers left Tabaro and moved to the vicinity of Mamo sometime between 1800-1820.

So far as I have been able to determine, legal title to the local land was first obtained subsequent to a government survey conducted in 1938 (document in the possession of Pedro Poito, former Capitán Gobernador of Mamo). However custom seems to have recognized certain traditional rights in the land prior to this time, and it is possible there was some legal basis for this, although no documentary records have been found which would support such a claim.

Mamo is reached by a dirt track from Soledad, eighty kilometers (48 miles) to the east. Most communication however, is over a similar dirt track which runs twenty kilometers (twelve miles) south to the shore of the Orinoco at Palitar or Taguache.

At the present time the Mameños are dispersed in numerous settlements scattered throughout the area, as listed in Table VIII (also see Map VI).

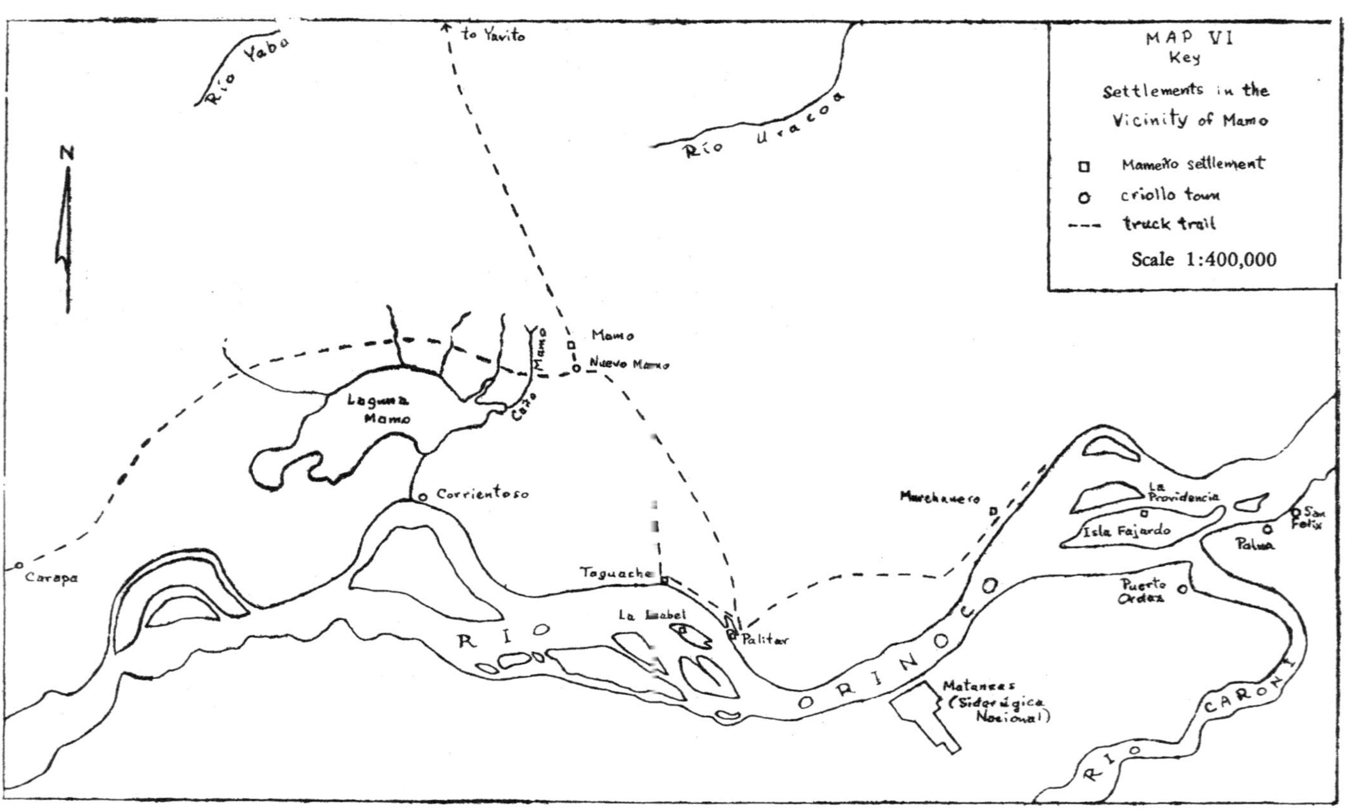
MAP VI
Key
Settlements in the
Vicinity of Mamo
Mameño settlement
criollo town
truck trail
Scale 1:400,000
N
to Yavito
Río Yaba
Río Uracoa
Mamo
Nuevo Mamo
Caño Mamo
Laguna Mamo
Corrientoso
Carapa
Taguache
Palitar
RIO ORINOCO
Matanzas
(Siderúgica Nacional)
La Providencia
Isla Fajardo
Puerto Ordaz
Palua
San Felix
RIO CARONI

TABLE VIII

POPULATION OF MAMEÑO SETTLEMENTS

Settlement	*Population*
Mamo (propio)	140
Palitar	135
Taguache	23
Isla La Isabel	20
Marchanero (est.)	57
Yavito	63
TOTAL	438

Within each settlement houses tend to be clustered together compactly, rather than scattered randomly as is the case in Cachama.

In spite of their dispersion, however, the inhabitants of these various settlements still consider themselves Mameños and view the settlements as subordinate to the home community. This they generally refer to as *"propio Mamo,"* a term which I will adopt in this study to distinguish the *settlement* of Mamo, or the home village itself, from the *community* of Mamo which is an affective and social entity that includes all the settlements listed above. In addition numerous Mameños now resident in various criollo settlements or in the towns such as San Félix, Matanzas, and Ciudad Bolívar are properly included as members of the indigenous community. It is estimated that something like 100 Mameños are currently living in the towns. This estimate is based on a list of relatives reported by respondents to the census which was conducted in Mamo.

Chapter 6

ECONOMIC FACTORS

THE MAMEÑOS are and always have been essentially farmers. Fishing has long provided an important secondary source of food, and in recent years the development of the Guayana industrial complex near the confluence of the Caroní and Orinoco rivers has opened up a third potential source of subsistence. Each of these and their ramifications will be discussed in turn.

The village of Mamo itself is located on the southernmost edge of the Mesas Orientales. At this point there is a rather abrupt escarpment which drops off about 50 m. to the Llanos Bajos (popularly known as the "Costo del Orinoco"). The Llanos Bajos are a flood plain which parallels the course of the Orinoco, ranging from 20-50 km. (12-30 miles) in width. The Mesas around Mamo are much like those of Cachama—with sandy or stony soil, covered with a savanna vegetation of coarse grass. *Matas,* scattered groves of scrub and trees, seem to be more frequent in this vicinity. As is true nearly everywhere, the savanna is unsuitable for agriculture throughout most of the year. Even during the rainy season its cultivation is limited to patio plants—a few fruits, vegetables and flowers which are nurtured along in the vicinity of the house. Due to the nature of the savanna it seems that, even with modern technology, it could be made *permanently* productive only with the use of mechanized equipment and advanced techniques of conservation.

However, numerous springs and streams emerge from the foot of the escarpment, presumably marking the level at which ground water is to be found under the mesa. These drain across the Llanos Bajos to the Orinoco. Even where there is no surface water this low-lying soil often remains moist the year around. As a result soil and vegetation conditions are very similar to those found along the river bottoms which are cultivated in other Karinya communities. (Technically perhaps, the Llanos

Bajos could be considered one immense gallery forest paralleling the Orinoco, but there is actually considerable variety in conditions of soil and vegetation. Some higher and drier localities even resemble the still higher savannas of the mesas.) Here as elsewhere, the principal problem is that of providing drainage for the fields so that they will not be too moist for the crops.

Although manioc provides the staple crop in Mamo, a number of other plants are important, such as bananas, pineapples, xanthosoma, yams, squash. Maize seems to be raised mostly for poultry feed.

Twenty kilometers south, several settlements have grown up where the shores of the Orinoco provide rich silts for cultivation. Most of the crops which are important in Mamo are grown here for individual consumption, but in addition considerable surpluses of maize and beans are produced for sale. Emphasis on these crops, with their relatively short growing season, seems to be associated with the cyclical nature of cultivation along the great River. At the onset of the rainy season the Orinoco rises and floods all but the highest spots, generally reserved as house sites. Fields can only be worked for the seven or eight months of the year when these flood waters recede to the main channels of the river.

Thirty-three kilometers north of Mamo the Río Yabo has cut a steep-walled channel into the surface of the mesa. The slopes of this channel are rich and moist. Numerous Mameños living in the community of Yavito produce quantities of manioc and manioc bread, plantains and bananas, pineapples, squash, "yancín" (dasheen or *danchi, Colocasia esculenta*), papayas and sugar cane.

The people of Mamo were always familiar with the potentialities of these areas, but they did not begin to exploit them until they were forced to move out of *propio Mamo* in search of fields or wage labor elsewhere. Since that time, however, these three localities have been exchanging foodstuffs. The differences in cultivated crops have meant a slight degree of specialization. Furthermore Yavito is deficient in fish and game and has long traded its surplus vegetable products with the other two areas, particularly *propio Mamo,* for dried fish and game to satisfy their protein needs.

There appear to have been no significant changes in any farming practises during this century. A few important crops such as the mango and "yancín" are undoubtedly of recent introduction, the latter probably coming from Trinidad or British Guiana. During the last few years the Ministry of Agriculture had introduced a heavier-yielding annual cotton, but it has become important only along the Orinoco. Most other recently introduced crops, such as pigeon peas, sesame and the like are grown mostly as curiosities. With the exception of annual cotton, the new crops arrived independently of the major forces stimulating culture change.

Nor have recent developments had any effect on patterns of land use. The farmer in Mamo continues to cultivate the swampy lowlands, the one in Yavito continues to clear the slopes of the Río Yabo, while their fellow tribesman maintains his fields on the banks of the Orinoco. There has been no attempt to exploit the savanna, nor even any indication of a desire to do so. There is no need to look to the savanna, for there is still far more cultivable land available in the more fertile low-lying areas than could ever be exploited by all the local men. In short, traditional ways of farming have continued because there is no population pressure, there is no land hunger. In the absence of pressures toward change, change is unlikely.

But farming in Mamo really represents only half the subsistence picture. Fishing is of nearly equal importance in its contribution to the diet. The lakes and streams which are scattered through the Costo del Orinoco are rich with a never-ending supply of fish, since any vacuum produced by human exploitation is rapidly replenished from the Orinoco itself. The adult men living in Mamo and along the Orinoco spend about as much time fishing (4-5 hours every other day) as they do cultivating their fields. They actually eat more fish than they do manioc bread (though their *total* intake of vegetable foods is greater).[1] The Río Yabo on the other hand, is extremely deficient in fish, and as mentioned above, the inhabitants of Yavito exchange their surplus vegetable produce with the inhabitants of Mamo for the latters' surplus of dried fish.

Hunting is not particularly important in any of these localities, except for aquatic species, which do constitute a lesser, but nonetheless significant addition to the diet. The most important of these are the *baba (Caiman sclerops),* several species of turtle, and a variety of wading and swimming birds.

It becomes clear from the above that the Mameño is closely integrated with his natural environment and dependent upon it. He must clear the forest and brush while at the same time paying close attention

[1] In fact, the importance of fishing among the Mameños is so great, it has suggested that perhaps the importance of fishing to basic subsistence has not been adequately emphasized among the largely riparian tribes of the Tropical Forest area of South America. It may be that fishing is far more important among many of them than is hunting. Certainly it can be far more productive.

to the amount of available water whenever he plants a field. He is dependent upon local fauna, particularly aquatic fish, reptiles and birds, as a major source of proteins in his diet. In addition timber is often cut for building purposes, wood is collected for firewood, moriche fronds *(Mauritia flexuosa)* are cut for their fibers, used in weaving hammocks, and both moriche and temiche *(Manicaria saccifera)* fronds are utilized for roof thatch.

Under the Pérez Jiménez regime (1950-57) laws were promulgated to "protect the natural resources" of the nation. These laws forbade the cutting of any timber without a permit, and according to the Mameños, this also applied to the removal of leaf fronds from palm trees. Likewise, no game could be hunted, nor fish caught, without first securing official permission, even if one was only obtaining them for his own use. Presumably these restrictions applied to Indian and criollo alike, but the Mameños seem to view this period as one of increased harassment at the hands of the criollos.

Their annoyance at these restrictions was even greater because they ran counter to an important concept in Mameño ideology. They believe that every stream or lagoon has its *amo* or "master" who controls the fish and other aquatic species which are to be found there. One's success at fishing or hunting depends upon the favor of the *amo.* This spirit never begrudges good fortune to a man if he is only seeking to feed his own family. But if the enterprise is designed to make money, if it is a commercial operation in any way, they believe he is doomed to failure in one way or another. What most rankled the Mameños about the conservation laws was that in all instances a permit was required. "How was a man to feed his family?" when he could be arrested for nothing more than catching a few fish for his own dinner table.

As a matter of fact, the local cacique did finally succeed in obtaining permits for these most essential subsistence activities. But although a unit of the National Guard was maintained locally to enforce such laws as those relating to conservation, it was necessary to travel to Ciudad Bolívar to obtain the permits. Under the Betancourt administration, however, conditions became much more tenable. There are no national Guardsmen present in Mamo, but the respective government agencies do send officials around periodically to facilitate the distribution of permits to the local people.

Livestock are of minor importance to the Indian community, although some of their criollo neighbors maintain herds of cattle and horses. Criollo cupidity seems to be the major factor inhibiting the possession of livestock. As one informant ruefully put it, "Most of us don't want to buy cattle because in three or four months a cow disappears. The *médico* (or curioso) can have cattle because he's a *médico* and people respect him" (because of his supernatural power). A few people have horses, but these are rarely kept in Mamo; rather they are pastured somewhere else, at a distance from the community.

For most families the only livestock that are at all significant are pigs, burros and chickens. Pigs are raised mostly for sale, chickens for their eggs which are eaten, or to be sold. Nearly every family owns at least one burro which is used for hauling —water from the spring, crops from the field, and a variety of items between Mamo, Yavito and the Orinoco (in spite of the fact that pickup or truck transportation is usually available, for the cost of hiring motor transportation may be exorbitant).

Traditional cultural activities do make it possible to exploit some other sources of income, but they are of minor importance in the total picture. Thus both curing and midwifery can be lucrative for a few individuals, but obviously one or two such specialists are adequate to meet the demand. Craft production appears to have been more important in the past than at present. The one surviving potter has moved to the city and no longer makes pottery. While several men know how to make baskets, only one still supports himself with this specialty, and he provides most of the needs of both Indians and the local criollos.

Wage labor is both familiar to the Mameño and an economic activity of long standing. Manuel María Macadito tells how he was employed at a cane plantation in Yavito about the turn of the century. A few years later, probably in 1910, he was working as a *cargador,* under contract to haul goods such as cane sugar, xanthosoma, and cowhides to the shores of the Orinoco.

With the dispersal of the Indians from *propio Mamo* circa 1912, a number of young fellows went out to seek their fortune elsewhere. Several of them signed on with *sarrapia (Coumarouna punctata)* contractors who transported them to the vicinity of Puerto Suapure on the lower Río Caura. Just as in rubber collecting and similar enterprises, they usually made barely enough to pay off expenses and debts. Nonetheless, some people like Antonio Martínez spent several seasons in the sarrapia harvest, apparently lured on by the prospect that the next time they would strike it rich.

Ordinary day labor has always been a convenient means of earning extra money. One can almost always find some one who needs help in his fields. Probably wage labor first became important when the Indians began to move away from Mamo. Particularly along the Orinoco, the rapid rise of the flood waters at the beginning of the rainy season means that a great deal of labor must be expended within a relatively short period of time in order to harvest the crops before they are inundated. These conditions produce a "harvest season" that is more comparable to that of temperate regions than is usually the case in tropical agriculture. Extra hands are always in demand at this time, and particularly the younger or single men who have yet to establish fields of their own, are attracted to this sort of employment. [I know of only three married men who frequently engage in field labor for others, while there are at least seven unmarried men who are generally so employed. Before industrial employment drew them away, (see Table IX), the principal income of many more younger and single men undoubtedly depended on opportunities for field labor.]

Day laborers are employed both by Indian and criollo farmers. But among the Indians themselves there is a fair amount of mutual labor exchange. This helps one another out while saving the expense of hiring work done. Mutual labor exchange is not used as much in the fields now as it is in tedious household tasks, such as the preparation of manioc bread, or with respect to the catching and distribution of fish and game.

Industrial Development and its Consequences

WHEN PEREZ JIMENEZ was in power a grandiose scheme was conceived for the development of an industrial nucleus in Venezuelan Guayana. Two North American corporations were currently in the process of opening up extensive deposits of iron ore which had been discovered in the mountains of Guayana, and were trans-shipping ore from facilities which they had constructed on either side of the mouth of the Río Caroní. The Falls of the Caroní, only a few miles upstream, offered great potential as a source of hydroelectric power. It could be expected that further mineral and natural resources might be developed as an initial industrial complex became established.

With this end in mind the Corporación Venezolana de Guayana was organized, and agreements were made with several Italian companies, first to build the Caroní Dam which would provide 300,000 kw of hydroelectric power, and then the Siderúrgica Nacional, the national steel plant at Matanzas on the Guayana shore of the Orinoco.

Needless to say, all this industrial activity provided great stimulus to the local economy. Urban concentrations such as Puerto Ordaz and San Félix sprang up, while people from all parts of the country flocked to the new area in search of jobs. The Mameños did not permit these opportunities to pass them by unaffected. Several of the younger men obtained employment on the construction crews, both at the Caroní Dam project and at the national steel plant. Unfortunately, most of these men were laid off as construction was completed. However, some had secured positions with the operating crews of the Matanzas steel plant, and as this neared full completion in 1962 more and more jobs were opening up. Most of those who had previously been laid off were being reabsorbed in the labor force for the steel plant.

This employment is not limited to unskilled laborers. Since Venezuela lacked men trained in the proper skills to maintain and operate the new industrial complex, many of the new employees were given on-the-job training in the requisite skills. Thus some of the men from Mamo have worked into positions as lathers, crane operators, and electricians. Table IX lists those whose principal income at present is from employment which is dependent upon the Guayana industrial complex.

The "No. of years employed" represents the total number of years, as most of the men listed were laid off about 1958 and did not go back to work until 1960-62. Several of those listed as presently unemployed are actually engaged in other activities, such as farming or school teaching. At least two of those listed in this category quite clearly state that they have no desire to return to industrial employment. Nonetheless, the fact that they have had this kind of first-hand contact indicates that they are not free of the direct impact of this industrial development. For similar reasons two criollos are listed because they are married to women from Mamo. They thereby serve as a source of acculturative influences for their conjugal kinsmen. Of even greater importance is the influence their employment will have on their children, since the latter are still considered to belong to and have rights in the Indigenous Community of Mamo, and since they too have frequent opportunity for interaction with their kinsmen who reside there.

TABLE IX

MAMEÑOS EMPLOYED IN INDUSTRY

	Name	*Occupation*	*Nº of years employed*
1.	Francisco Reyes	crane operator	5
2.	Jesús Pérez	electrician	5
3.	Adolfo Tempo	welder	4+
4.	Juan Ñávarez	electrician	4
5.	Miguel Guillén	"gatero" (lift driver?)	4
6.	Evarito Vera	mechanic	4
7.	Pedrito Pariche	lathe operator	2
8.	Joaquín Brito	carpenter	11 mo.
9.	Teodoro Avendaño	electrician	3 mo.
10.	Antonio Pariche	"caldero"	3 mo.
11.	Andrés Vera		4
12.	Juan Francisco Vásquez		4
13.	Pedro Damián Pariche		
14.	Leopoldo Rodríguez	laborer	4
15.	Santos Rodríguez	laborer	1
16.	Ramón Isidro Pariche	laborer	occasional
17.	Pedro Trinos Reyes	longshoreman	occasional
Presently unemployed (1962)			
18.	Crispín Tempo	mechanic	
19.	Ricardo Reyes		
20.	Fernando Martínez	crane operator	
21.	Francisco Ñávarez		
22.	Francisco Chiroco		
23.	José Pariche		
Criollos married to Mameñas			
1.	Darío Romero	laborer	4+
2.	Urbano Suárez	longshoreman	occasional

The indirect impact of industrialization on local economic patterns has been even more far-reaching. Since the river has always been the principal highway of communication in this area, cultivation along the Orinoco had always been oriented more to cash sales of a portion of the crops than was true in localities which are some distance from the river. But the development of urban concentrations at several points along the lower Orinoco has created great demand for staple grains such as maize and beans. To a lesser extent there has also been increased demand for certain vegetables, such as squash, watermelons and "yancín." Recently the Ministerio de Agricultura y Cría has attempted to stimulate the textile industry by introducing a superior variety of cotton. At least one farmer on La Isabel tried it out seriously in 1961-62 and harvested nearly two tons.

To date this kind of cash cropping is restricted to the islands and shores of the Orinoco itself, but Fernando Martínez, the progressive schoolteacher of Mamo, envisions the local farmers playing an increasingly important role in providing foodstuffs for the workers of the growing industrial complex just across the river.

Through direct employment in industry, through increased cash cropping or merely through the general increase in economic activity, family income in terms of actual cash in hand has increased somewhat. Particularly where there is direct employment in industry, the increase has been marked. Naturally there has also been extensive broadening of economic opportunities. It is likely that even more individuals could enhance their present earning capacity, were they sufficiently motivated to do so. Even women are presented with opportunities to earn a regular cash income. Several girls from Mamo are employed as domestics by city families, and some are considering the possibility of studying for commercial positions.

Industrial development and rapidly expanding economic opportunities within a broad spectrum of activities has stimulated some outright emigration to the towns. I estimate that something on the order of 100 Mameños were living in a town at the time of our study, with about 60 per cent of the emigres being women! Although most were living in San Félix, one or two were said to be in the vicinity of Ciudad Bolívar and a like number in the El Tigre area. One youth was even living in Caracas where he was attempting to further his education. It is true that emigration has its beginnings much earlier (see CHAP. 8 on community). The fact that there was already an established pattern made it relatively easy to respond to the attractions of new industrial cities. While it is legitimate to speak of increased emigration sparked by the industrial growth of the last decade, it must be emphasized that these people did not all emgirate from *propio Mamo.* They left from nearly all the localities where Mameños have been and still are resident, and they left and are continuing to leave over a period of years. Thus, although the picture is one of significant emigration, it has not been particularly disruptive of the community as a whole.

Actually emigration by itself represents no more than half the picture. It might be more accurate to describe the present situation as one of increased spatial mobility. There is continual movement from Yavito to Mamo, from Mamo to "the Islands," or from Mamo to the towns; and back again. One side effect of this mobility has been the development of boarding as an institution. Pedro Poito, former governor of Mamo, boarded a young woman who claimed to be ill and her three children for several months while she "recovered." She appropriated most of her husband's wages from the Matanzas plant to pay for room and board as well as treatments. Likewise Fernando the village schoolteacher paid a portion of his monthly salary to his parents in exchange for room and board. A similar situation is found in one or two households in Palitar.[2]

Larger incomes and the generalized stimulation of local economic activity has also meant increased availability of a great many material goods and foodstuffs. The well-dressed teenage girl in Mamo is indistinguishable from her city cousins—even to putting her hair up on giant rollers (bouffant hair styles were currently the rage), and a trip to the city meant an opportunity for a permanent. Weekly paychecks among the industrial workers have permitted increased consumption of liquor. Both distilled spirits and beer are popular. Some of the well-to-do families have invested in kerosene refrigerators in which they can keep their beer cold. (At least one enterprising family also sells ice which they freeze in their refrigerator.) Radios are becoming a fairly common item, and most recently the industrial workers have started to invest the equivalent of a month's pay or more in battery-powered transitor stereophonic phonographs! On a more mundane level no house is without

[2] See Chap. 8: FAMILY for a discussion of how older patterns of economic interdependence within the extended family have been adapted to the new economic conditions.

a small kerosene stove which is admittedly a luxury item, since it is used only at the beginning of the rains when heavy uninterrupted downpours make it difficult to secure firewood. The most important food items which are bought with some regularity from local merchants are powdered milk, green coffee, and *papelón* (raw cane sugar), although, as indicated above, considerable quantities of grain and starchy vegetables are purchased directly from the producer. Undoubtedly the government's recent installation in propio Mamo of a generator for electricity and the drilling of a well for water will also have numerous repercussions on the local economy.

It is striking, however, that Mamo lacks two of the most desired symbols of "progressiveness" in Cachama —"zinc" roofing and bicycles. Undoubtedly their lack is directly related to local conditions. Since Mamo is distant from any highway, transportation of metallic roof sheeting would probably bring its cost up to exorbitant levels. Again, the lack of paved roads and extensive areas of sandy or stony ground militate aginst adopting the bicycle as an efficient means of transportation. The burro remains superior. To date a step upward would mean investing in a pickup or truck (as some criollos have done).

So far I have discussed the changing economic situation mostly in terms of its economic effects, although I have implied the existence of certain correlative social influences. The more important of these will be taken up in succeeding chapters, but discussion of one seems appropriate at this point. The growth of industry and towns along the Guayana shore of the Orinoco has produced an interesting modification of residence pattern. In addition to those who have emigrated directly to the towns, a considerable number have become "suburbanites," commuting to work from their place(s) of residence. For several decades the Mameños have been scattered about the area, living in numerous settlements such as Yavito, Taguache and La Isabel. Apparently, in many cases there were no more than one or two Indian families in a given settlement. As industrial employment opened up a few men moved to the towns, but the majority settled in Taguache and Palitar. These two settlements are so located that one can easily reach Matanzas within a half hour by motor launch. Palitar in particular had been an insignificant cluster of houses prior to this time, but in 1962 there were 44 houses, three stores, and a school in Palitar Adentro, and several more houses in Palitar Afuera. About 40 per cent of the residents are Indians from Mamo. Several individuals there own motor launches including two Indians and one criollo married to an Indian. At least one

Indian launch and the latter criollo launch make daily trips to Matanzas. A lucrative addition to their income is obtained by selling passage to other workers who lack their own means of transportation. The situation in Taguache is similar, although since it is several minutes further upstream, fewer industrial workers have settled there.

However, these men are not only daily commuters. A number are weekend commuters as well. Only a half day is worked on Saturdays. As soon as paychecks are distributed at noon, the workers return to Palitar by launch. There three or four of them seek out a pickup truck and arrange for transportation to *propio Mamo,* where they generally arrive early in the evening. Some, like Leopoldo Rodríguez, maintain dual residence in the two settlements. Evarito Vera came each week to visit his convalescent wife. The remainder constitutes a variable group which changes from week to week, mostly sons or nephews or cousins of persons resident in *propio Mamo,* who merely want to visit their kinsmen for the weekend.

Saturday night there is usually a dance at the "Casa Grande," the home of Gregorio Pariche, which is the focus for many community activities. Drinking begins during this time, but does not become serious until the dance ends at about 11:00 o'clock. From 11:00 until dawn the workers, accompanied by some of their local friends, dissipate some of their week's wages by drinking, singing, and generally "whooping it up." Sunday is generally a quieter day, although the activities of the night before may continue at a slower pace. About mid-afternoon the workers return to Palitar for another week at the factory.

Although some aspects of this pattern, such as heavy drinking, might be considered evidence of social disorganization, the integrative aspects appear to far outweigh them. The commitment to the community of Mamo, the desire to return frequently to visit family and friends, tends to reinforce the ties of industrial workers with their natal community. They are willing to undergo added expense, just to be able to dance, sing and drink with kinsmen and friends, even though they could dance and sing and drink just as much or more in Palitar or San Félix. For that matter, residence in Palitar appears to have been chosen precisely because it is that point along the north bank of the Orinoco which has the most direct communication with *propio Mamo.* Thus commuting, both daily and weekend, reflects the current strength of Mamo as a community, and in turn it serves to reinforce interpersonal ties within the group, as well as personal commitment to the community as a whole.

Comparison and Conclusions

IT IS CLEAR THAT the Mameño occupies a much more bountiful environment than does his Cachaman cousin. Arable land is abundant and there is no population pressure threatening future expansion of agriculture. Fish and aquatic game are also abundant, enabling the Mameño to eat quite well. In Cachama there are, practically speaking, neither fish nor game. All available arable land is being cultivated, forcing the Cachaman to look to the less attractive savanna land which is also more expensive to cultivate. The Cachaman does not eat nearly so well.[3]

At the same time, living in the *cabecera municipal,* or in proximity to the Orinoco river, has subjected the Mameño to considerable surveillance and control over his use of natural resources by government authorities. For some reason the Cachamans have not been subjected to the same kinds of controls, even though on the face of it they are more accessible. Perhaps the difference reflects a distinction in Indian-criollo relations in the two communities.

Livestock is unimportant in both, although the Mameños do keep a few head of smaller livestock such as pigs and burros. It appears that livestock may have been somewhat more important in the past, although there is no evidence that it was ever a vital part of the Karinya economy.

Likewise, craft specializations appear to be dying out in both communities, since most craft items can be obtained more cheaply and with greater facility in the towns.

Whereas wage labor is a long-standing practise in Mamo, it seems to represent a new development in Cachama. The Mameños have been living in close proximity to criollos for a long time. Presumably it was always possible to obtain employment with the latter. Particularly after the dispersal of Indians from *propio Mamo* (ca. 1912), does wage labor appear to have become well developed. In Cachama neither the opportunities nor the necessity of seeking wage labor were very great until the development of the oil industry in that area during the 1940's.

There is more than just a time difference represented here. During the many years he was engaging in wage labor the Mameño had an opportunity to familiarize himself with criollo culture. The Cachaman had

[3]Observable differences in energy expenditure among the children of Cachama and Mamo may be a direct expression of the differences in *kinds* of food consumed in the two communities.

no such opportunity. When employment in Guayanese industry opened up, neither the idea of working for wages, nor the necessity of moving in a criollo milieu were unfamiliar to the Mameño. He quite quickly and naturally took advantage of these opportunities. But the Cachaman was not familiar with wages, nor was he intimately acquainted with criollo culture. He had little motivation to seek employment in the petroleum industry, and only now is he becoming accustomed to wage labor as a means of economic enhancement. Even so, a relatively independent occupation, such as working in the gravel, remains more attractive for many young Cachamans.

The fact that many of the industrial workers from Mamo have been trained in one or another skill may represent nothing more than historical accident, but I prefer to consider it otherwise. Most Mameños are literate, whereas most Cachamans are not. Mameño values also emphasize education, "civilization," and sophistication. Skilled labor or commercial employment is considered to be more "civilized" than unskilled labor or working a field "in the hot sun." Undoubtedly the success of Mameño workers in obtaining skilled labor positions is due to this cultural "drive to civilization." While this is also expressed as a value in Cachama, it does not seem to run very deep. There is little integration with other values attitudes, and there is a minimum of appropriate behavior to support this point of view.

The development of the two industrial complexes in the vicinity of these two communities have both had numerous indirect economic effects. In both cases cash cropping has been stimulated, though it has become a much more significant part of the local economy among the Mameños. But again, familiarity with the criollo way of life has facilitated a sizable emigration to the towns, something which is almost alien to the Cachamans, in spite of the latter's greater proximity to urban settlements. In fact, while the Cachamans are tending to move back to the tribal lands, the Mameños appear to be increasing their mobility, even though they continue to maintain affective ties with the home community.

An increase of income in both groups has meant increased consumption of purchased goods. In Cachama changes in *patterns* of consumption have been relatively modest —macaroni and canned fish, bicycles and "zinc" roofs. But in Mamo the major changes have been changes in patterns of consumption— "cityfied" hair styles and dress; consumption of beer; investment in appliances, be they kerosene stoves, or refrigerators, or stereophonic phonographs; and such new food items as powdered milk. Yet such items of material progress seem to be less important as status symbols in Mamo than are "zinc" roofs in Cachama.

One difference which appears striking on the surface turns out not to be when examined more closely. There are at least four *kioscos* or small stores in Cachama, none in *propio Mamo.* In Mamo doña Marta of the Casa Grande does sell such things as soda pop, beer, ice cubes, etc. But most of this sort of business is in the hands of the criollos just down the hill in Mamo Abajo. Their stores are of long standing and sufficiently well stocked that they would create stiff competition for any new commercial enterprises. Having no need, the Mameños have not developed any local stores. But in Cachama there was less direct competition, which provided local individuals with an opportunity to set up their own stores.

The major distinctions between the two communities are that in Cachama subsistence continues to be based for the most part on traditional activities. The most significant changes have been directed to these traditional subsistence activities, e.g., the introduction of cash cropping, and the cultivation of the savanna. Most alternative occupations remain secondary and subsidiary. In Mamo there has been less change in traditional subsistence patterns, although there has been some intensification of crop production. Instead, many of the younger men have shifted to a wholly new and different occupation, that of industrial worker. This in turn has brought both economic and social changes in its wake, which presumably will become greater in ensuing years. Cash cropping and increased consumption have developed comparably in the two communities, but there have been more significant changes in *patterns* of consumption in Mamo. Perhaps most striking of all is the fact that contact with industrialization has introduced centripetal tendencies among the Cachamans, whereas it has stimulated centrifugal movement among the Mameños.

CHAPTER 7

KINSHIP

THE PAST THIRTY years in Mamo have witnessed an almost complete shift from the speaking of Karinya in everyday conversation to Spanish. In fact, children today no longer learn Karinya at all. As a consequence Karinya kinship terms, which were in a process of change in Mamo, were arrested part way through that change, before the system could reach a new equilibrium. Today it has been replaced by the ordinary Spanish terminology. Nevertheless, we were able to obtain several sets of Karinya terms from different informants. On the basis of this data it is possible to sketch out a very interesting, though incomplete, pattern of change.

The traditional system (male speaking) is diagrammed in Fig. VII. It is based mostly on the data obtained from an 85-year old informant, although most of the terms indicated by him are supported with information obtained from a 70-year old man.

No female informants of comparable age were available, and all of the systems obtained from younger informants indicate various kinds of modifications had already begun to occur in the system by the time they were learning it. Nonetheless, it has been possible to partially reconstruct the traditional female-speaking terminology on the basis of present data, the known traditional pattern, and comparison with male-speaking terminology (see Fig. VIII). Terms for parallel cousins do not appear in Fig. VIII, but presumably they were traditionally the same as those for own siblings.

The same conventions are used in these diagrams as for the Cachama system, viz. where there are both address and reference terms for an individual, the former appears on the upper line, while the latter is indented one space on the lower line. Alternate address terms appear in parentheses.

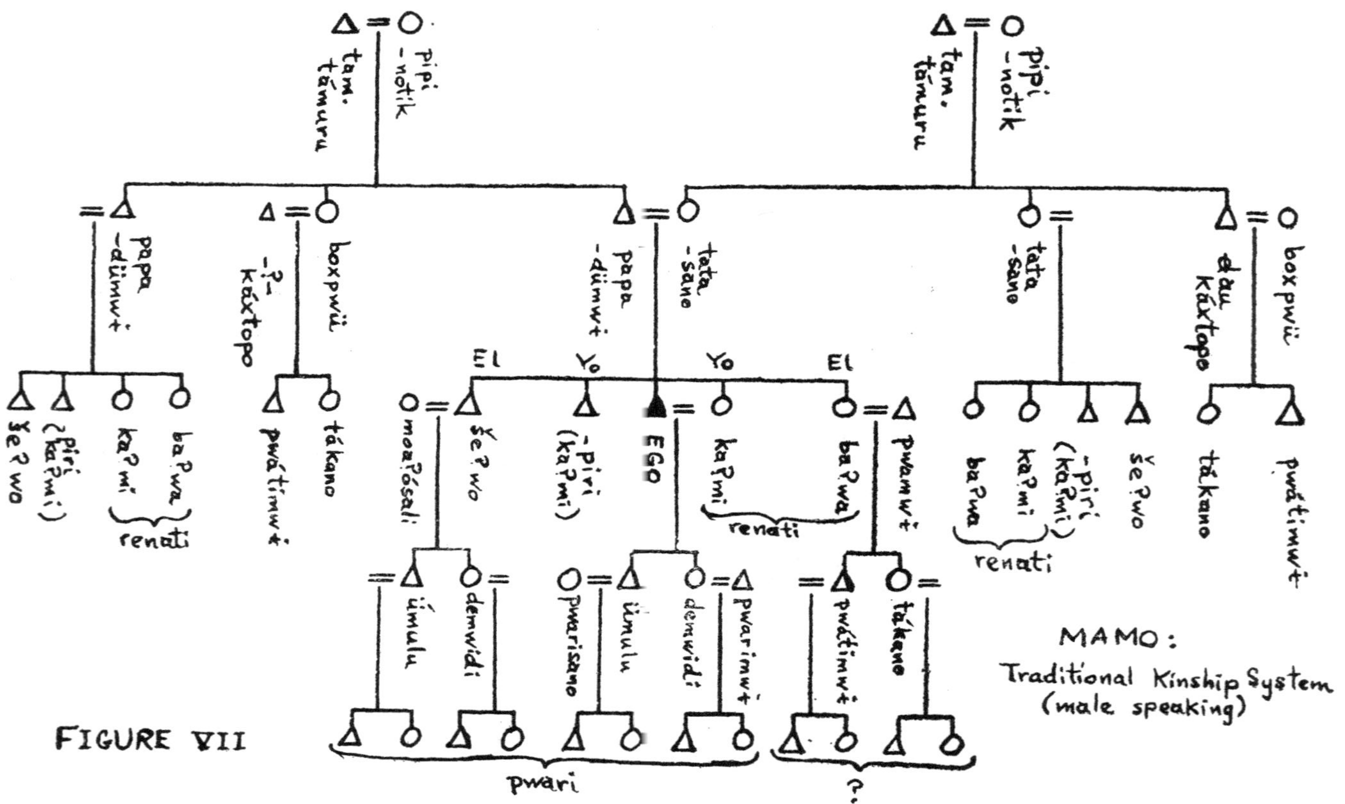

FIGURE VII

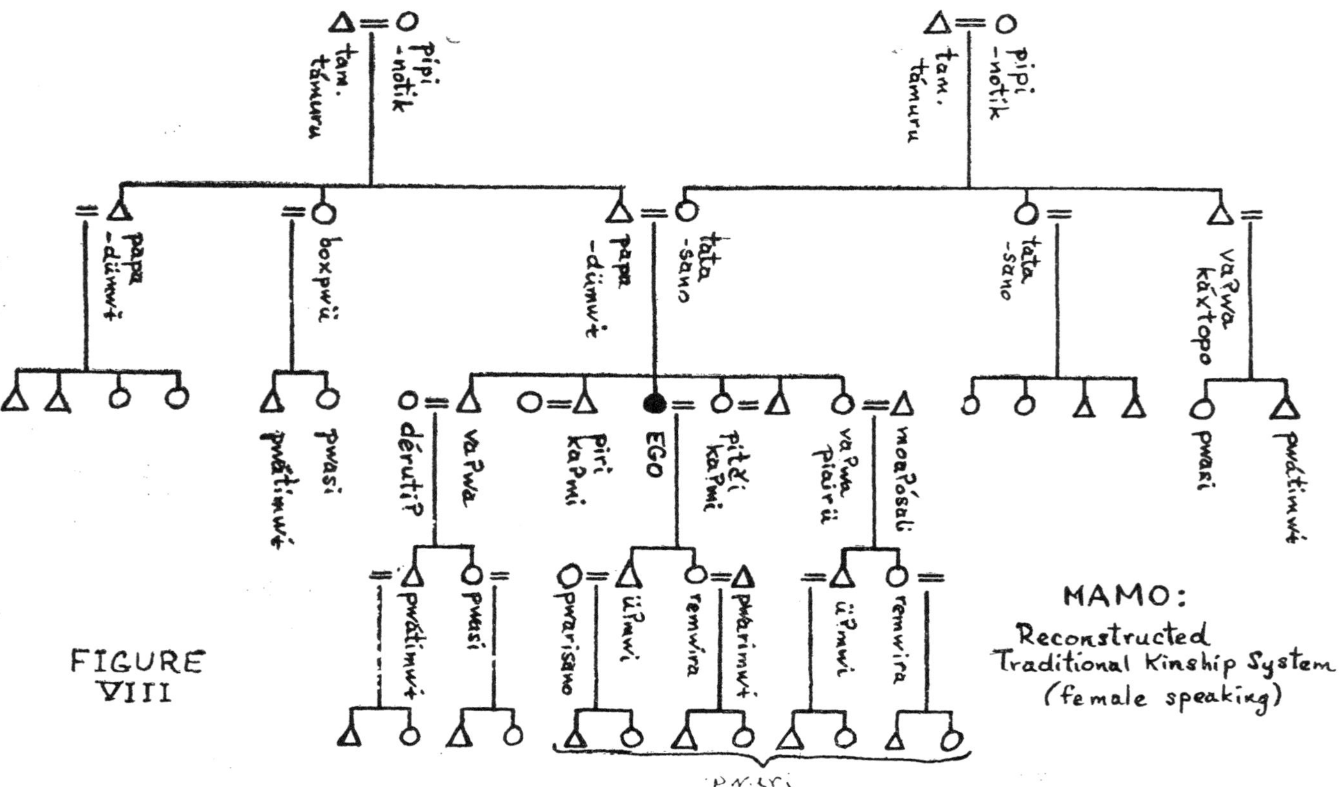
pipi
-notik
tam.
támuru
pipi
-notik
tam.
támuru
papa
-dümwɨ
boxpwü
papa
-dümwɨ
tata
-sano
tata
-sano
vaʔwa
káxtopo
pwasi
pwátimwɨ
déruti?
vaʔwa
piri
kaʔmi
EGO
pitči
kaʔmi
vaʔwa
piairü
moaʔósali
pwasi
pwátimwɨ
pwátimwɨ
pwasi
pwarisano
üʔmwi
remwira
pwarimwɨ
üʔmwi
remwira
MAMO:
Reconstructed
Traditional Kinship System
(female speaking)
FIGURE
VIII

In all cases where it can be identified, the first person possessive prefix *a-* has been separated from the root morpheme. In practise it is invariably attached to the following terms: *-notik* (FaMo, MoMo); *-sano* (Mo, MoSi); *-dümwï* (Fa, FaBr); *-piri* (YoBr, FaBrYoSo, MoSiYoSo); and sometimes to *támuru* (FaFa, MoFa), *renati* ("sister"), *boxpwü* (FaSi, as in *athanbóxpuli*), and *káxtopo* (MoBr).

It is not clear what the collateral terms may have been on the +2 generation in the traditional system. Only two informants (70 and 52 years old) were able to give us these collateral terms and in both instances they were generational. Is it safe to assume that the +2 generation was *originally* bifurcate merging? One could argue either way, but the limited available data seem to favor the latter conclusion.[1] The traditional system in Cachama was bifurcate merging on this generation. Presumably both communities once shared a common culture. Furthermore, in Cachama the present system is generational on the +2 level. It would be reasonable to expect a similar process to have taken place in Mamo, even though we have only been able to record the end product.

The +1 generation was clearly bifurcate merging in the traditional system, but my three youngest informants (52, 50, 37 years of age) all indicate an extension of *káxtopo* to FaBr and of *boxpwü* to MoSi effectively equating these two terms with the Spanish "tío" and "tía," and thereby transforming the terminology to the lineal type.

Data for the −2 generation is inadequate to draw any conclusions except that *pwari* include the offspring of all *children,* both own and classificatory.

As is the case in Cachama, the −1 generation appears to be the most resistant to change. As long as Karinya terms remained in use the bifurcate merging pattern prevailed.

It is the 0 generation which presents the greatest difficulty for analysis. The traditional pattern was one of Iroquois cousin terminology. The two female informants (52, 50) agree in describing a system of Eskimo terminology. The data from our male informants (aged 70, 37), however, indicate a more complex pattern of change in which the terms for male cousins became Hawaiian, while the terms for female

---

[1]GILLIN (1936: 85-97) claims the kin system of the Barama Caribs, which is very similar to the Karinya, is generational on the +2 and −2 generations (cf. p. 94), and also diagrams it that way. But in his two listings of terms he fails to indicate that the terms apply to any other than PaFa or PaMo and their *own sibling of same sex.*

cousins remained Iroquois. In spite of the internal contradictions here, it is nonetheless clear that kinship terminology in Mamo was being modified in the direction of a system which would be more consistent with cognatic descent. The recent substitution of Spanish for Kàrinya terms has served the same purpose. We will see below how the present patterns of independent nuclear family residence, combined with kinship responsibilities and claims which are equally distributed on a bilateral basis have made a lineal system of kinship functionally the most appropriate for this community.

Some Comparative Comments

AS FAR AS I was able to determine, conjugal kin are the same in Mamo and Cachama, (see Fig. III) except for WiSbCh, but the data are too sketchy to extract any significance from this.

Several terms are problematic since they seem superfluous. Given the remainder of the terms in the kin system, there seems no reason why it could not function perfectly well without these problematic terms. One of these is *renati,* a male-speaking term for sister or female parallel cousin, without distinction of relative age. At first this was taken to be a recent innovation, but there is evidence of a respectable time depth for it among the Callinago, whose kinship system includes many cognates with that of the Karinya (cf. TAYLOR 1946). Among the latter the term has come to be applied to both parallel and cross cousins, which is further evidence of the importance of cognatic descent. Cross cousins were traditionally called *tákono,* a term which includes the sister's daughter. With the extension of *renati* to cross cousins, it was only natural that it would be applied to sister's daughters as well, and this is exactly what took place in Cachama. In Mamo for some reason, this did not occur. Rather *renati* was restricted to kinswomen of Ego's own generation, in spite of the fact that it never completely replaced *tákano,* which continued to be used both for cross cousins and sister's daughters.

This represents only one of several instances of a common phenomenon in Karinya kinship — a tendency toward the extension of kinship terms, usually from closer kinsmen to more distant relatives. Thus in Cachama the term *piri* (YoBr, f.s.) underwent a process of extension and came to mean simply "brother." Effectively then, *piri* in Cachama is the female equivalent of the male-speaking *renati* ("sister").

Several times it has been mentioned that sister's children were equated with cross cousins in the traditional kinship terminology. This appears to be a survival of a former practise of preferential sister's daughter marriage. Contemporary Karinya deny the possibility of marrying this kinswoman, although four such unions were encountered in Cachama. There is considerable comparative evidence to support the probability of this practise having occurred among the Karinya in the past. GILLIN (1936: 95) sums this up as follows:

> A further peculiarity of the (Barama) system is to be noted in the provisions made permitting the marriage of a man with his sister's daughter, a type of marriage which has also been reported from the Carib Tamanak, Macusi, Galibi, Island Carib, Cumanagoto, Chayma and Palenke... Among the Barama Caribs a man calls his sister's daughter takano ("marriageable" or cross cousin), and a woman calls her mother's brother iyao, the term which she uses for all men whom she may marry.

In short, sister's daughter marriage appears to have been a widespread custom among the Cariban tribes of northern lowland South America. I have already pointed out that both Callinago and Barama kinship systems are closely related to that of the Karinya. Thus, it is more reasonable to suppose that the latter were like their linguistic relatives in practising sister's daughter marriage than to argue that they were distinct in this respect. Two factors probably led to the present obsolescence of the custom. Firstly, where preferential sister's daughter marriage is consistently practised it leads, in the second and all subsequent generations, to actual cross cousin marriage as well (i.e., sister's daughter is also the mother's brother's daughter, see Fig. IX). Not only does this explain how sister's children come to be equated with cross cousins, but it makes it a virtual necessity where this is a common form of marriage.

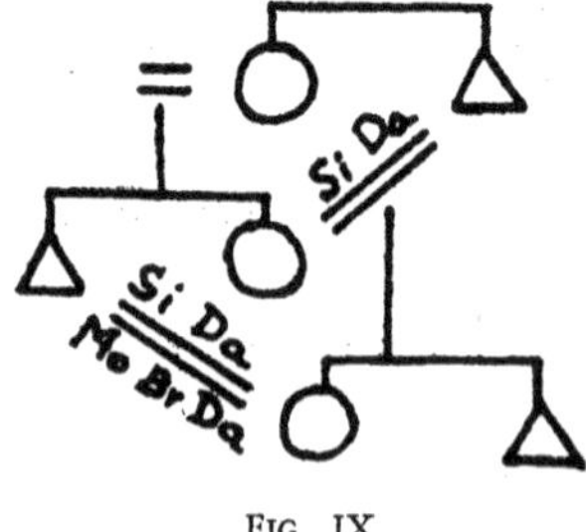

FIG. IX

Under these conditions sister's children would be practically non-existent as a distinctive class of kinsmen. Only when crosscousin marriage *ceased to be common* would they re-emerge as such, and at this time they might very well be considered inappropriate spouses, even when union with a cross cousin continued to be permissible.

Secondly, most Cachamans denied the propriety of marrying a first cousin (although four with cross cousins and five with first parallel cousins were recorded). In contrast the Mameños raised no objections to this type of marriage, even though only one such case was encountered among them. In Chapter III it was pointed out that this attitude is probably an accomodation to criollo values as well as Roman Catholic doctrine, and may not represent a very profound objection on the part of the Karinya. Nonetheless, close kin marriages having become infrequent for other reasons, it is convenient to explain their nonoccurrence in terms of the demands of the dominant culture.

The question might then be raised, why did close kin marriages become infrequent? Murphy's explanation (1960: 91) of a tendency to observe an incest tabu between all co-residents is not satisfactory for the Karinya, since all the evidence points to preferential matrilocality in the past, particularly when sister's daughter marriage would have been prevalent. Rather, the explanation in this case seems to rest on the recent shift in Mamo to neolocal nuclear family residence. This has led to the equivalence of cross and parallel cousins and has thereby militated against either as a potential spouse. A similar end result has come about in Cachama through increasing emphasis on the ambilineal ramage.

With descent and kinship ties becoming increasingly bilateral, there has been an appropriate shift in social organization, although with conflicting tendencies toward an ambilineal or bilateral system. It can be expected that the ultimate result will be bilateral, with either ambilocal, or more likely neolocal, residence. The latter tendency is stronger partly because the Karinya are not much interested in their own lineage and genealogy. Some cannot even name their own grandparents.[2] An ambilineal type of social organization is much more likely where there is interest in genealogy and where account is kept of one's ancestors in both parental lineages. A bilateral organization is also favored because of criollo influence. All other factors being equal, we would expect the influence of the dominant culture to be the deciding factor in such a change, as in fact it has been in Mamo, where the Spanish terminology (which is associated with bilateral descent) has wholly replaced the

[2]These difficulties, the common tendency to equate incorrectly certain Karinya terms with Spanish terms, and the fact that change has produced different perceptions of Karinya kinship structure among different individuals may be taken to explain the discrepancies between the present discussion of kinship and that reported by WILBERT (1957).

Karinya. In Cachama the present trend is toward ambilineality. Currently there is no evidence of a shift to independent nuclear families with neolocal residence. But should such a pattern emerge, I would expect to see a rather rapid transition to bilateral descent.[3]

---

[3] In a bi*lateral* system the emphasis is horizontal. "Descent" is less important than "kinship affiliation." Generally, each individual begins with himself at the center of his kinsmen and traces his kin ties outward on *both* his mother's and his father's sides. Closeness or distance of relationship to Ego is emphasized more than lineage ties or descent from a common ancestor. Under these circumstances the group of persons included as kin will *differ* for every individual except siblings (or occasionally spouses).

In ambi*lineality* the emphasis is vertical. Kin ties are based on descent from a common ancestor, but such descent may be traced through *either* males or females (usually some of each). In fact, Ego often has an opportunity to choose which of several kin groups (that of any *one* of his four grandparents, of either of his wife's parents, etc.) he wishes to affiliate with (see FIRTH 1957; and MURDOCK 1960). This is in contrast to unilineal descent where one is allowed no choice in affiliating with a particular line of descent. Ambilineality also contrasts with bilateral reckoning in that kinsmen of various degrees will be members of the *same* kin group.

CHAPTER 8

FAMILY

KINSHIP IN MAMO plays a role which is quite different from what it must have been in the past. It no longer serves to define marriage rules except for incest restrictions. It is incidental to residential practises, and apparently it has narrowed its scope in terms of defining descent. Nonetheless it continues to be important in some contexts, which will be examined shortly.

MARRIAGE

AS WAS INDICATED in the preceding chapter, marriage between kinsmen is extremely unusual in Mamo today. Only one case of cousin marriage (with a mother's sister's daughter) was discovered. Out of a total of 65 current unions, there was no indication of one with any other significantly close kinswoman.

Formal marriage is much more common here than in Cachama. I counted three civil marriages and five church marriages, in addition to nine couples who were married in both ways. This means that 26 per cent of the conjugal unions had been formally and legally consummated. The majority, nonetheless, are united only by consensual union. Although there is no discrimination against these latter individuals, there *is* a certain amount of prestige attached to formal marriage. It is one of those practises that are considered to be indicative of one's superior level of "education," "humanness" ("somos *cristianos*"),[1] and civilization. It

[1] Apparently the early missionaries instilled the idea that pagans and non-Christians are only half human. By definition then, a *cristiano* is a human being.

is clear that this is not the only factor which determines the form of the conjugal union. Opportunity for formal marriage is also important. The great majority of formal marriages are to be found among those who live in *propio Mamo*. Fifty-six per cent of the couples living there have been formally married. The next highest proportion is to be found in the several neighborhoods along the shores of the Orinoco, but there the percentage is only 28. Most of these were either former residents of Mamo, or else are accustomed to return there on the occasion of community fiestas — the only time when a priest is present to conduct baptisms, confirmations and weddings. In recent years a few of the young people have travelled to San Félix or Ciudad Bolívar in order to be married by the civil authorities. Consistent with the general custom in eastern Venezuela, children whose parents are formally married take their father's surname, while offsping of consensual unions take their mother's.

The commonest reason for marriage is "falling in love," although direct sexual attraction plays some part, too. Any boy who is unlucky enough to impregnate a girl may find himself faced with considerable pressure to marry her. A few individuals seem to take other factors into consideration, such as marrying a girl of the right family (the younger daughters of the wealthy local *curioso* are being eyed from this point of view), or finding the proper wife to further one's career (an attitude of the ambitious Mameño schoolteacher).

While a couple of girls consummated their first conjugal union at 11, most do so between 12 and 21 (see Table X). The mean age at marriage for girls is about 16. The mean age appears to have declined slightly from what it had been in the past, reaching a low of 14.3 years in the 20-29 age group. In the 10-19 age group (which includes only those individuals under 15 who are actually married) the mean age at marriage has risen to something over 15. The exact figure cannot yet be calculated, since three girls between 15 and 19 are still unmarried.

Among boys, the responsibilities of a conjugal union come somewhat later, between 16 and 26, or even older. For them the mean age at first conjugal union is about 22. This too has been dropping slightly, it is only about 21 among the 20-29 age group. It is unlikely that the mean age will drop below 20, however. In the 15-19 age group only one-third of the youths have married; and there are eight bachelors, aged 26 or over.

Although marriage among Mameño men is often delayed for economic reasons, this is a criollo pattern rather than an Indian one. Per-

TABLE X

MAMO: AGE AT *FIRST* CONJUGAL UNION

Present Age	*11*	*12*	*13*	*14*	*15*	*16*	*17*	*18*	*19*	*20*	*21*	*22*	*23*	*24*	*25*	*26+*	*Total*	*Mean*	*Mode*	*Range*
Men																				
10-19**						(1)*	(2)	1 (1)	1								6	17.5	18	16-19+
20-29						2	2	1		5	(1)	3	1			(4)	19	20.9	20	16-26+
30-39			1					1	4	1		1		1	1	3 (2)	15	20.9	19	13-26+
40-49							1	1				1				5 (1)	9	23.7	26	17-26+
50+				1		2	1	1	1			1		1	3	8 (1)	20	22.8	26	14-26+
TOTAL																	69	22	—	13-26+
Women																				
10-19**	1		2	1	2	1 (1)	(1)	1 (1)									11	15	—	11-18+
20-29		4	3	7	4	1	2		1								22	14.3	14	12-19
30-39		2	1	1	3	1	3										11	14.8	14/17	12-17
40-49	1	1		3	1		3		1		1						11	15.5	14/17	11-21
50+			1	4	1	1		1	2		2	1				(1)	14	17.6	14	13-22
TOTAL																	69	16	14	11-22

* Figures in parentheses refer to unmarried individuals.
** Unmarried youths younger than 15 are not included.

manent bachelorhood is even more of a criollo pattern. Such individuals occur with some frequency among the latter. There are eight that can be so characterized in Mamo, but not a single individual belonging to this category was encountered in Cachama. In a sense, the emergence of one criollo pattern, emigration in search of wage labor, has inadvertently resulted in another, delayed marriage or permanent bachelorhood.

Wage labor, whether in the fields, or employment in Guayanese industry, is much easier to assume for a few days, weeks or months, than is the task of clearing and planting one's own field. Wage labor brings more immediate cash returns without necessarily tying one down. Most young men appear to prefer remaining economically independent as long as there are no matrimonial obligations to consider. Most will eventually marry, though it is unlikely that three of the four over 30 (aged 51, 48, 37, 35) will ever do so, as they appear to be mentally retarded.

First unions of women do not appear to be very stable (see Table XI). Of 66 women, thirty or 45.5 per cent have had more than one conjugal union. In part at least, this is because of the high proportion of unions with criollo men (see Table XI). A good many Indian girls are seduced by criollos during their teens. Sometimes this results in a conjugal union, sometimes the girl is abandoned by her "lover." No distinction between these two situations has been made in our tabulations, since in most cases the girl will be abandoned after the birth of her child. Of 19 unions between criollos and Indian women under thirty, less than one-third are still living with their criollo consort. It is significant, too, that in the 20-29 age group, where the proportion of unions with criollo men has been the highest, eleven women out of 21 have had more than one union. The only age group which exceeds this proportion is that 50 and over. In this latter group many of the second unions have been consummated by widows who set up housekeeping with another man after the death of their first mate.

Bearing out the generally unstable and temporary nature of unions with criollos is the stability of male unions. From a total of 62 men, only 18, or 29 per cent, have had more than one conjugal union. Many of these second unions were consummated by widowed older men (six out of 13). Only five of those under 40 have been married more than once. Among the men, too, there is a much lower frequency of unions with criollas, only seven, although the greatest number, three, are to be found in the 20-29 age group.

Table XI

MAMO: *NUMBER* OF CONJUGAL UNIONS

Present Age	*MEN*						*With criollos*	*WOMEN*						*With criollos*
	1	*2*	*3*	*4*	*5*	*6*		*1*	*2*	*3*	*4*	*5*	*6*	
10-19	1	1					1	7	1					2
20-29	15	1					3	10	8	3				12
30-39	12	1		2			1	7	2			1	1	3
40-49	6	1	1				1	6	4	1				3
50+	10	9	2			1	1	6	8		1			3
TOTAL	44	13	3	2	0	1	7	36	23	4	1	1	1	23

FAR AND AWAY the majority of Mameño households are nuclear, composed of the nuclear family or modifications which are consistent with a nuclear family residential pattern. Of a total of 59 households thirty consist of nothing but the nuclear family, ten others are conjugal dyads (adult spouses without children in the household). A few others consist of maternal or paternal dyads, or conjugal dyads with one or more grandchildren attached. Thus a total of 44 (75 per cent) can be considered as belonging to the "nuclear family type." The remaining fifteen households do not show any particular pattern, except that a variety of kin ties may be utilized in establishing residence. Presumably these vary according to individual circumstances. Thus, of nine extended families four are matrilineal, two are patrilineal, and three are organized on an ambilineal basis. In addition there are three sibling joint families. Interestingly enough, neither polygynous households nor polygynous unions were encountered in Mamo. Though there is one instance of probable polyandry, the personalities of the three individuals involved clearly indicate this to be an exceptional situation.

Consistent with this pattern of nuclear family households is the fact of male neolocality as the predominant rule of residence. Out of 81 adult males thirty are neolocal in residence. Only a couple of these showed any indication that kin ties might have played any role at all in their choice of residence. Almost all can be considered *wholly* neolocal. The next most popular residential pattern is male patrilocality, with twelve being strictly patrilocal (nine are still single) and eleven more in patrivicinal residence. Only ten can be classed as uxorilocal and the remainder are scattered according to a variety of kinship ties (mothers, siblings, sons, etc.). The shift to a bilateral kinship system has been due in part to increasing importance of the male role in familial economics. Thus male neolocality or patrilocality is an expectable residential pattern. Even greater confirmation of increased importance of the male is to be seen in the overwhelming proportion of female virilocal residence (40 out of 72, or 56 per cent). Only fourteen have adhered to a matrilocal principle (eleven matrilocal, three matrivicinal), while nine more can be classed as having followed a patrilocal one.

The picture which we get from these statistics is one of a good deal of individual independence; male dominance, at least in the economic sphere; and complete absence of a cyclical pattern of household organi-

MAMO: RESIDENCE *

			Matri-	Uxori-	Patri-	Viri-	Sorori-	Fratri-	Filia-	Filio-	Neo-	Other
-local	Male	50+		3	1		2			2	15	
		30-49	1	3(6)	3			2			10	
		15-29	4	4	8		1	1			5	3
	Female	50+			1	12		1	1		1	1
		30-49	1			14					2	
		15-29	11		5	14(3)						1
	Child.	-14	178(2)		3		2	1				w. grand-parents: 11 other: 4
-vicinal	Male	50+					1	1	1			
		30-49	1		5		1	2				
		15-29	1		3							
	Female	50+					1					
		30-49	1		2		2					
		15-29	3		1		1					

(Numbers in parentheses refer to criollos).
* The classification of residence utilized here is based on FISCHER (1958).

zation. Rather than a process of household growth and contraction as children marry, bear their own children and move away to set up their own household, we instead find children leaving the household at or before marriage. In some cases young people leave their natal household before marriage in order to pursue various economic opportunities. The usual practise today is to set up an independent neolocal household immediately upon contracting any type of conjugal union, although the location of various kinsmen, particularly if they are conveniently situated to an attractive economic resource (fertile fields, good fishing, industrial employment), may also be important considerations. Usually however, initial residence in the vicinity of a kinsman is abandoned by the age of thirty, as witnessed by the fact that 83 per cent of neolocal males are older than this.

It is assumed that residence formerly had a uxorilocal bias, resulting in localized matrilineages and matricentered clans. This assumption is supported by data from other Karinya communities (cf. discussion of the family in Cachama, above), as well as other closely related Cariban-speaking groups (e.g., Callinago and Barama River Caribs). What happened to these patterns in Mamo? Some fifty years ago a serious dispute arose between the Mameños and their criollo neighbors who had assumed control of local political affairs. Naturally the Mameños lost out. With conditions unbearable at home, there was a gradual exodus for the next twenty years or so. I did not collect detailed information on the nature of this exodus, but from my notes at least eight different localities have been identified where these emigrants settled (Yavito, Cardoncito; Taguache, Palitar, Providencia, Corralitos-Marchanero, Los Perros, Isla Grande —only the last was already inhabited by Karinya at the time), and there is evidence that they scattered to still other localities. If the matricentered clan still existed in Mamo up to this time, the period of emigration certainly marked its end. Emigration was by individual men or nuclear families seeking work, or new fields to cultivate.

The nuclear family was now on its own, and it became increasingly dependent on the husband and father. It is probable that most agricultural labor had been undertaken jointly by the women of the matricentered clan. But the principal attraction in the emigration of the nuclear family from Mamo was economic opportunities for the male head of the family. Furthermore, the new conditions would have meant sending one's wife to work alone in the fields. Thus the male members of the household assumed a greater proportion of the field labor, and in time came to be the principal productive agents. The fact that Mameños feel they should respect their fathers even more than their mothers undoubtedly stems from this period. The necessity of dealing with criollos on one's own also encouraged the shift to Spanish as the everyday language.

The new residential pattern at first had the effect of placing matrilineal relatives at a social distance equivalent to that of patrilateral kinsmen. The earlier pioneers, however, appear to have served as contacts for kinsmen who moved later, but with a de-emphasis on the exact nature of the individual kin tie. Thus there were numerous instances where informants reported having followed brothers or fathers to a new locality, and several cases can be observed today of a like attraction to the vicinity of a brother-in-law or sister. In this way the shift to neolocal or ambilocal residence, and the use of Spanish, also paved the way for transition to a cognatic kinship system of Eskimo type.

FERTILITY

THERE IS EVIDENCE of increasing fertility among the women of Mamo. Those who are fifty or older gave birth to an average of 5.6 children, of which 5.1 were born alive. Seventy-one per cent of those born alive reached the age of fifteen. In the 30-49 age group the number of births per mother rose to 7.8, with 7.3 being born alive. If we exclude two women who appear to be infertile, the number of *live* births per mother becomes 7.8. However, the number of miscarriages also rose slightly over that of the next older group, from 0.4 to 0.5 per mother (the proportion of women suffering one or more miscarriages seems to fluctuate around the ratio 1:4 in all three age categories). Of 167 children born to these women, 77 per cent reached the age of 15. In the 15-29 age group twenty-nine women have each borne an average of 3.6 live children, while the rate of miscarriage is only 0.3 per mother. It must be emphasized that for the most part these women are still in the first half of their child-bearing period. The total number of miscarriages will undoubtedly rise somewhat, but on the other hand, the present number of births per mother suggests that they are well on the way to equalling or surpassing the number of births per mother in the 30-49 age group. While some of these children probably will not reach the age of 15, only 6.8 per cent of this youngest age group have died to date.

Table XIII

MAMO: FERTILITY & CHILDHOOD MORTALITY

Mothers Present Age	Nº	*Nº pregnancies*		*Mortality*			
				Infant		*Childhood*	
		Births	*Miscarriages*	-6 *mo.*	6 *mo.-1 yr.*	*1-5 yrs.*	*6-15 yrs.*
50+	16	82	7	8	3	4	5
30-49	23	167	12	11	4	4	2
-29	29	103	10	2	1	2	2
	2*	10*					

* Union of criolla and Indian.

Causes of Death
(as reported by informants)

Age	Cause	-6 mo.	6 mo.-1 yr.	1-5 yrs.	6-15 yrs.
50+	mozozuelo	5			
	fever		1	1	
	gastroenteritis			1	1
	fever & vomiting			1	1
	measles			1	1
	whooping cough	1			
	ulcers		1		1
	grippe	1			
	unknown	1	1		
30-49	mozozuelo	4			
	gastroenteritis		2	1	1
	fever	1		1	
	fever & vomiting		1		
	whooping cough	1	1		
	diarrhea	1			
	worms			1	
	"attack"				1
	evil eye	1			
	unknown	3		1	
-29	gastroenteritis		1		1
	fever & vomiting				1
	fever	1			
	grippe	1			
	whooping cough			1	
	worms			1	

The decrease in infant and childhood mortality is due in part to the presence of a *Medicatura Rural* clinic in Mamo Abajo, and to extensive campaigns of immunization against the commoner infectious diseases such as whooping cough.

Gastroenteritis remains the most important cause of deaths in infancy and early childhood. While cleanliness is a somewhat greater virtue in Mamo than in Cachama, there remain innumerable opportunities for small children to come into contact with filth, the major source of the disease germs. The presence of numbers of domestic animals (especially dogs and swine) probably contributes to the spread of this disease.

Not a single case of *mozozuelo (tetanus neonorum),* which used to be the single most frequent cause of infant death, was reported by the mothers in the 20-29 age group. Again the presence of the clinic, which provides some prenatal care, as well as instruction to local midwives, may be partially credited with this achievement. In part, it is due simply to an increasing awareness on the part of midwives of the importance of care and cleanliness in the delivery of infants. One Mameño midwife has lived in the towns (San Félix and "El Tigrito") a good deal and has become rather sophisticated about techniques of midwifery. She has had considerable influence on the practises of her sister, who is the principal midwife in Mamo for Indians and criollos alike. While they do not understand the cause of *mozozuelo,* the midwives are careful to sterilize knife or scissors in flame before cutting the umbilical cord, which is also cauterized after cutting. It is worth noting that childbirth in this community lacks the folk remedies and magical observances which are designed to facilitate labor in Cachama. The technique of the midwife consists mostly of massage of the mother, giving her something to pull against for leverage, etc. In cases of very difficult birth resort may be had to prayers to the appropriate Christian saints. Thus the whole complex of practises associated with childbirth is criollo rather than Indian in character.

It is probable that superior dietary conditions have been of even greater importance in reducing childhood mortality than improved hygiene. The diet includes a high proportion of animal protein. Fish is consumed in considerable quantities nearly every day, and is supplemented from time to time with other game. Powdered milk, which is available in the stores of Mamo Abajo, constitutes a regular purchase among the Indians, and cheese is also bought frequently. In addition to regular consumption of powdered milk at home, 22 of the children between five and ten years of age were being supplied with a daily ration of fortified milk at the clinic.

The superiority of the diet is obvious among the children in terms of both physical energy and personality. Small children, even infants, are active and play vigorously. They are also much more expressive of their emotions. Laughing and crying occur freely without the necessity of excessive stimulus. Undoubtedly the same diet which produces this excess energy and expressiveness also contributes to better health among the children and a superior resistance to disease.

In part this superior diet is due to location. All local streams are tributary to the Orinoco which up to the present time has provided an unlimited supply of fish. But the increase of fertility among women aged 30-49, with a concomitant decrease in mortality among their offspring suggests that other factors such as a better standard of living, further improvement in the diet, better hygiene, etc., have also played a significant role.

ORGANIZATION OF THE FAMILY

THE DIVISION of labor within the family is more clearly defined than is the case in Cachama. The man is the real breadwinner in Mamo. In addition to conducting all hunting and fishing, he undertakes the majority of field labor. Women may help their husbands in the fields, but it is not primarily their duty to do field work. They merely assist in these chores. Naturally, where the man is employed as an industrial worker, his income is the major economic resource for the family. In all but the last activity boys usually help their fathers.

Household chores and care of the children are primarily the woman's responsibility, be they cleaning fish, cooking, or washing and mending clothes. Girls usually help their mothers. Men may, however, lend a hand with certain chores, such as cleaning fish (which they, after all, have caught), or in heavy tasks such as grating and pressing manioc.

Tasks which are ancillary to operation of the household, like going for water, collecting firewood, and caring for livestock, seem to be pretty equally shared between the sexes as well as between adults and older children. Usually the responsibility for one of these tasks is assigned to a particular individual in each household, but identity of that individual will vary from one household to the next.

There is very little surviving craft activity here. Craft production is no longer significant for supplying family necessities, except in the case of hammock weaving. Nowadays familial division of labor is little concerned with the necessity of assigning responsibility for craft production.

In economic terms both husband and wife serve very important functions within the family. For the most part their roles are complementary and interdependent. A man would have a hard time of it trying to live alone; a women would find it even more difficult, since she has been for the most part divorced from a directly productive role. Not only has the male increased in economic importance within the family, but he has retained significant control of familial finances through the relative isolation of Mamo. Although there are no overt objections to women dealing independently with outsiders, there have been so far few opportunities for them to do so. They are free to trade in the local stores, but itinerant traders only began to visit the area during the time of our stay there. The few local *mongueros* are interested in buying the crop from a whole field, which is clearly the man's province. Travel to the towns usually requires several days. Because of household duties, small children, etc., women are not always able to accompany their husbands on these trips. Thus, sale of hammocks or purchase of staple or luxury items for the household are mostly in the hands of the men. Even should the woman accompany her husband, he likely handles most such transactions out of habit and greater familiarity with the town. In the case of industrial workers, it is they who bring home the wages. Even though their wives may force them to hand it over when they reach home, they can usually contrive to spend at least part of it before arriving there. In nearly every instance, then, it is the man who controls and directs the economic activity of the family, and this is in the face of increased freedom and independence on the part of the woman.

This increased freedom is evident in many ways. In the first place the woman in Mamo is hospitable, friendly, even outspoken. She does not hide on the approach of strangers, nor refuse to speak to outsiders in the absence of her husband. On the contrary, she is more likely to offer her visitors a seat *indoors,* and bustle off to the kitchen where she prepares coffee for them. Women are perfectly free to go anywhere within the neighborhood, though this is understandable since the houses are usually grouped in a compact cluster. Although they usually go in groups of two or three, women are also free to go to the store in Mamo Abajo, to the Spring at El Jagüey to do their washing or fetch water, to go into the woods to collect ripe cashew fruits, or even to the fields —all without the express permission of their husbands. Many of the women who live in Palitar would sometimes accompany their spouses downriver to work in the morning, then continue on to San Félix where they spent the day shopping. In the afternoon they would return with the launch, which picked up the men at the Matanzas plant on its return. Of course, in these latter cases, even though the women had full freedom of action during the day, they did so with the express knowledge and permission of their spouses.

In *propio Mamo* some of my best informants were women; there was no hesitancy about giving all kinds of information, much of it volunteered, to an outsider. In fact, a number of the local women could be described as dominant personalities. Not that they henpecked their husbands, but they certainly were not the sort which would accede meekly to whatever demand of their mates. This is a combination of personality traits which would be extremely unusual in Cachama.

PATTERNS OF CHILD CARE

CHILDREN BEGIN to be disciplined almost as soon as they learn to walk. It is felt that they can understand what is right and wrong, even though they may not yet have learned to talk well. Proper etiquette is considered very important, and they are early taught not to listen to adult conversation, not to walk in front of an older person, and to ask the blessing of their godparents whenever they meet. Children also ask a blessing of their parents before leaving for school, and before going to bed at night.

Young children seem to have pretty free run of the town, so long as they do not go out of sight (and earshot) of the houses. By the age of five they wander freely from one end of town to the other, although parents do forbid them from wandering out into the woods. Smaller children (as young as three) also go almost anywhere in town, but usually in the company of an older sibling. The principal factor inhibiting freer exploration seems to be timidity, and lack of self-assurance when away from their mothers.

By the age of seven most children are charged with caring for younger brothers and sisters. They can be seen almost any hour of the day, when they are not in school, carrying a smaller child on their hip.

However, they are never given the responsibility of the smaller child for the whole day. A part of their time is free for their own play. Even children as old as ten are not kept busy the whole day, although their duties and responsibilities are more extensive.

In general, parents are strict with their children, most of whom are well-behaved. In Palitar, however, criollo influence seems to be greater and techniques of child discipline are less effective. Mothers are continually screaming at their children. They will turn on them without warning and scream at them to do this, do that; or don't do something else. As a result, children are much greater crybabies than in any other Karinya group. They were observed to scream continuously for ten, twenty or more minutes. Another difficulty in Palitar is the inconsistency of parents. One striking example occurred during Carnaval when there was a good deal of tomfoolery among the children. One minute a mother would be yelling at hers not to throw water or powder at each other, yet a few minutes later she would be giving them money to buy powder, filling balloons with water for them, or even throwing water herself![2]

Attendance at school is greatly emphasized among the Mameños. Nearly every child attends for two or three years between the ages of 7 and 15. During the week attendance at school and study of one's lessons take up a good deal of the child's day. By the age of 12 or so girls are assuming the responsibility for a great many household chores, while boys will be charged with such tasks as going for water, putting the burro out to pasture in the evening and fetching him in the morning. While their tasks tend to restrict the girls' freedom, the nature of boys' responsibilities do not prohibit them from continuing to do much as they please. The difference between the two sexes in this regard is functionally important, since girls tend to contract a conjugal union much earlier than do boys.

What is perhaps most striking about relations between the sexes is the fact that there is never a point where restrictions are imposed on contact between them. The relationship between teenage boys and girls is quite free, and not unlike that which obtains among North American teenagers. The boys are constantly teasing the girls, who generally seem to enjoy the attention, although they sometimes attempt to retaliate. Especially during Carnaval, the greatest proportion of water throwing and dumping powder in each other's hair was being done by the teenagers. Girls are perfectly free to visit any house in the settlement alone, and

[2] After this study had gone to press a paper by Levine (1966) came to my attention which suggested a more definitive explanation for this behavior.

their mothers may also send them on an errand to the store in Mamo Abajo.

In the evenings their freedom of movement is somewhat more restricted. They are, however, permitted to sit together outside the door of their house, where they will be visited by several boys. This way they feel more or less left to themselves while still being kept under the watchful eye of parents or grandparents.

The combination of freedom and responsibility which girls face here has probably arisen as a useful but chance adaptation to current patterns of youthful marriage and neolocal residence. Among males delay of marriage permits them to get established economically and to develop sufficient maturity to set up their own independent household. Since it is independent, girls often cannot fall back on parents, sisters, or mother-in-law for asistance and emotional support. The duties and responsibilities which are more and more assigned to them from the age of seven on prepare them for their roles as housekeepers after marriage. Free social interaction with the opposite sex develops self-confidence and enables a girl to learn appropriate responses to a broader range of personalities than if she were restricted to social contacts within her own family and kinsmen. When she does leave her family to marry and set up her own household she is better able to cope with unfamiliar situations, even though she may lack close kinsmen to fall back upon for practical and emotional support.

In spite of the general mistrust of and dislike for criollos, a good many Mameño girls have been seduced by criollo men in the last fifteen or twenty years. As noted above, only a few of these have resulted in permanent unions. It seems that the general attitude of freedom and independence of action for women has had a good deal to do with the development of this problem. It is highly unlikely that most criollos who attend dances in Mamo or otherwise seek the acquaintance of the Indian girls have any other objective than getting as many "kicks" as possible. They have no intention of establishing a permanent relationship. But the girls of Mamo, accustomed to a free and open relationship with the Indian boys of the community tend to be the same with the criollo. When they become pregnant their criollo "lover" flees his responsibilities and they are left with a fatherless child to rear. Thus, what is adaptive in one context can be dysfunctional in another. Fortunately familial and kin ties remain strong, so that parents or siblings can be called upon to aid in caring for and educating these children.

This is not to imply that sexual liaisons do not occur between Indian youths. They undoubtedly do occur, though the Karinya are much less preoccupied with sexual exploits as a proof of one's manhood than are the criollos. Besides, such sexual liaisons are much more difficult to discern where both parties are Indian. The young Indian cannot so easily escape his responsibility in the event he impregnates a girl. He cannot go back to his own community and boast of his exploits. He cannot seek refuge among his own kinsmen, for they will all be faced with pressure from the community. He might try to escape to the towns, but this would result in virtual exile, since he would certainly be unable to return so long as the girl remained single, while his family would still have to face pressures for him to marry from the girl's family, as well as from the community at large. The simplest course is a consensual union, which in most instances proves to be stable.

The implications here are all too clear. Where there is sharing of common values and commitment to the *same community of interest,* openness and freedom of heterosexual relations is possible. Even though this may lead to clandestine liaisons, the likelihood of abuse is slim as long as there is no possibility of escaping the responsibilities which one incurs. Both parties will suffer social pressure or even ostracism at the hands of the community. But where, as in the case of the criollo "lover," one of the parties has no interest in the values of the other, has no commitment to the community of interest, and can very easily escape any of the responsibilities which may be involved, then the likelihood of abuse is not only possible, but highly probable.

Kin Groupings

THERE ARE no *corporate* kin groups larger than the nuclear family or household. The matrilineage and clan have long since disappeared. Rather than developing into ramages they have been replaced by a kindred type of organization. Each individual has certain compelling obligations to his parents, siblings, and children, and in addition, feels that he *ought* to give occasional gifts to his grandparents in recognition of his kin ties to them. Naturally the composition of these personal kindreds varies for every individual except siblings. However, upon marriage one also assumes similar obligations towards his spouse's kindred. Although this might represent nothing more than the intersection of two personal kindreds in which one spouse may act to fulfill the obligations of the other, even though technically he has no personal commitment to the spouse's kindred, it seems much more consistent with actual values and practise in Mamo to refer to this as a "conjugal kindred." In this case the composition of the personal kindred differs for every individual except *spouses.*

In discussing the family in Cachama the long-standing custom of sharing fish, game and produce within the matricentered clan was found to be in decline. Not so in Mamo! The shift to neolocal or ambilocal residence and straightforward bilateral descent meant merely a bilateral extension of such obligations. As it was explained by Santos Chiroco, a boy's family helps him clear his first field, and then he gives them a share of the produce. When he gets married his parents-in-law and brothers-in-law also help him (with clearing or expanding his fields), and in return he also shares some of the produce with them. An even clearer example comes from the almost daily distribution of fish to members of one's kindred. One day Juan Guevara was cleaning a big mess of thirty or forty fish which he had caught that morning. Luis Martínez was trying to buy some fish which he could salt down and take back to Yavito. He approached Juan who told him, "I don't have any to sell. I only caught enough for *sancocho* (the stew pot). I have to send some to my mother, my *suegra,* my brother,. . . There's not enough here for me to sell." The next day Juan didn't fish, but he was provided with a batch from his brother's catch. So cooperative sharing provides for the needs of everyone with kindred affiliations.

Grandparents are on the periphery of this network of exchange. They do not receive regular gifts, but Manuel María Macadito proudly reported that even his grandchildren "may give me Bs 6" *when he visits them.* Every time he visits those grandchildren who live in "El Tigrito" (which is not very often) they pay the costs of the trip.

The rise of wage labor and industrial employment have only served to strengthen these kindred obligations. Instead of giving their parents food, children who live in the towns, or whose principal income is in wages regularly give cash to their parents, which can in turn be spent on food and clothing.

Perhaps the outstanding example of the accomodation of this traditional practise to new socio-economic circumstances is provided by the Reyes family (Fig. X). All the children on the first line are adult, married or employed, and economically independent. The children on the second line have not yet reached adulthood. Otulio lives with his sister Irenes whose husband is employed at the steel mill at Matanzas. She has assumed full responsibility for Otulio's support, and therefore rarely sends money home. Manuelico and Aurora live in San Félix with their sister Teodora in order to attend higher grades in school. Teodora's husband also works at Matanzas. Since she is keeping her two younger siblings, and fully supporting Aurora, she only occasionally sends money home. Ricardo, who is a teacher in Chaguaramas, and Francisco, who works for the steel company, are responsible for the support of brother Manuelico. Francisco sends Bs 30-40 a week to Teodora. He also sends money home from time to time, when he feels he can (Bs 20, 30, 10). Ricardo is paid monthly in Soledad, and passes through San Félix both

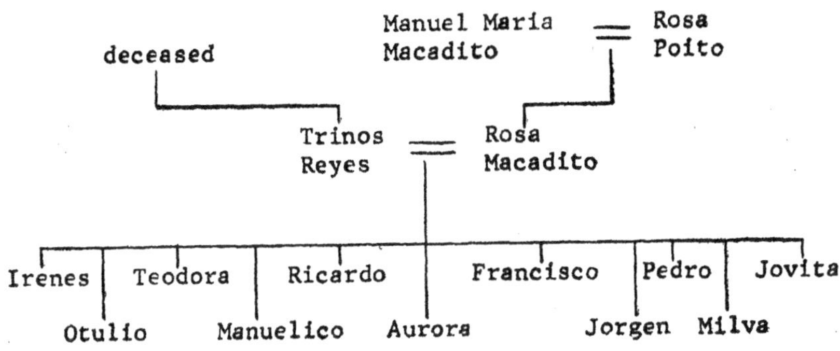

Figure X

going and coming, at which time he leaves money with Teodora. He usually doesn't pay any cash to his parents, with whom he is "boarding," but he brings provisions with him when he returns from Barcelona. Sometimes he brings clothes —a shirt, a dress, etc., for his parents.

Pedro isn't regularly employed. He works wherever he encounters a job. But whenever he can he sends a little bit home, although he doesn't help much in the support of the students. Jovita, whose husband is employed at the steel plant, sends money (Bs 5-10) or provisions to her parents on a more or less weekly basis.

Trinos and Rosa also take or send things to their children from time to time —manioc bread, *dulce de merey,* produce from the field, etc.

Although the grandchildren don't send regular gifts to their grandparents, Trinos and Rosa live next door to them and they spend much of the day together. Trinos and Rosa generally do share with them some of the money received from their children. This indicates that a child's obligations to his parents remain strong throughout life, whereas those to his grandparents are always relatively weak.

Summing this situation up, we find that old patterns of kinship have disappeared, old forms of familial organization have been grossly modified in Mamo. But this has not meant a complete loss of cultural integrity. While these aspects of the culture have moved closer to criollo patterns, *they have not become identical with them.* New forms of kin organization have emerged in the conjugal kindred; old patterns of kinship behavior, such as mutual exchange between kinsmen, have been adapted to them; and these have been reinforced, rather than weakened, by the introduction of new economic opportunities, such as wage labor and industrial employment.

COMPARATIVE COMMENTS

COMPARING MAMO to Cachama certain similarities stand out: a decline in marriages between close kinsmen, the disappearance of procedures which provided traditional sanctions for the marital tie (making the consensual union the most common form of marital alliance), more frequent unions with criollos, and an apparent decrease in the stability of marital unions. The decline in marriages between close kinsmen is due to the rise of an ambilineal ramage organization in Cachama, whereas in Mamo it is clearly the result of a shift from the old matrilineal organization to the bilateral nuclear family with male dominance.

In both communities "falling in love" is the most common reason given for contracting a conjugal union, though at least some Mameños seem to take a more hardheaded approach to marriage by weighing the advantages and disadvantages of a particular union. Consistent with such attitudes is the prestige attached to a formally contracted union (whether civil, religious, or both). In Cachama formal marriage carries little or no prestige with it, and the consensual union remains the general condition.

The 20-29 age group seems to have been most susceptible to unions with criollos in both cases. In Cachama this has come about both because of increased contact with the towns and because of increased tensions between neighborhoods within the community. Nonetheless the incidence remains relatively low —only about five per cent of all conjugal unions. In Mamo the incidence is greater— 11 per cent of all unions in the 20-29 age group, or 17 per cent of the women. The Mameños have always had more criollo contacts, but the current increase in unions seems to have begun with the introduction of a school some 25 years ago. Unions with criollos will probably continue to be frequent among younger people in both communities. In Cachama the same reasons will prevail. In Mamo, however, employment in the Guayanese urban-industrial complex will probably raise the incidence of criolla unions among men, and likely will produce unions which are more stable than those contracted with criollos from the vicinity of Mamo.

In Mamo the stability of the conjugal union seems to be directly related to the proportion of criollo unions. Thus any change in the number or nature of criollo unions will affect marital stability. In Cachama there has also been considerable instability in unions between *Indians*. This seems to be related to the general disorientation and social disruption which accompanied the arrival of the petroleum industry in that area. As the Cachamans become accustomed to these new conditions it can be expected that the conjugal union will again become more stable, although it may never regain the stability that it had in the past.

Surprisingly, there is little difference between the two communities in the age of marriage for girls. Youthful marriages are not uncommon; the mean age at marriage appears to have declined somewhat in recent years, though it is possible it has begun to climb again in the very youngest age group.

There is greater contrast in the age of marriage for boys. In Cachama boys range two to three years older than girls at marriage, and of course they are attached either to the girl's or their own family for a time after marriage. This allows them to adjust to their new state before assuming full adult responsibilities. But in Mamo where consummation of a conjugal union means full responsibility for an independent household, boys tend to put off marriage until considerably later, usually their early twenties, when they are more secure economically (and also more mature emotionally).

The household in Cachama, with its continuing matricentered bias, tends to be cyclical in character, with daughters maturing, marrying and bringing their husbands to live in the household, starting their family; and only later setting up their own independent household. Even then residence often continues to be matrivicinal for many years. The apparently high proportion of virilocal females is in part misleading, though it may reflect some recent undermining of the traditional matrilineally biased extended family. In Mamo the household is neither matricentered, nor extended, nor cyclical. Whatever its former characteristics, it is now composed of a single nuclear family, children tend to leave it at or before marriage, and residence is usually neolocal, even though a variety of kin ties may be utilized in establishing residence in specific instances. In all cases, however, these are merely links which put one in contact with certain advantageous conditions such as good farm land or an opportunity for industrial employment. Consistent with the importance of the male in economic pursuits, the Mameño household is centered on and dominated by the male.

Health conditions and rates of reproduction are superior in Mamo. In the 30-49 age group average number of live births per mother is nearly eight, while in Cachama it is only just better than seven. The death rate among infants and children is also lower in Mamo than in Cachama. The contrast is not due so much to differences in availability of medical attention and medicines, but rather to a basic difference in diet and the conditions under which medical attention can be obtained. Greater protein consumption and a generally more balanced diet contribute to better health and greater energy among the children of Mamo. Secondarily, conditions of medical attention are more acceptable at the local clinic. Furthermore, midwives appear to be more hygienic in their techniques of assisting at childbirth. This appears to have produced a significant decline in deaths related to childbirth, with not a single case of *mozozuelo* reported by mothers under thirty. In Cachama there has been no significant change in the rate of deaths during early infancy and an actual *increase* in the number of cases of *mozozuelo.*

The division of labor in the Cachaman family is clear, yet there is often considerable overlap by the two sexes who help each other with their daily tasks. Craft production is still fairly important for local consumption, and the women are weaving even more hammocks than formerly, due to increased demand among urban criollos. In Mamo male activities are more strictly limited to that sex, since they often necessitate travel (hunting and fishing), heavy labor (wage labor), or commuting (industrial employment). Craft production has all but disappeared. Care and maintenance of the household is first and foremost the woman's responsibility. Only those tasks which are *ancillary* to the operation of the household continue to be shared by the sexes, or divided up without reference to sex.

In spite of increased self-assurance and independence of the female in Mamo, the woman remains subordinate to the man due to their geographical distance from urban areas and the fact that the man is more than ever the family breadwinner. In contrast, the woman remains subordinate in Cachama because of traditional patterns of *social* isolation, and reticence with strangers.

The emotional link of a child with its mother is strongest in Cachama. Ties to the father are secondary and relatively unimportant. Discipline is never harsh and is wholly neglected until the child is six or seven years old. Even so, children are rarely hyperactive or extroverted. There is evidence that newer attitudes toward discipline are beginning to appear in Cachama, but they have not affected the majority of parents as yet.

There is no question that children are close to their mothers in Mamo as well, but they are also expected to exhibit love and respect for their fathers. There discipline is begun at an early age, but children are much more active, and considerable freedom is allowed so long as they remain within sight and hearing of the settlement. Social adjustment comes earlier because children become acquainted throughout the settlement at an early age.

In both communities school attendance has provided a somewhat greater degree of freedom for children of both sexes, but in Cachama girls remain more restricted than boys. Teenage girls are carefully watched until their marriage. In Mamo free and open social interaction between teenagers of both sexes has probably facilitated a healthy transition to the roles of an adult, but it has also made the Mameño girls more susceptible to the amorous advances of insincere criollos.

The greatest contrast between the two communities is to be found in the nature of their kin groupings. In Cachama an ambilineal ramage organization has replaced the putative earlier matrilineage, though it has retained some of the corporate functions of the latter. The ramage remains strong as a focus for social interaction, even though certain current trends (such as failure to share cash income within the ramage) could conceivably undermine it. The residential clan has been superseded by the neighborhood in functional importance, particularly as a focus for political loyalties. Yet the clan has not become wholly extinct, for it continues to be important as a basis for affiliation with one or another neighborhood.

Mamo lacks any sort of corporate or exclusive groupings, whether based on kinship or residence. Residence in a particular settlement is tied primarily to economic considerations, and changing economic conditions may provoke a change in residence. Rights and responsibilities toward kinsmen are extended bilaterally in the form of a personal or conjugal kindred, and obligations to the kindred are taken very seriously by most Mameños. Rather than weakening this kin grouping, changes associated with recent urban-industrial influences have been integrated into established patterns of kindred behavior and have actually served to reinforce this type of organization.

Summarizing the changes which have occurred in the areas of kinship and family organization, we can say that in Cachama the impact of the petroleum industry and increasing contact with criollos has been disruptive. A certain amount of disorganization occurred in the family. Kinship ties have become increasingly cognatic, but are tending in the direction of ambilineality rather than bilaterality. Broader kinship and community organizations have become increasingly fragmented. It would appear that the present strength of the ramages and neighborhoods has resulted more as a reaction to social disorganization on other levels than for any other reason. Even the ramage has resulted from increased flexibility in exploiting existent kin ties, the new flexibility undoubtedly resulting from frustration in attempting to hew closely to the traditional patterns of residence and kin affiliation. In short, the ramage proved more adaptive under contemporary conditions than the former matrilineage.

In Mamo on the other hand, kinship structure and family organization have adapted very well to the changes brought about by development of Guayanese steel and other industries. To a considerable extent this was made possible because many of the changes which have occurred in Mameño social organization had already been completed before the people of this community were exposed to industrial conditions. The result has been even greater strengthening of the Mameño family and kindred organization, which has in turn produced greater self-assurance and a more tightly knit community.

CHAPTER 9

THE COMMUNITY IN MAMO

MAMO IS A well-integrated community whose members maintain strong ties of loyalty no matter where they reside at the moment. Although there may have been a period of disorientation and loss of integration in the past, Mameño unity seems never to have undergone serious disorganization. Today the community is stronger than ever, and in sharp contrast to the fragmented situation of the neighboring criollos.

The head of the community is the *gobernador,* generally referred to in the traditional manner as *"cacique."* Older informants can trace the line of caciques back to General Chiroco who gained his title in the Five Years War and became cacique after that time. No one is very certain how caciques were selected in those days, but from the time of Cipriano Castro (1899-1908) through the rule of Gómez (1908-1935) the cacique was appointed by the state government and he ruled by their consent. The cacique in Mamo during this whole period was Pedro Pariche. It seems fairly certain that he could not have remained in office without the approval of local criollo políticos (led by Pedro León) as well as those in Barcelona, the state capital. Apparently the same policy of appointment continued under the presidencies of López Contreras and Medina, since Pariche continued as cacique during their administrations. In the brief period between the end of Medina's administration and the dictatorship of Pérez Jiménez democratic principles seem to have been promoted at all levels of government. The method of election was instituted in Mamo, and four different individuals were elected to succeeding two or three year terms as cacique or gobernador. However, the dictatorship of Pérez Jiménez seems to have offered at least the opportunity to return to the former system of appointment by the state government. One Mameño, Pedro Poito, took advantage of this opportunity, journeyed to the state capital in Barcelona, and had himself appointed gobernador. He continued in this capacity until 1962 (see discussion of the aftermath of his leadership, below).

Traditionally the cacique played a rather paternalistic role. People came to him with their problems. He took care of those in need. He played a major role in underwriting the town's fiestas, providing food, drink, music, fireworks, etc. (Pedro Pariche is still critical of recent gobernadores who "couldn't even put on a decent fiesta.")

The cacique also served as a center for group action. It was he who called all the people together in cayapa to build a house or clear and plant a field. Although no informants mentioned the fact, it is likely he received gifts or regular payments of tribute from the people of the community. Excess income of some sort would be necessary to meet the numerous additional expenses required of the cacique. Today the governor receives no remuneration for his services, but much less is expected of him in his official capacity.

In the past, when dealing with outsiders no one spoke out except the cacique. He handled all outside relations, and in fact was one of the few who even spoke Spanish. A number of people in Mamo maintain this situation continued unchanged up until the last 15 or 20 years. The fact of having lived dispersed among the criollos for 40 or 50 years and the present self-assurance of most Mameños when dealing with non-Indians belie this assertion and strongly suggest that it has not been true for at least two generations.

The governor is assisted in his duties by a "second," who mostly runs errands and serves as a messenger. In addition he has delegated some authority to *comisarios* whom he has appointed in some of the settlements that are dependent from Mamo, such as Yavito and La Isabel. The comisarios serve a minor judicial function, hearing and attempting to settle petty disputes. All major matters (such as murder, incest, stealing livestock, etc.) would bypass even the governor and be referred to municipal or district authorities. It is not clear on what basis a comisario is appointed, nor what his term of office is. The present governor has never made such appointments and his predecessor was vague as to the criteria which are used, even though it was he who made the present appointments. A large settlement like Palitar lacks a comisario, while neighboring Isabel, with only five houses and 20 inhabitants, has one. The distinction may be that Yavito and La Isabel are predominantly Indian, whereas Indians make up only about half the population of Palitar. Clearly the governor of the Indigenous Community of Mamo could not have jurisdiction or authority over any criollos unless they were actually occupying Indian lands. (In practise his jurisdiction is rather tenuous even in the latter circumstance).

However, final authority over all Mameños living in these several settlements remains vested in the governor, though he rarely has either the need or the opportunity to assert himself. Such authority does not arise from the fact that all are Mameños. Those who move to the cities, or to another Karinya community, or who lose themselves in a criollo community on the Guayana side of the Orinoco are no longer subject to him. Likewise the settlement of La Providencia on Isla Fajardo is sufficiently distant from Mamo and has been out of contact with the home community for so long, that it no longer feels itself to be a part of it. The governor no longer has any authority in La Providencia because the people never refer any problems or bring any matters of concern to him. Nor are they motivated to return to Mamo for other reasons, such as a fiesta. Effectively they have achieved the status of an independent community.

Relations with Criollos

MAMO WAS ORIGINALLY settled by Indians and remained mostly Indian for nearly a century, but gradually a few criollo families moved into the area and some of them settled in the Indian community itself.

When Gómez came to power in 1908 political opportunists found that unqualified support of his government often netted comfortable rewards in the form of appointment to local office, with all the perquisites and influence with are usually associated with corrupt administration. In return for their unquestioning support they were assured permanent political tenure. One such was Pedro León, who came to Mamo about the time Gómez assumed control of the government. Pedro León appears to have been a typical local caudillo. He took control of local government out of the hands of the Indians. He moved the criollo segment of the population out of *propio Mamo* and founded a new settlement about a kilometer away at the foot of the mesa. He moved the prefecture and the jail to Mamo Abajo and built a separate church there.

Like most criollos before him, Pedro León was more interested in livestock than he was in farming. The trouble was that his livestock included hogs. The Mameños were used to cattle and had fenced their fields for them, but hogs were a new factor. It wasn't long before they got into the conucos and decimated them. The Indians didn't know what to do. They complained to Pedro León, but no action was taken. They presented the case to the judge of the district in Soledad, but received no satisfaction. So the cacique ordered the Indians to kill every pig they could find, and leave them in the fields to rot. Pedro León called in the officials from Soledad. The Indians were severely rebuked, some informants even say they were beaten with the flat of a machete. In any case they were sorely humiliated before Pedro León and in the eyes of their criollo neighbors.

From this time on relations with the criollos have been anything but smooth. The latter wanted to run the Indians out. They said the Indians were too poor to own livestock, and they would confiscate animals belonging to an Indian without paying compensation. Fences around Indian fields would be breached so that wandering livestock could get in. The poorer criollos put their conucos on Indian land without asking permission or offering to pay for use of the land. To this day the only way to get a criollo off Indian land is to buy him out, and even then this does not prevent his clearing a new field somewhere else on tribal property.

Beginning with the incident over the pigs, some Mameños left *propio Mamo* and moved to other areas where they would not have to protect their crops from swine and other livestock. Continuing harassment from criollos led more and more individuals to forsake the community over the next several decades. Some went to other Karinya communities such as Isla Grande, but most of them seem to have scattered at first. In time, however, clusters of Mameños grew up at Yavito, Cardoncito, Los Perros, Taguache, Palitar, La Isabel, Marchánero, and La Providencia. In spite of their dispersion, most of these settlements never lost their ties with *propio Mamo* and they continue to feel themselves a part of the community today.

Things took a turn for the better when the Gómez regime came to an end. Pedro León seems to have lost control of Mamo under López Contreras, and a survey was made of community lands. Apparently, however, the majority were unhappy with the survey, feeling that the cacique had allowed them to be given less than they laid claim to. A second survey was effected in 1958, although the boundaries do not coincide exactly with those of the earlier one. This time copies of both surveys were obtained, together with a map, and these are now in the possession of the community.

Possession of a copy of the survey has considerably reassured the Indians about their rights over the land and several families had returned to *propio Mamo* during the three and one half years from 1958 to 1962. Still others were contemplating a return, and there was some idle talk of a "get-tough" policy toward criollo squatters.

For a time after the decline of Pedro León the criollos remained dominant in local affairs. They succeeded in obtaining a school which was installed in Mamo Abajo nearly 25 years ago (probably under López Contreras). Later they secured a wireless telegraph station and a dispensary of the Medicatura Rural, though the former was undoubtedly connected to the detachment of Guardia Nacional which was stationed in Mamo during the Pérez Jiménez regime.

Nonetheless, while the Indians were strengthening their position by securing new land titles, drawing people back to *propio Mamo,* and getting involved in local politics, the local criollos were gradually losing out. Municipio Mamo has always been overwhelmingly rural, with the 167 inhabitants counted in Mamo Abajo in 1950 constituting less than ten per cent of its total population (Vila 1953: 193). Apparently it was administratively impractical to maintain a distinct municipio centered in Mamo. In 1955 it was consolidated with adjacent Municipio Carapa and the prefecture, the municipal records, the jail, and other administrative paraphernalia were removed to Carapa 40 kilometers away. Everyone in Mamo, criollo and Indian alike, was outraged at this development. Seven years later in 1962 there was still determined talk of bringing the municipio seat back to Mamo. Nonetheless, this loss also stimulated numerous fears that the wireless station or the clinic would be the next to go.

Indian Leadership

TO A CERTAIN extent the Indians have jumped into the breach. Loss of the prefecture may not have been due to inadequate criollo leadership but certainly no outstanding leadership appeared among them to prevent its loss. The Indians seemed to feel this very keenly, almost as if to say, 'The criollos took it away from us, and now they've lost it for everyone.' It may be an underlying attitude of this sort which has stimulated them to seek several benefits for Mamo which both they and the criollos can enjoy.

The most recent of these was the bringing of electricity and a municipal water supply. In 1960 or 1961 a commission from the Indian community of three young people and the governor went to Barcelona specifically to request these utilities. It was principally through the insistence of this commission that the Comisión de Fomento agreed to drill a well and install an electrical generator for lights. The well was drilled in January 1962, the generator arrived in April, but their installation had not been completed before we left Mamo.

Before this the Indians had succeeded in obtaining their own school in Mamo Arriba, in spite of the fact there had been a school in Mamo Abajo for many years. The school is a matter of great pride for the Indians. It serves as a kind of community status symbol, eloquent testimony in their minds of their present enlightened condition as "educated," civilized human beings. By having a school of their own they are able to set themselves off somewhat from their criollo neighbors. Certainly possession of the school has enhanced community integration in Mamo Arriba. Even the children of Indian families who live at the foot of the mesa walk the extra distance to attend this school, rather than mix with criollo children. Indirectly this school has probably benefitted the criollo community as well, as it relieved some of the pressure on what appears to be an overcrowded facility in Mamo Abajo.

The major difficulty was in keeping a teacher for their new school. For nearly three years the Indians struggled to find one who would stay on permanently, without much success. There are few who really desire to teach in a rural school. The fact that it was an Indian school made it even more unattractive. The Mameños finally hit upon what promises to be a satisfactory solution to the difficulty. One Mameño youth who was continuing his schooling in San Félix expected to complete his course of study within a few months. The Indians determined to ask for his appointment as village schoolteacher as soon as he was free. If anyone would stay in Mamo as a schoolteacher it would be the son of one of the leading families. In the meantime his brother Fernando, who had also had some teaching experience, filled in the job and seemed to be doing creditably.

Fernando himself is an interesting phenomenon. He attended the school in Mamo Abajo for five years before setting off to seek his fortune. He was employed in a variety of unskilled jobs throughout the state of Anzoátegui and in Ciudad Bolívar for several years, but managed to enhance his education a little during this time. He tried to start a school for the children in Cachama, but failed because parents there refused to contribute to the expenses of the school. In 1957 he obtained employment in the Siderúrgica Nacional at Matanzas where he learned to operate a crane. He was laid off at the end of 1958 because the Italian company which employed him had fulfilled its contract. Fernando then returned to Mamo where he worked at farming with his father.

During this time he got involved in politics and became very interested in doing his part for the welfare of his community. This attitude had something to do with his assuming the job of schoolteacher until his brother could take it over permanently. Fernando could have picked up his pay for schoolteaching in Soledad, but preferred to make the longer trip to Barcelona every month "because this gives me an opportunity to visit some of the government offices there and make known the wants and needs of Mamo," or to check up on the progress of some promised improvement. If he found something lagging he could then exert a little pressure for them to speed up their work.

In spite of his youth, Fernando is clearly respected by other members of the community, even those who are three times his age. He is intelligent, vocal, and a forceful debater. Even though his only official capacity was that of village schoolteacher, he is important as an informal leader of the community. It is curious that another young person was elected cacique or governor early in 1962, even though Fernando was present at the time. Yet he continued to exert more leadership and influence than those who held formal office. Fernando was constantly discussing his ideas and projects with other members of the community. When a community meeting was held it would be formally opened by the governor before Fernando took the floor and led the discussion.

Even where Indians and criollos met jointly to discuss the progress of the new utilities projects with party officials, it was Fernando who dominated the meeting. Not only did he reemphasize the needs of the two communities for lights and water, he brought up the subject of the bad condition of the road from Soledad to Mamo. After the meeting, various people, both Indian and criollo, scolded the latter for not speaking up themselves, since such improvements are as much in their interest as that of the Indians.

It would appear then, that the criollos are losing control of local politics through lack of dynamic leadership and failure of the majority to give support to the leadership which does exist. The Indians on the other hand are not only united behind their leaders, but their leadership is dynamic and energetic.

The schoolteacher is only the most outstanding of these. Several others have also assumed significant roles in the Indian community. Most of these are young, but they are actively supported by the elders, those people who one might expect to assume leadership roles. A number of these youthful leaders belong to the Pariche family. Invariably one or another of the teenage Pariche girls will be chosen as secretary or treasurer of a local committee, be it the local arm of A.D., or merely a group collecting funds to underwrite the fiesta of the patron saint. Gloria and her brother José Pariche were members of the commission which traveled to Barcelona to petition for installation of lights and water. By all reports it was the insistence of these young people which finally brought success. Now José is being trained to operate the electric generator and he will be in charge of it for both the Indian and criollo settlements. Their older sister Juana is also very vocal and takes an active part in the discussion of all matters which might affect the community. Her opinions are mature and judicious and they are respected by all in the community. Undoubtedly the influence of these members of the Pariche family is in part due to the prestige of their mother Doña Marta who actually wields a good deal of authority, even though she holds no formal office. Doña Marta is so subtle and diplomatic in her control that an outsider would hardly be aware of her true importance.

But this certainly is not the whole picture. Vicente Chiroco is another young man who commands considerable respect. Some he has inherited from his father, since both of them are believed capable of offering effective prayers over the sick. Some is because he has married a Pariche girl. But a good deal of his leadership potential is due to his inherent good sense. One of Vicente's brothers might also become important in the youthful leadership of Mamo should he return from Caracas where he is pursuing his education. He has expressed considerable concern with the future of the community, and especially relations between Indians and criollos. Finally I should not neglect mention of Emilio Ñávarez, the youthful governor who was elected to that post at the beginning of 1962. Most of the people in the community agreed that they had chosen Emilio because he was young, and particularly because he can read and write. They felt they had been exploited enough by people who had been able to take advantage of an illiterate cacique.

Emilio was not perhaps the most effective governor possible but he certainly marked an improvement over his predecessor. He approached his responsibilities with energy and enthusiasm. He was conscientious and sincerely interested in working for the future welfare of the community. Perhaps his only faults were a slight lack of maturity and a hesitancy to assert his authority, which probably arose from his relative youth.

Then too, the present functions of the governor are considerably modified from those of the old-fashioned cacique. Traditional paternalism disappeared even before the office was assumed by an individual who is younger than most of the adults he represents.

The governor no longer serves as the center for dealing with outsiders. Most individuals deal with anyone at any time, irrespective of the governor, and for the most part wholly without his knowledge. The only time he really serves as such a center is when official delegations from the state government visit the community. Even so, hospitality usually centers in the Casa Grande of Doña Marta, and Fernando the schoolteacher likely will spend more time hosting such delegations than will the governor himself.

The governor does still appoint his subordinates, such as the "second" and the *comisarios,* but neither he nor they are often called upon to settle disputes. Emilio did take an active role in trying to straighten out a case of incest which occurred during our stay in Mamo, but the incident was sufficiently serious that it was referred to the municipal authorities in Carapa where it was finally settled, though hardly to the satisfaction of the Mameños. We observed the handling of several other problems which arose during the three months we were there, some of them serious. For the most part they either settled themselves, or no satisfactory solution was worked out, mostly because Emilio felt hesitant to assert his authority.

The governor is also formal leader in community meetings and on public works projects. For a couple of Sundays he called together all the men in the community to help in clearing the line of boundary markers which delimit the lands assigned to Mamo by the federal surveys. Nearly everyone called upon turned out or had an acceptable excuse for not doing so. There was considerable public outrage against the one or two who refused to participate, principally because they were felt to be flaunting the whole community.

Whenever necessary a meeting of the whole community is called by the governor. No household would neglect to be represented. It is more difficult to get representation from the outlying settlements, but sometimes a special effort is made to include them, too. Technically community meetings are chaired by the governor, but following opening preliminaries in which the purpose of the meeting is explained they follow a course of free discussion. Several people may talk at once and even talk at cross purposes. Nearly everyone speaks freely as they are moved to do so. Women and young people often have as much or more to say as the elder men. Yet such meetings seem to move to a satisfactory conclusion without too much difficulty. If they are dominated or controlled by anyone it is by Fernando the schoolteacher. Even he is very diplomatic in guiding the course of discussion, although his influence is usually clear in the decisions which are made.

At one such community meeting it was proposed that each man contribute Bs 1 per week, and the women Bs 0.50 per week to underwrite the expense of the fiesta, which was to be held five and a half months later. Nearly everyone agreed enthusiastically, even though there was no indication of pressure to sign up with the plan. A couple of individuals even offered to contribute more than requested. The enthusiasm expressed here was not only one of support for the community, but pride in it and a desire to contribute to its enhancement by organizing a good fiesta.

Although the governor may on occasion contribute a large sum to the expenses of a fiesta, he is never expected to assume all the costs of every one. Cayapas are no longer held for individual benefit, although Emilio does sometimes call together all the men of the village to work on projects which are of *community* concern. Even in these instances any refreshment, such as a bottle of aguardiente, is provided by some "public-spirited" citizen, rather than the governor.

The latter is, of course, in no position to regale the rest of the community with food and drink, either on the occasion of a public project or a community fiesta. He receives neither remuneration nor the tribute which was paid to his old-time predecessors. Indeed, a number of people maintain that the governor *should receive* a salary. The feeling is that this is a responsible position, and one that deserves to be paid. They argue that such salary should come from the federal government. This attitude is consistent with what one finds in most criollo communities throughout Venezuela, for here as elsewhere people no longer consider such things to be their own responsibility.

In many ways the Mameños have learned to exploit state and national governmental machinery to their own advantage, which is only another way of saying they have learned the political ropes in Venezuela. They have found a considerable amount of truth in the Biblical promise, "Ask and it shall be given to you." Those who are both faithful and aggressive politically are most likely to obtain what they ask for. The Mameños are sufficiently educated and sophisticated that they are not only aware of national politics, but they can and do take an active role in them. The majority have been staunch supporters of the A.D. party since the 1940's. Apparently the Pariche family was sufficiently outspoken that one of their number, a curioso, was arrested on charges linked to the latter profession in an attempt to intimidate local support for A.D. During the Pérez Jiménez regime most supporters had sense enough to keep quiet, but their sentiments did not change, and with the overthrow of Pérez Jiménez they enthusiastically threw their support behind Rómulo Betancourt who was elected president of the republic from the A.D. party. In striking contrast to Cachama, his picture was displayed on the wall of nearly every home, and most Mameños could talk somewhat intelligently about their reasons for preferring Betancourt and his party.

The Mameño schoolteacher was a leading light here, as elsewhere. He served on the local committee of Acción Democrática, which became so active that it often acted independently of the municipal committee to which it is technically subordinate. During our stay in Mamo Fernando spent as much time on politics as he did teaching school. He studied political literature, engaged in political discussions, organized local committees for political action, drummed up local support, etc. When A.D. planned a nationwide census to prove the breadth of their popular support, Fernando not only organized the local census committees, but had completed the census two weeks before it was to have officially been taken. Because of his activity and enthusiasm he soon became known at district headquarters of the party in Soledad. When party officials from the state or the district visit Mamo it is Fernando who to a large extent serves as host, guide and spokesman for both Indian and criollo communities. He was one of three delegates from the whole district who attended the state party convention in Barcelona. Fernando has been sufficiently successful politically that he is considered something of a threat by opposition groups (see below). He is serious about devoting even more time to politics, in fact would like to make it a full-time occupation. If the political climate of Venezuela remains fairly stable, it is likely that he will yet make his mark, at least on the state level. Such success would undoubtedly have considerable repercussions in Mamo, since, even if patronage should disappear completely from state and local government (which is unlikely), they would still have a vocal spokesman who could speak in their favor to decision-making officials in the state and federal government.

Affective Ties to Mamo

RARELY IS THERE an attempt to conceal or deny the fact of being Indian; though at the same time no one seeks to emphasize it. There has been no thought of trading on the Indian heritage to gain personal or group advantage. But in general Mameños are proud of their Indian ancestry. There is no sign of shame or self-deprecation when they announce, "Somos indios *kari?nya,* caribes orientales." Yet in Cachama *indio* is avoided in preference to *indígena,* and *Cariña* has replaced *caribe.*

A Mameño openly remains a Mameño wherever he may go. He feels that he belongs to the tribe, that he is a member of the community, and this tie is only rarely lost. One belongs to Mamo because that is where his ancestors lived. The ties of the "abuelos" are felt to be binding on their descendants. Then too, one's kinsmen are almost all Mameños. The tie of kinship to one's parents and uncles, siblings and cousins provides a strong centripetal force binding one to the community. As was indicated in the preceding chapter such kin ties have not only remained strong, but have actually been readapted and strengthened in terms of contemporary conditions. The wide dispersal of Mameños has not been as effective in weakening such kin ties as one might expect. Finally, binding people to Mamo is the fact of their birth there. There is an almost spiritual tie to the place of one's birth, and particularly a "contagious" one to the spot where one's *maruto* (placenta) is buried. (This last factor even provides an important, though much weaker, bond between the criollos and their birthplace in Mamo.)

Affective ties have also been maintained through the particular configuration of the community itself. The paternalism of Pedro Pariche, the old cacique, had a good deal to do with maintaining the loyalty of the Indians through the long and difficult period between intensification of criollo hostility *circa* 1912, and the renewal of Indian aggressiveness in the economic and political spheres from the late 1940's to the present. In addition to the various aspects of paternalism mentioned above, Pariche also created strong affective bonds throughout the community by rearing numerous orphaned children. He claims to have fostered 29 such orphans. Many are now deceased, but we did succeed in verifying a number of them through other sources. Even after leaving the caciqueship Pariche maintained strong personal interest in the welfare of the community. Since the only church was in Mamo Abajo he had another structure built in Mamo Arriba to serve the Indian community. Unfortunately it was taken over shortly afterward for use of the school, and the images of the saints were moved into a back room. Even so, Pariche never fails to visit this "church" and pray to the saints whenever he returns to Mamo from his fields on La Isabel.

Frequent return to *propio Mamo* is another indication of the sentiment maintained by most Mameño Indians. Any major fiesta, such as that of the patron Santa Rosa on August 30, or Holy Week, or Los Muertos is an occasion when people congregate from their various places of dispersal to mark the celebration. A priest visits the local churches only on the occasion of the Fiesta of Santa Rosa and on July 16, Día del Carmen, the fiesta of Mamo Abajo. These are the only times that baptism, confirmation, and marriage can be performed there. What is striking is not only that the majority of Indians prefer to have these ceremonies performed in Mamo, but that they will wait for the occasion of the Fiesta of Santa Rosa to do so, clear indications both of their continuing identification with Mamo and of their antagonism toward the criollo community.

Even life crises are preferably endured in Mamo rather than elsewhere. Return for marriage has just been discussed (though consensual unions may be entered into at any time). The traditional girls' puberty ceremony has disappeared, but many mothers still prefer to bear their children here with the moral and emotional support of mothers, sisters and other close kinswomen. There is almost a conviction that children ought to be born in Mamo, no matter where their parents are presently residing, which in turn continues the affective tie between an individual and the place of his birth.

THE PEOPLE OF MAMO express their affective sentiments for the community, their approval of it, their support for it through adversity and success in many ways. Approval of and support for such things as the promised utilities installations and the Indian school constantly arises in daily conversation. Nearly everyone feels it not only a right but a duty to send his children to the school in Mamo Arriba.

Support for Fernando, the other youthful leaders of Mamo, and for the political activities of various members of the community is not often expressed in the same type of generalities. But it comes out clearly in expressions of approval for particular activities, or decisions which have been made, or ideas which have been expressed by these individuals.

In fact there is a free and open current of interpersonal relations among everyone resident in Mamo. To a considerable extent it also reaches out to the other settlements dependent from it. There is a continual round of visiting between neighbors, irrespective of kin ties. There is a continual flow of gossip on matters of concern to the community, though there is a tendency to avoid topics which *might* be prejudicial to it. There is talk of the school, of seeking more aid from the state government, of protecting oneself from the criollos, or perhaps preparations for an upcoming fiesta or about the game which is currently in season.

Two fairly serious matters were discussed quite thoroughly in this informal fashion while we were in the community. One concerned a case of father-daughter incest. It involved a repeat by a man who was the only Indian anyone could remember ever having committed such an act. There was considerable concern over how this would reflect on the community, and a very definite feeling the guilty party should be punished. The first time he had committed incest was when Poito was governor and no one did anything to punish him that time. But as Emilio Ñávarez, the present governor, expressed it, "The first time you can repent, but the second time is too much." Local outrage was enhanced by the fact that the perpetrator had extensive kin ties throughout the community, and all of his kinsmen were particularly eager to see him punished. The community itself probably would have worked out a satisfactory means of dealing with the case. However, because of its seriousness it was referred to municipal authorities in Carapa. There it was decided that since the man was only living in consensual union with the girl's mother and actually only a *social* father to her, the easiest solution was *legal* marriage to the girl. This solution was patently unsatisfactory to the Mameños, but it is clearly evocative of their present respect for the law that they made no attempt to secure further satisfaction.

Another problem which produced a good deal of informal activity arose over the "Rockola" (jukebox) in Palitar. Several women, mostly wives and mothers, began to complain that the factory workers were splurging their wages at the "Rockola." Not only were they playing the infernal machine, but they were consuming entirely too much liquor, which was bought from the establishment. Too much dancing with unattached girls led them astray from their wives and families, and besides there was more than a suspicion that some of these girls were prostitutes. For a time there was a good deal of furor over this, particularly after some of the men became over-inebriated, abused their wives, and squandered their whole week's wages at the "Rockola." Rosa Macadito was on the verge of forming a women's committee and forcing the governor to take action. She was actively supported by a half dozen others, and there was a fair amount of tacit sympathy among those who had no direct concern. Before any definitive action could be taken, however, the whole community was distracted by a much more serious disturbance over the activities of the former governor, which will be discussed below.

Not only is "grapevine communication" effective in Mamo, but integration of the community is clearly expressed in other ways. Cooperative economic exchange is a basic pattern of kindred relationships. Paralleling this is a pattern of neighborly exchange within the settlement. From time to time the woman of the house will send a dish of *prepared* food as a gift to one or another of her neighbors. This gift will be reciprocated within a few days. Such exchange occurs continually. Hardly a day goes by that one does not see a child bearing a small dish of food to some other part of the settlement. In economic terms these are unimportant. The portions usually are no larger than one serving, and they will usually be consumed by one or two persons in the receiving household. In *symbolic* terms they are extremely important. They express the friendship and respect of the giver, and they serve to reaffirm the common ties between the two households, even in the absence of bonds of kinship.

There is considerable concern with maintaining an appropriate community image, which is one reason there was so much outrage over the instance of incest committed by an Indian. That was most un-Indian behavior, even though "You have to expect it from criollos, they'11 live with... just about any female..." Much of the concern with proper etiquette, which is instilled into children at such an early age, is also explained in terms of what is "right" for the Indian community. Maintenance of a distinctive and genteel community image serves as a boundary marking device. It is one way of setting themselves off from the criollos. In their own minds at least it also makes them morally superior to the latter.

Even though there are no moral overtones connected with the consumption of alcohol, inebriation may lead to behavior which is considered unseemly. Most wives and mothers object to intemperate drinking, both because of the expense involved, and because of the abuse which they sometimes suffer from inebriated husbands. No older man of respect is a heavy drinker, although some of the younger leaders such as Vicente Chiroco and Fernando often become drunk on weekends. Perhaps this is tolerated as a part of the weakness of youth.

Few women have succeeded in asserting any control over the alcoholic excesses of husbands or sons. Not so Doña Marta Parlche. She long ago convinced her husband never to drink anything stronger than beer and that only very occasionally! But she didn't stop there. Doña Marta, who is a very real though *covert* leader in Mamo, is greatly concerned with the image of the whole community. She is aware that inebriated men often act foolishly, and this has led her to become a sort of community temperance officer. She realized that the only way to control drinking is to control the source of supply. As a consequence she stocks a considerable amount of beer and aguardiente "for my family's use." Whenever drinking begins it is always possible to obtain liquor from Doña Marta. But when it becomes evident that the men should consume no more intoxicants, she discovers that she has "just run out." I know from personal experience that this is a ruse, since on two or three occasions I was able to obtain beer from her after other parties of men had been told there was no more to be had. True it is that liquor can be obtained in Mamo Abajo, but usually by this time the men are in no condition to get down the hill to replenish their supply. Even though Doña Marta may be acting illegally, local liquor consumption is controlled much more effectively than if everyone were left to bring in their own supply. While drinking has not been stopped (and it would probably be impossible to do so), it has certainly been controlled, and the community image has been protected if not enhanced.

Another instance of this concern for the community image occurred when a group of ARCistas hit town one Saturday evening. The ARCistas are a splinter group which broke away from Acción Democrática in 1961. They had come looking for Fernando, presumably to pick a political fight, since his sympathies were well known throughout the district. Fortunately he was away that weekend. Finding Fernando absent, they danced with the girls for awhile, then discovered there were North Americans in the audience. Evidently they decided that the latter would do almost as well as their original objective. A couple of them buttonholed us and launched into a harangue on how the present government had sold out to millionaires and foreign imperialists. How the State Department could topple any government they didn't like. How Yankee Imperialists are taking all the wealth out of the country. I changed the subject to the Alliance for Progress, thinking this might meet more with their approval, but it only stimulated fresh criticisms.

What happened in the next few minutes was a master stroke of diplomatic skill. Doña Marta and several men of the community had been listening to the discussion. When it gave signs of getting heated, two or three of Doña Marta's teenage daughters and granddaughters suddently appeared and invited the strangers to dance. Two of the men called me aside and "suggested" that this would be a good time to go home, if we wanted to. "Not that anything could happen here. These fellows are opposed to the government. *But we're all here. We are backing you up* (dando espaldo). If you prefer to talk to them, you are perfectly free to go ahead and do so."

At this moment one of the respected elders of the community came strolling down the street. Eloy Guevara said, "Here comes José 'los Santos. He's looking for you." All the while these things were taking place Doña Marta was hovering inconspicuously in the background. She never said a word, but it was quite evident that she had been directing the whole maneuver.

Here again there was a clear concern for the image of the community. What would we think if they allowed insults or violence to occur to us? What would we think if they, who were our friends, didn't back us up? How sincere would their professed support of the Betancourt government be if they didn't put these interlopers in their place? The fact that such action was taken is strong evidence of the identification with and loyalty to Mamo as a community, a community which commands a distinctive pride in its members. The fact that the intruders were dispatched so smoothly, without their being aware of what was taking place, is not only a credit to Doña Marta's diplomatic skill, but further testimony to the general feeling that insults, violence, or a scene of any sort would be detrimental to the image of the community as a whole.

For some time before our arrival in Mamo there had been increasing misgivings on the part of many individuals about the behavior of Pedro Poito who had been governor since 1955. He drank too much, he frequently borrowed money without repaying it, he neglected many of his responsibilities as governor, and what was most serious of all, he failed to speak out for the community interest. Individual dissatisfaction was evident, since Poito found it increasingly difficult to get anyone to respond to his orders, or to pay attention to him at all. Yet no one spoke out against him, for there was unwillingness to do anything which might undermine the community or destroy its unity.

A month or so before we began the study of Mamo Poito called a community meeting, said he was tired of his responsibility, and declared he wanted to resign. The community took him at his word, accepted his resignation, and elected Emilio Ñávarez to replace him, mainly because he was young, intelligent, and literate. All of these were traits which Poito either lacked, or about which there was serious question.

From the moment of our arrival Poito sought to gain our sympathy and support. Though his story about being tired of the governorship never changed, it soon became evident that he was sorry to have given it up. When drunk he sometimes intimated that he felt he had been *relieved* of the office by the community. Meanwhile the townspeople began to be more openly critical of Poito and his behavior than they had been while he was governor.

Still they sought to avoid any open antagonism. When Doña Marta raised a question about the disposition during Poito's term of office of funds paid by the state as rent for the school building, the whole matter was quickly dropped. Everyone seemed to feel that it would only create an unpleasant situation, without ever seeing the funds restored. The general attitude seemed to be "Let bygones be bygones." "Let sleeping dogs lie," and avoid internal friction, particularly where no good was likely to come of it.

Of course, Poito could not but be aware of some of the criticism directed toward him. Adding to his feeling of insecurity was the fact he had always supported the national U.R.D. party, in spite of the overwhelming allegiance of other Mameños to A.D. One night while drinking with Fernando, Poito taunted him,

"Go ahead and denounce me (for my political loyalties)."

"Why should I denounce you? You can have your own opinion."

"Go ahead and tell, you're a *huevón* and government bootlicker (adulante), anyway."

Such insults were too much to bear. Fernando leaped at Poito, who grabbed him by the throat. The two were separated, but their families entered the fray to defend their respective honors. Then someone accused Poito of being armed with a knife. Poito's daughters spoke out in their father's defense, but the women of the Casa Grande demurred that he had neglected his duties and misapropriated funds while governor. At this point the women took over the fray in earnest and screamed profane insults at each other while the rest of the community arrived to see what was going on. Personal slurs replaced political insults and the women were on the verge of coming to blows before onlookers stepped in and broke the whole thing up.

Everything was in an uproar for several days following this outbreak. The principals on the two sides would have nothing to do with each other. Poito accused Doña Marta and Rosa Macadito of having conspired against him. Though they had certainly done no such thing in the past, this affair brought them together as they recounted the events of the fight, lamented Poito's many failings, and discussed what ought to be done about him.

The Chiroco-Guevara family had stayed out of the fight, but the next day they assigned themselves as Fernando's bodyguard and hustled Poito back to his territory when he sallied forth to continue the argument.

Now that hostility toward Poito had come into the open nearly everyone began to express their feelings about him. "It's Poito's fault the whole thing happened, the way he'd insult the community whenever he was drunk." Since it had all come to a head that fateful night, everyone suddenly discovered that everyone else had long harbored the same thoughts about him. Dissatisfaction and criticism which had formerly been kept to oneself was now found to be shared throughout the community. Even with open conflict the community remained united, except for the outcaste Poito and his family. Those few who were not openly critical preferred to remain silent, rather than join Poito's side.

The whole dispute was settled formally by the *comisario* from Mamo Abajo. He talked to various witnesses and participants individually, then called them all together to pronounce sentence, which was a mild rebuke to Poito —telling him when he gets drunk not to get involved with other people. This satisfied no one. Hostility remained great, and Poito felt himself on the defensive. At the end of the week he and his family packed up and moved out completely, "without saying goodby to anyone."

As soon as the Poitos had left, a noticeable stillness settled over the community, as though people suddenly found themselves with a good deal of food for thought. After a time they gathered in small groups, where they quietly discussed the situation. The affair was settled, yet it had damaged community unity. The loss of even one individual through anger or hostility was a serious matter. It damaged the community image, it left unpleasant feelings, and it could have been dangerous. There was always the chance of a community split and the rise of factionalism with continued unpleasantness and infighting.

Under such conditions the community certainly could not concentrate on its own best interests, and would probably be much more vulnerable to inroads from without than when it could present a united front.

Reality of the Community

IT SHOULD BE eminently clear from the points which have been discussed here that the Mameños are bound together as a community by affective ties of pride, loyalty and long tradition. They function effectively as a group, and attempt at all costs to avoid internal dissension and division within the community. Though the functions of the cacique have changed in this century, the present governor remains an integrative symbol and rallying point. His strength as a leader can be enhanced in direct proportion to his aggressiveness on matters of community concern. Yet a weak governor does not necessarily mean a weak community, for Mamo is presently blessed with a surfeit of capable leadership. At times the informal actions of individuals who hold no formal office is more important than the formal action of the duly elected governor.

Open and continued hostility in relations with their criollo neighbors has doubtless contributed to Indian integration. In any society clear-cut problems or enemies which are easy to identify are generally effective in bringing together opposition and promoting solidarity in response to a clearly recognizable threat. In Mamo the first reaction to criollo hostility was retreat, and this lasted for a generation or more, although the Indians never lost their unity in face of this threat. The past fifteen or twenty years have seen them take up the offensive, adapting to the external situation better than the criollos, and making use of some aspects of the criollo way of life to enhance their own. While local political structure deteriorated in the hands of the criollos, the Indians have gradually encroached on criollo roles in local politics. It is they who are revitalizing this structure at present.

They have learned how to operate effectively within the given framework of Venezuelan government and politics on both local and state levels. To date they have been successful in securing a variety of advantages for Mamo, and undoubtedly they will continue to do so in the future.

The drive which has led to such success is centered in the more youthful segment of the community, though there are also some older people who clearly understand such matters. More important, however, the youth enjoy the full support and encouragement of their elders who are also progressive and forward-looking, though not quite so energetic.

The Mameños have always been loyal to their community, but undoubtedly it is their present success in dealing with the contemporary world that has reinforced their pride in it and enables them to admit straightforwardly their identity as Indians.

Consistent with their close identification with the community, the Indians of Mamo are most concerned with maintaining a "proper" image of it. Group ties are strengthened by *symbolic* extension of behavior which is characteristic of the kindred. Considerable care is taken to encourage behavior which would be of credit to the community —be it personal etiquette, moral behavior, or working for community betterment; and to avoid actions which would be a discredit— such as drunkenness, brawling, and irresponsibility.

There is considerable effort to avoid open hostility, dissension, or anything else which might destroy group unity and tear the group apart. In fact, maintenance of a united front is a strong social value here. Even when discord does arise, the tendency is to stick together and keep splintering and factionalism to a minimum. To date such responses to internal conflict have been successful in meeting the situation, even on one or two rather serious occasions. Though the conflict was not always resolved, the unity and integrity of the community were preserved, which after all is a far more important consideration.

Comparative Comments

THOUGH MAMO differs from Cachama in almost every regard, it is perhaps in the realm of community organization that it is most strikingly different. As pointed out in Chapter IV, Cachama can hardly be said to represent a true community. Rather the group has been torn into several factions by dissension, suspicion, hostility, and lack of communication between neighborhoods. Though neighborhoods are only separated by distances of from one to five miles, (one and one-half to nine kilometers) they are entities unto themselves wholly independent of each other. Today they are the largest socially and politically functional units. One is a Cachaman only in residence, but it is the neighborhood which commands most of his loyalties.

Leadership has also deteriorated in Cachama. The hereditary cacique has lost his control of the community. Elected governors are extremely vulnerable to the vagaries of local public opinion. Almost anyone who can rally a few sympathizers around him can emerge as a short-term leader.

In Mamo on the other hand, one is first and foremost a Mameño. Residence in a particular settlement is a secondary and relatively unimportant fact. Even though one may live ten, twenty, or more miles from *propio Mamo,* which makes direct contact relatively infrequent, affective ties, social, political, and ceremonial loyalty remain strong. One important factor making for the difference may be that in Cachama people are more conscious of the threat from within, which tends to tear the community apart, whereas in Mamo the threat is identified as a criollo threat from without. This actually promotes community integration, binding people more closely together.

CHAPTER 10

VALUES

CERTAIN VALUES of the Mameño are readily evident in his conversation and in attitudes which are expressed in his daily activities. First and foremost is his aspiration to achieve the state of being "civilized" *(civilizado).* This is a complex matter which includes wearing shoes; the adoption of criollo house dresses by the women (though a few older men still retain the traditional Karinya kilt); burning a light all night long; being genteel, hospitable and well-mannered; being respectful of others; and being able to consider oneself *cristiano* (a term often used interchangeably with, and as a near synonym for *civilizado*). In contrast with the Cachaman's self-consciousness and sense of shame about his present condition, the Mameño is proud of the state which he has achieved.

Being *culto,* having *fundamento,* an attitude of good manners and respect for others, is one aspiration which is valued in and of itself, irrespective of its connection with being "civilized." Time and again we would hear a Mameña mother cautioning an unruly child, "Tenga fundamento." Education also receives great emphasis, as we will see below, since this is considered one of the most important means of achieving "civilization" and of ensuring that one will be able to retain this state.

Naturally, many other values are not so self evident, and must be got at through more intensive means. For this purpose we again utilized the values interview. The same series of questions which had been employed in Cachama was administered to a representative cross-section of Mameños. Satisfactory answers were obtained for all questions.

Because of the difference in character between the two communities the contrast between the two representative cross-sections should be immediately evident. The following six individuals were interviewed:

Semi-traditional:

Santos Chiroco	70 years old, man of honor and respect in the community, a praying curer.
"Tata" Rosa Poito	75 years old, respected because of her age, a "lazy thinker" ((difficult to interview).

Median types:

Juan Guevara	37 years old, father of 6, reads and writes, a man of strong opinions.
Cristina Pariche	20, mother of three, reads and writes, rather shy "lazy thinker" (difficult to interview).

Progressive:

Inés María Macadito	52 years old, towndweller, midwife, egoistic and aggressive.
Fernando Martínez	29, single, village schoolteacher. Has inferiority complex over his marked shortness. Has had five years of school, plus additional self-improvement. Very broad world-view. Has had much experience in the towns, shows great deal of criollo influence. Active in community affairs, and national politics. Respected by almost all members of the community as a leader, although he holds no really formal position other than that of schoolteacher.

We were fortunate that during our stay in Mamo Inés María Macadito arrived for an extended visit. She was born there, and most of her family still lives in Mamo. Although she still considers herself an Indian (at least in the context of the community of Mamo), she has been living in towns like San Félix and "El Tigrito" for a number of years. Inés María was interviewed as a representative of the progressive orientation —one who was reared according to traditional Mameño values, but who has since become strongly oriented to the towns.

The sample for Mamo is more complete than that for Cachama principally because the factor of age is less important than in the latter community. One of the most progressive Mameños is a middle-aged woman, whereas a girl barely out of her teens ranks no more than an "average" type. Strictly speaking, there are no true traditionalists in Mamo, the two listed as semi-traditional are practically the most conservative to be encountered there.

Possessions and material prosperity. There is striking uniformity in the items which are considered essential for the home. Every respondent but one (Cristina) lists a bed, though several homes actually lack this item of furniture. Only two (including Cristina) mention hammocks. Tables and benches or chairs are listed by half the informants. The women tend to list *corotos* (pots, pans, and kitchen utensils) and basic foodstuffs (such as salt, garlic, lard, coffee, etc.) near the head of their enumeration, whereas the men invariably place them last. Indicative of a typical aspiration for better things is Cristina's desire for glasses to be kept in the *sala* (the living room, as opposed to the *cuarto* or sleeping room). The jug filled with drinking water is generally kept in the *sala* and possession of a set of individual drinking glasses to be displayed near the water jug is greatly desired.

The things considered important by the progressives are no different in kind from those listed above, but they do indicate a somewhat higher standard of aspirations. Inés María considers a (kerosene) stove essential, while Fernando sees both a refrigerator and a radio as necessary items. Indicative of his feelings of inferiority at still remaining single he prefaced his answer to this question by emphasizing that "The most important thing a house needs is a wife..."

Luxury items, made possible by an increase in individual or family income include such things as pressure lanterns or electric illumination and a variety of ornaments for the interior of the house — mirrors, pictures for the wall, potted plants, etc. The women (with the exception of Inés María, who is a town dweller) appear to consider kerosene stoves as luxury items. Indeed, they are used that way in Mamo. They are reserved for the initial part of the rainy season when firewood is damp and hard to burn. Cristina evinces a practical desire to invest in chickens and livestock, but she would also like to obtain a glass-fronted cupboard. The progressives again have higher standards, electric lights and running water to be among the first luxuries one would obtain. True to her urban orientation, Inés María would go all the way and build herself a cement block house, with a zinc roof. Then she would furnish the inside not only with a variety of ornaments, but with cupboards and a wardrobe as well (in Venezuela these tend to be portable items of furniture, rather than being built into the house).

Nature of the family and intrafamilial relations. The general feeling seems to be that the principal obligation of a man to his wife and family is to provide for their needs —food, clothing, etc., even in unusual circumstances, such as being away from home for a period of time. Some of the women go on to stress that the man should be aware of his family's needs without their having to be brought to his attention. Perhaps this is consonant with the ideally quiet and retiring feminine role. Along with the attitude of providing for the family there is considerable emphasis on being industrious and hardworking. The ideal husband should be affectionate, considerate, generous with what he earns, content, and faithful. He should not beat his wife, and he should avoid fights with other men. There is also a strong value placed on cooperation between husband and wife in many of their undertakings. First and foremost as a cooperative endeavour is the rearing of children. But in addition to speaking for the wife and defending her in all matters, one should counsel with her on family affairs and should take her advice into consideration.

Likewise a man's principal obligation to his children is to provide for them, to care for their needs. He is generous to them, watches out for their best interests and teaches them to be industrious, to avoid quarrels, not to be lazy or shiftless *(vagabundo).*

The proper role of the wife is to be obedient to her husband as well as affectionate and loving. Obedience means quiet submission to the husband's wishes, for the woman who is shrewish, argumentative or talks back *(cachorra)* is universally deprecated. (There is general disapproval of behavior which is *cachorro* in either sex, but there seems to be more concern with its occurrence among women, probably because it is a frequent characteristic of criolla women).

A mother's care for her children is considered so basic that it is almost assumed in several of the responses. Emphasis tends rather to be on giving advice and counsel to one's children, and on the need to discipline them, but by scolding rather than corporal punishment, which is reserved only for the most serious misbehavior. It is also the special obligation of the mother to instruct her daughters in the various duties around the house and to prepare them in other ways for their future responsibilities as wives and mothers.

There is overwhelming agreement that the most desirable characteristics among children are obedience, and respect, for their fathers above all, their parents in general, and their elder siblings. Unlike the Cachamans, the Mameños believe that one can begin to teach a child proper patterns of behavior at quite a young age. "They know, even if they can't talk yet. The older they are the better behaved they should be, for they can understand (their parents') advice better." Politeness, decorum, and "good behavior" are stressed from the earliest age in most families. Some, but by no means all, individuals indicate agreement with the old North American value that "children should be seen and not heard."

Girls in particular should be assigned certain household tasks by the time they are seven or eight, and they may be given the responsibility of caring for younger siblings before that time. Boys on the other hand may be allowed a much more carefree existence, allowed to roam about the village, and even to wander into the nearby woods by the age of seven or eight. In actual practise, small girls seem to range from one end of the village to the other about as freely as do the boys. Nonetheless, it is true that the former seem to settle down to helping around the house sometime before they reach puberty. It is very strongly emphasized that girls should never leave the vicinity of their homes unaccompanied. Again, in practise this applies only to areas beyond the village, and even in the latter case, two girls of approximately the same age may be sent to the store or the dispensary in adjacent Mamo Abajo.

By the time a girl has reached her teens she should be assuming household tasks without any direction from her mother; she is expected to continue to respect her parents and pay attention to the advice which they give her. Especially after she has reached puberty a girl should take care never to go out of sight of her house alone. She should be polite, kind, and attentive to her friends, but at the same time demand politeness and respect from male acquaintances.

A teen-aged boy on the other hand should express his affection for a girl in which he has a serious interest (the *novia*), but at the same time respect her. "He should behave even better than she."

Like the girls, teenage boys are expected to respect their parents and their peers, and to treat everyone with politeness, kindness and affection. This last value recurs over and over again in any discussion of interpersonal relations. Good manners and decorum are expected in all dealings with others.

There is but one point of differentiation between the three subtypes with respect to the proper behavior of children. Only the semi-traditionalists emphasize that teen-age boys should share with their parents game and other things which they obtain on their own. That this distinction is not significant, however, will become clear in our discussion of the proper relations between married adults and their parents-in-law which appears below.

When queried specifically about methods of discipline most informants respond with an answer which contrasts with that given above to characterize the ideal parent-child relationship. This time the emphasis is on corporal punishment, although there are also numerous implications that a good deal could be accomplished through verbal disapproval and scolding. Only urban-oriented Inés María continued to maintain that corpooral punishment "is not a good way to punish them." This is probably a personal idiosyncrasy since I would expect a higher incidence of this type of discipline among urban families. Even among the others there is a definite feeling that corporal punishment should not be severe. Every respondent was careful to limit it to whipping of the shins or lower limbs in order to avoid really hurting the child.

There is little distinction in the *potential* freedom of the two sexes during childhood. By three or four they are fairly free to roam the village, although parents feel they should check in at home every hour or so, but mothers tend to be quite liberal in measuring such periods of time. By the age of seven or eight it is expected that they will be kept busy with schoolwork or chores at home, although theoretically children of this age are less restricted in their freedom about the village. Teenagers may be allowed to spend several hours in the evenings sitting outside one or another house in the village and visiting with other teenagers under the discreet eye of an elder person. Inés María, speaking in terms of her urban environment, contrasts markedly with the values of the other Mameños on this point. She would permit her children to leave the house only for a few *minutes,* a half hour being the maximum time, and then only when several children are together. Girls, under no circumstances, would be allowed to leave the house alone. Thus, the conditions of urban life may be seen to be a great deal more restrictive when it comes to the rearing of children.

The principal emotion one should have for his parents is that of love, combined with concern for their well-being. Respect is also important, but there is little feeling that a child should fear his parents. Children should help their parents, cure them if they are sick, protect them in the obligations which they have incurred, and support them in their old age. Generally the emphasis is on the father as the most important parent, although the younger respondents tend to discuss this value in terms of *both parents.* Again Inés María has a somewhat distinctive point of view on this question. She feels that while children love their mother, their primary emotion toward the father is one of fear. Undoubtedly this is more consistent with generalized criollo values and practises, whereas the other respondents essentially provide a picture of the somewhat distinctive Mameño orientation.

Family integration appears to be quite strong, and there is nothing in the expressed values to contradict this interpretation. All members of the family cooperate in numerous kinds of work, such as stripping moriche fibers in order to make a hammock, processing manioc, weeding the fields, or harvesting maize or beans. There is a difference of opinion as to whether families should eat together, but this difference is significant only as a reflection of the practises in the family of each respondent. The whole family might travel together to visit an acquaintance in another village or to the towns if the primary purpose of the trip is recreation and amusement. However, only one or two persons will undertake a trip if its primary purpose is a matter of business. Fernando expressed a rather unique opinion about family unity, which might be described as "cooperative specialization:"

> Depending on the opportunities which are presented, the members of a family have the duty to cooperate with each other. It's not good for a family to occupy itself with one single concern. Each should be doing his part to help the others, who are doing something else so that the first won't have to be concerned with that duty.

In Mamo the general practise at marriage is for the newlyweds to set up their own independent household. This means that one's primary duties and responsibilities are directed to the spouse, without the constant demand for interaction with other kinsmen. Most people feel that the wife's first interest is her own home, and that she should be, first and foremost, responsible and subordinate to her husband. Likewise for the man marriage marks the point of full independence from his parents. At the same time the married adult does retain certain very important ties with both his own parents and with those of his spouse. These ties entail certain continuing obligations, such as loving and respecting both parents and parents-in-law. Indeed, parents-in-law are to be treated just as one's own parents. Most respondents feel that one is definitely closer to one parent-in-law than to the other, but there is no significant agreement as to which one. One very important pattern that remains strong is the economic obligation which is felt toward both parents and parents-in-law. One should share not only the produce of his fields, but whatever fish and game he succeeds in obtaining. Presumably this is an old pattern that has remained strong here whereas it is in the process of breaking down in Cachama. But not only has it remained strong in Mamo, it has been adapted to changing socio-economic conditions by being redefined and reinforced. Today it is just as important for a person to share his cash income with these same relatives, and he does so willingly, without discriminating between parents and parents-in-law.

Individual maturation. The values expressed in this series of responses are striking in that all but one person indicate they consider it important for girls to learn to read and write, in addition to learning the tasks associated with the home. As he is a progressive schoolteacher, Fernando saw no reason why girls could not learn some skill which would enable them to obtain regular wage employment. For boys it is still more important to learn reading and writing, and even to learn a craft or a trade. Along with this, however, most respondents feel that boys should not neglect their training in farming, fishing and hunting.

Group organization, leadership, etc. If anything, an attitude of respect for others is a more fundamental value in Mamo than in Cachama. One should be respectful not only of relatives and compadres, but should respect other people in general, even if there is no particular social tie linking them to him.

The greatest amount of respect is focused on the father, Mamo lacks the matrilateral bias of Cachama, although the mother is nearly as important. As a matter of fact, there is some indication from the answers of the progressive respondents of a tendency toward treating the parents equivalently rather than singling one or the other out as more important. One should also treat his elders and his kinsmen with respect. In addition there is frequent mention of the community governor, compadres, community elders, and "the government." Several individuals mention that one should respect his peers, or even younger persons in order to promote a reciprocal attitude of respect. But with the one possible exception of a broadening of respect feelings for the parents, the replies of the respondents are quite uniform.

Respect is even more an important component of leadership. There is general agreement that a leader in the community should be a man who not only can be respected by everyone, but who is respectful of others. Beyond this he should be knowledgeable, industrious, and a responsible individual. The progressives stand out from the other informants by adding several additional requisites to the qualities listed above. They stress that he should be conscientious in his concern both for his own family and for the community as a whole. He should be well-reared with *fundamento* —being correct in behavior and patient in his dealings with others. And Inés María particularly emphasizes the importance of experience for successful leadership.

The role of the governor as official head of the community is viewed in very integrative terms by the people of Mamo. Their relationship with him is one of two-way reciprocation, with the emphasis being on what *they* can do for *him.* If he needs anything, one should perceive this and supply his need. If he plans to take a trip one should contribute to the expenses when asked to do so, for the trip is in the interests of the community. One should accede to the governor's requests, assist and support him at all times, and speak out in his favor whenever there is some disagreement or complaint. Only one respondent mentions that you just "tell the governor" when you need something. There was no indication in the series of answers of any significant distinction between the values orientation of the three sub-groups.

With the exception of Tata Rosa the respondents view the role of the governor in rather positive terms. They list numerous functions which he can assume in the interest of both the community and the individual. Generally, emphasis is on the community, with service of the governor to the individual being secondary in importance. The governor is responsible for keeping order and ensuring that justice is done, for seeing that houses and streets are kept clean and in good repair. He should provide that houses are built for those who have none, and should otherwise make sure that no one is in need. It is his responsibility to see that the community is represented whenever and wherever necessary. If its needs are greater than can be supplied from local resources, then it is his duty to appoint a commission to request these things from the state and or federal government (which is exactly what was done in obtaining lights and water for Mamo).

Likewise there is essential agreement concerning the obligations which the individual owes to his community. Primarily his duty is to assist the governor and to obey his mandate, performing whatever tasks are required of him. One is obligated to inform the governor of any matters which are of concern to the community at large such as a dispute between some of its members. One should strive to maintain accord within the community, for maintenance of the unity and integration of the group as a whole is among the highest values. Fernando carries individual obligations one step farther, arguing that one has the duty to "work for the welfare or benefit of the community... and the community will in turn aid the individual members."

When queried about the maintenance of law and order under conditions where the community would represent the only authority, our respondents tend to take a severe attitude toward anti-social behavior, which is emphasized more than the positive formulation of law and maintenance of order. A couple of respondents recognize the necessity of formulating a code of laws and setting up a court to judge cases of wrongdoing, but one of these would merely define these functions as duties of the governor or cacique.

Tata Rosa affirms that "The basic law would be to live tranquilly." Although she was the only one to put this value in positive terms, the continual Mameño emphasis on decorum, respect and politeness —a general smoothness of interpersonal relations— did emerge in several other answers with clear disapproval of such behavior as argument and dissension, fighting, making fun of other people, disobedience, answering back, and interrupting a conversation. Punishment for this type of misbehavior would be mild, one to three days confinement, but the important thing is the feeling that it can and ought to be punished. The two progressive representatives do not mention these points in reply to this question, although it is clear from other responses that they do share in this value. Perhaps this is indicative of a slight weakening of the value applying to smoothness of relations. Perhaps the progressives see this as desirable behavior, but do not consider it the sort of thing which one can coerce people to conform to.

Murder is considered by all to be the most serious crime. They would punish murder with anywhere from two to 20 years imprisonment. Rape, incest and robbery are also serious, and would be punished by from one to several years confinement. To judge from recent history in Mamo, few of these anti-social acts would present any serious problem as their incidence would be quite infrequent. Presumably the severity of punishment proposed by our informants is a response to the conditions they have seen or heard of in the cities, where it is apparently difficult to maintain law and order.

Change, progress, and contacts with non-Indians. There is full agreement that education is a valuable asset for any young man or woman. Almost everyone views it as a means of better employment. With an education you can earn your living with your head —in an office, in a business, as a schoolteacher, etc. Furthermore, education can enhance one's personal qualities. It increases your intelligence and enables you to learn more. It teaches discipline, good manners, to respect one's elders, etc. Education teaches you how to express yourself clearly, it provides better understanding of affairs which might affect you, and enables you better to protect yourself in legal matters. Finally, Fernando points out its value to the community whose "stability and progress... depend on the education of its youth. If they are educated they can advance the Culture of the tribe."

The major advantages of modern life are considered to be the vastly increased rapidity of communication, via letter and telegraph, and mechanized transportation. The public school, the local dispensary, and the present democratic government are other positive elements. Over and above the basic popularity of A.D. is the fact that the present government does not capriciously enforce the restrictive conservation laws which were imposed under the Pérez Jiménez regime. The administration of Betancourt was also responsive to local desires and requests. The installation of a well and an electrical generator in Mamo by the state government is seen as another positive achievement by means of which civilization is being brought to Mamo. In local eyes material betterment is seen in the increasing abundance of such items as radios, phonographs, refrigerators and similar mechanical contrivances. On the other hand jukeboxes are viewed with mixed feelings, for although they provide entertainment, they also take money away from the community, and they may serve as a base of operations for prostitution. The disadvantages brought by modern civilization are certainly much fewer, so far as the average Mameño is concerned, than are the advantages. About the only element for which there is a modicum of agreement is that relations between Indians and criollos are very poor, with the criollos insulting the Indians behind their backs and attempting to take advantage of them whenever possible. Beyond this there is no discernible agreement with regard to the disadvantages of modern life.

The ideal compadre is a person who is respectful of his compadre and generous to his *ahijado,* preferably an elder person, somewhat older than the parents of the godchild. There seems to be some feeling that compadres should be of equivalent economic status, since, "If your compadre is rich he cannot treat you as an equal." As in Cachama compadres have traditionally been criollos, but in recent years there seems to have been an increase of Indians who have assumed that role. Undoubtedly this is correlated with the fact that one does not forget who his compadres are in Mamo; and the *padrino-ahijado* relationship is marked by distinctive behavior. The preference for an Indian would also reflect an attempt to reinforce the feeling of community in Mamo.

However, the progressives show little concern with the racial and cultural background of their compadres. In Fernando's response this is probably a reflection of his idealism; whereas for Inés María it undoubtedly results from the fact that there are few available Indian compadres in the urban environment in which she is living.

Religion. Religion to the Mameño means Catholicism. But because of the limited contact with a priest (no oftener than once or twice a year) their beliefs are rather vague and generalized, and partake more of a folk cult than of the orthodox form of Catholicism. The most important thing to teach a child about religion is how to pray. He must know of the existence of the saints and that they can be prayed to in order to request things of them. A child is also taught to believe in and to love God. Beyond this there is little in the way of formal learning about religion. However, some respondents feel that the learning of good behavior and proper respect for one's elders is also a part of one's religious training. Again the strength of this particular value is evident, for it continually crops up as a qualifying factor throughout a broad spectrum of values attitudes.

COMPARISON AND CONCLUSIONS

IN GENERAL THE values system in Mamo has changed much more than that of Cachama, with the most conservative values in the former community being somewhat more progressive than the most recent changes in the values orientations in the latter. The distinctions between the two communities even extend to the representative types of individuals which can be discerned in a "typical" cross-section. In Cachama there is clearly a majority of "conservative" traditionally-oriented individuals, with a small but growing minority of "progressives." Furthermore age is an important determinant of one's values orientation. None of the older people in Cachama can be considered progressive, while a proportionally larger number tend in that direction with increasing youthfulness. In Mamo on the other hand, there are no true conservatives. The most conservative element is best described as "semi-traditional." Although all those who belong to this group are older, age is not really a significant factor in Mamo. Far more important is degree of contact with criollo and urban ways of life. A middle-aged urban dweller is best classed as "progressive." Midway between the semi-traditionalists and the progressives we distinguished a median type for purposes of discerning values orientations. These are people who are rural dwellers, who have had some education, but are relatively unacquainted with traditional lore. They stand out neither as being particularly conservative, nor as holding truly progressive ideas. On the basis of their responses to the values interview, however, they would appear not to be particularly distinct from the "semi-traditionalists," and to all intents and purposes the two categories could as well be lumped together.

Possessions and material prosperity. Although the Mameño standard of living is somewhat higher than that of Cachama, their level of aspiration far exceeds that of the Cachamans. Whereas only the younger progressives of Cachama mention beds as necessities and no one specifically mentioned other items of furniture, the Mameños invariably consider a bed an essential piece of furniture along with tables and benches. The Mameño progressives move somewhat further along the same continuum and add a refrigerator and radio. Again luxury items in Mamo such as electric lights and running water are in advance of the aspirations which are considered attainable in Cachama. The majority of individuals would use enhanced economic conditions to increase their consumption. In Cachama three respondents also indicated a concern to increase production. There was no comparable concern in Mamo, but presumably because it is not necessary in that community to work out an elaborate scheme in order to obtain an increase in income. This is within the reach of every individual who is willing to seek employment in the towns or in the new industrial complex that is growing up nearby in Guayana.

Nature of the family and intrafamilial relations. Some basic Karinya values appear to remain in both communities, but some striking changes have also taken place, particularly in Mamo. In the latter case, however, change has not meant replacement of the old by the new as much as a reworking of the old as an adaptation to the new.

Ideal relationship between spouses is strikingly uniform in the values systems of both Cachama and Mamo, but there is an equally striking difference in their opinions concerning the proper way of rearing children. The pattern in Cachama is one of laxity, with little discipline being imposed before middle childhood. In Mamo on the other hand respect and obedience are instilled at an early age, and proper behavior is reinforced both with verbal and corporal punishment. Respect and politeness are considered important qualities of personality in both communities, but there is greater emphasis on them in Mamo, where they are at the same time considered to be applicable more extensively than just to kinsmen and friends, and also to be applied more intensively.

While the mother is the most important parent in Cachama, it is the father in Mamo. Love and respect are the most important emotions one should feel for his parents. In both communities it would appear that increasing contact with criollos, rather than development of progressive attitudes *per se,* have also resulted in the idea that one should fear his parents, particularly the father. The evidence from Mamo indicates that this is not an *inevitable* consequence of a more progressive and broader world view. Likewise a restrictive attitude (as opposed to an increase of discipline) toward one's children would appear to be linked to urban contacts or living in an urban environment, rather than being directly linked to the development of a progressive point of view.

In terms of daily tasks there is little distinction between the activities which a family might undertake together in either community. But familial integration would appear to be greater in Mamo. This is partly because Mameño families tend to amuse themselves more together, but primarily because of the very strongly emphasized pattern of economic and social reciprocity which is maintained between a married couple and the parents of both spouses. An old pattern of sharing natural products has been elaborated to include sharing of cash income and other economic goods. In contrast, the traditional pattern has broken down in Cachama, and there is no indication that new economic goods such as cash income are even considered comparable to the traditional ones.

Another difference between the two adaptations is that Mamo has not broken down as a community, and consequently those values which reinforce community integration are those which remain strong. There is every indication that the traditional Karinya pattern was more like that to be seen in Cachama (minus intense factionalism, of course). Evidently in the course of trials and difficulties with their criollo neighbors, the Mameños discovered the present pattern of behavior, which proved to be more adaptive for the world in which they are forced to live. Along with community integration there has been a further elaboration of familial integration. Undoubtedly, maintenance of a broader base of support has also proved advantageous in dealing with the trials of the modern world, whether they be unscrupulous criollos, or adaptation to developing industrialism and urbanization. The greater emphasis on the father in Mamo had undoubtedly resulted from the necessity for the man of the family to deal with this new world for the family as a whole.

The Cachamans have not yet hit upon such a felicitous series of adaptations, and consequently they suffer from factionalism and community breakdown. While families have remained strong, they remain matricentered, and there is no indication of an increase of familial integration. In fact, some of the patterns which have served to reinforce familial integration in Mamo not only have been neglected in Cachama, but have actually begun to break down themselves.

Individual maturation. The contrast between the two communities is quite clear here. In Cachama the most important training which should be given a child relates to his future role as a subsistence producer. Even the progressives do not consider formal education particularly important in this regard. In Mamo on the other hand, formal education is valued for both boys and girls, since it is felt that this could enable either sex to obtain a lucrative position in wage employment. At the same time, hower, there is no feeling that training in subsistence skills should be neglected. Obviously the difference in attitude is directly related to differences in expectable opportunities and in past experiences at wage employment.

Group organization, leadership, etc. As was stated above, the emphasis on a two-way attitude of respect in Mamo has been significant in maintaining community integration and ensuring a broad base of support for both individual and community. Cachama has not developed this kind of mechanism for the maintenance of community integration, but there is some indication of an attempt to reinforce and exploit the compadrazgo with this end in mind. In Cachama there is confusion and disagreement about the functions of the governor. In Mamo there appears to be essential accord about his tasks, and particularly concerning the responsibilities of the individual in assisting him. Informants even evinced a willingness to contribute to expenses incurred by the governor in pursuit of community business. Not so in Cachama where the general attitude is a selfish one oriented to the advantages that can be obtained from the governor, at the same time that patterns of economic redistribution through the community leader have disappeared completely. There is some opposition to contributing toward the governor's expenses, and some Cachamans even hold that he lacks any right to demand compensation from tribal members. This particular point of view is clearly a reaction against exploitation of the office by past governors, or accusations of exploitation directed to them. The progressive attitude toward office-holding in Mamo indicates an increasing concern with the quality of the officeholder and his services to the community.

The data concerning severity of sanctions directed to anti-social behavior are somewhat contradictory, for sanctions are severe in Mamo, where internal harmony has remained strong. Perhaps sanctions against anti-social behavior were traditionally severe among the Karinya, but I doubt that this was the case. It seems more likely that the causes for this attitude have resulted from a feeling that with progress comes disorganization and lessening control over the individual. In Cachama this is derived from personal experience within the community. In Mamo it is perhaps a reaction to poor relations with the criollos, and almost daily accounts of lawlessness and violence in the towns and cities.

Change, progress, and contacts with non-Indians. Formal education is valued by both Cachamans and Mameños, but in Cachama it is considered to be useful primarily for men, and then almost entirely in terms of enhanced employment opportunities. The Mameño agrees that an education can be advantageous in obtaining employment, but he does not limit such advantages to men, women too can benefit by being literate. But the value of education does not stop here, it provides the means to attain progress and "civilization" which are desirable ends in themselves. Generally "progress" and the changes attendant upon it are viewed favorably though almost everyone has one or two reservations. Only the conservative element in Cachama seems to harbor strong feelings of opposition to recent changes.

Religion. "Religion" to most men in Cachama refers to curing and the activities of the curioso with respect to the supernatural. Women and the younger progressives, however, are oriented instead to formal Catholicism. The Mameño makes a clear distinction between the activities of the curioso, which are practically limited to curing, and "religion" which is the local folk expression of Catholicism.

Here as elsewhere in the values orientations we see a progressive continuum beginning with the older conservatives in Cachama, proceeding through younger conservatives, older and younger progressives. The values of the semitraditionalists and median-types in Mamo generally represent a stage beyond that of the Cachaman progressives. Finally the Mameño progressives represent the most advanced attitudes which have been developed from the broadest background of experience with criollo and urban environments.

IV

CONCLUSION

CHAPTER 11

THE CONFORMATION OF CULTURAL CHANGE

THE PRECEDING exposition has presented two situations of cultural change among different communities of Karinya in Venezuela. At the present one of these is in direct contact with the petroleum industry, the other profoundly affected by nearby development of the national steel industry. Extensive changes are taking place in both communities; yet it has been shown that there are striking differences in the changes which have occurred and which are occurring in them. Such differences involve all aspects of change, from the specific details to rates of change and, what is most important, the very nature of the changes impinging upon the two communities.

This concluding section will examine the forces which have stimulated change, and the reasons for the differences between the two communities. From there we will proced to a more speculative level suggesting what might have happened had conditions been somewhat different. Knowing what we do about the contemporary Karinya, in the midst of culture change, an attempt will be made to make some predictions about what can be expected in the future. As a science, anthropology must be able to make valid predictions. The attempt here is in the spirit of a modest contribution to that end.

FORCES CONDUCING TO CHANGE

IT HAS BEEN shown that both Cachama and Mamo are presently undergoing processes of cultural change. Anyone who visits either community, even briefly, cannot but be aware of this fact. But it is not enough to say that change is taking place, or even to describe such changes *in extenso.* What has brought such change about? Why has change occurred? A vague explanation would be that these communities are "becoming modernized" or that they are "in contact with Western civilization." But these still do not answer the question, Why did change occur when and how it did? It is not even satisfactory to reply that the Karinya are becoming acculturated to Venezuelan criollo culture. Why didn't they do so before? Even more critical in this regard is the question of why change is different in the two communities. To explain the *specific* changes which have been identified in the preceding chapters it is necessary to seek *specific causes,* which can be shown to be in more or less direct correlation with each other.

I dislike the simplistic explanations and assumptions of the economic determinists, and yet economic factors appear to have been important in both instances under discussion here. It should, however, be quite evident by this time that these were not simple forces, but rather that they were considerably complicated by other factors: family structure, inter-ethnic relations, political personalities, and the degree of community integration, to name some of the more important ones.

In order to facilitate exposition these specific forces will be presented in modified tabular form along with the particular changes which each has brought about.

CACHAMA

Forces for Change	*Changes Brought About*
Economic:	
Developing oil industry and rise of towns.	Greater variety of material goods; new economic opportunities.
New economic opportunities: wage labor, work in gravel, cash cropping.	Increase in available cash.
Increase in available cash.	Increased consumption of new material goods.
Increased consumption of new material goods.	Growing participation in, and affective commitment to the larger economic sphere.

Family:	
Internal drift of kinship designations.	Alteration of kin organization.
Influence of Spanish kinship patterns.	Idem.
Change in residence pattern and family organization.	Idem.
Restriction on warfare and trade.	Male activity rechanneled to agriculture, increased male dominance in fields and household.
Increased male dominance.	Possibility for mature men to establish neolocal residence. Matriliny gradually replaced by ambilineality and ramage organization, but with continued matrilineal bias.
Individual character of new economic opportunities.	Incipient weakening of family.
(Reasons unknown).	Neighborhood replaced clan as functionally most important territorial unit.
Neighborhood replaced clan.	Personal and kin-group commitments to neighborhood reinforced, factional breaks coincide with neighborhood boundaries.
Community:	
Intrusion of oil industry, activities on tribal land.	Lessening confidence in ability of cacique to protect community from outside exploitation.
Suspicions of favoritism and misappropriation in distribution of right-of-way payments.	Resentment, factionalism, and community breakdown.
Intervention of criollo outsiders.	Increased factionalism and community breakdown.
Values:	
Perception of threats to familial solidarity.	Preference for severe discipline of children; desire to do things together as a family.
Community conflict and group disorganization.	Emphasis on past values, critical view of contemporary leaders (conservative reaction).
	Attempts to formulate new values more appropriate to present conditions (progressive reaction).

Naturally, values tend to change somewhat later than the modifications in economic practises, family organization, or social and political structure to which they are related. Thus we also find many people expecting the governor to carry on most of the traditional functions of the former cacique. Likewise there are frequent protestations concerning the desirability of formal education, but the values orientation of the Cachamans hardly shows them to have developed a very strong motivation to pursue it. In their eyes learning basic subsistence techniques remains by far the most important task of children and youths.

MAMO

Forces for Change	*Changes Brought About*
Economic:	
Forced to seek fields elsewhere.	Men replace women as principle producers; employment in wage labor.
Greater familiarity with criollo culture.	Ability to take advantage of new economic opportunities when presented.
Growth of industry in Guayana.	Employment in industry; increased cash cropping.
Increased income from industry and cash cropping.	Urban-influenced patterns of consumption, rising standard of living.
Family:	
Emigration from Mamo.	Adoption of Spanish in everyday conversation; extended family replaced by independent nuclear family units.
Nuclear family organization, Spanish speech.	Adoption of Spanish kinship terminology.
General maintenance of kin ties.	Development of bilateral kinship.
Economic reciprocity between all primary relativies.	Emergence of limited bilateral kindred.

Community:	
Maintenance of kin ties.	Continued identification with *propio Mamo.*
Return to Mamo for childbirth.	Idem.
Pride in tribal ancestry.	Idem.
Changes in national and state policy.	Modifications in caciqueship.
Continued identification with *propio Mamo.*	Growing individual motivation to assume leadership roles, and concern for improving community.
Values:	
Broadened world view.	Reworking of values system to adapt it to contemporary conditions.
Changes in various aspects of Mameño culture.	Generally consistent changes in values.
Continued distinctiveness of Mameño culture.	Maintenance of values system which is distinctive or "superior" to criollo values.
Feeling of possessing superior values.	Reinforcement of community integration.

WHY THE DIFFERENCES?

COMPARISON OF THESE two communities, Cachama and Mamo, presents us with a most interesting problem. These are two communities which presumably once shared a common culture. Much of this assumption is verified by characteristics of their contemporary cultures. Furthermore, traditions of original founders or early immigrants having come to both communities from Tabaro supports the assumption of past cultural similarity. This being the case, why or how did culture change take such diverse courses in these two instances? There appear to be several factors which have contributed to the different conformations assumed by change in each group.

One of these is the degree of isolation. The initial impression which one has of the relative isolation of the two communities is the exact opposite of what is actually the case. In the whole history since its founding, estimated to be about a century and a half, Mamo has never been isolated. Since sometime before European discovery the Orinoco river has been the principal highway between the Guiana coast and the interior of northern South America. From the earliest colonial days it was so used by the Spanish. At the time of Mamo's founding Ciudad Bolívar (then Angostura) had been the center of trade for a couple of centuries. Constant traffic up and down the great river meant that contact was possible not only with Ciudad Bolívar, but with the great variety of both Venezuelans and foreigners who traveled there to trade. The Mameños could not help but be influenced somewhat by such contacts, and occasional trips to Ciudad Bolívar undoubtedly made them more sophisticated than their fellow tribesmen from other communities.

At the same time these contacts remained at arm's length. The twenty kilometers (twelve miles) which separate Mamo from the Orinoco can easily be walked in three or four hours, but the distance is sufficient to discourage anyone who does not have a really good reason to make the trip. This means the Mameños have always had a certain amount of control over their contacts with urban centers and with new or sophisticated ideas. If they were interested they could travel to the Orinoco or Ciudad Bolívar where they would be in direct contact. If they were not interested they could effectively reject new ideas by staying at home. Even today this is essentially the situation in Mamo. Industrial development has not taken place in the community; for that matter there has been no significant development of any kind along the north shore of the Orinoco. If a Mameño is interested in employment in the steel industry he can go to Matanzas and apply for work. If he is attracted to urban living he can move to San Félix or Ciudad Bolívar. If he wants to pursue his education he can accompany some relative who is moving to the city. But if for some reason he rejects these things, or is not interested in them, then he does not have to face up to them. They remain almost out of touch, on the other side of the river, until he makes up his mind to pursue them. When he does so it is essentially on his own terms.

Cachama's present situation, with the principal highway of eastern Venezuela running right along one margin of the community, is a very recent development. Their present condition of intensive contact with the towns, with employees of the oil companies, with criollo entrepreneurs of various classes, etc., has all come about within the last twenty years. Throughout most of its history Cachama has been relatively isolated. The upper Guanipa river, on which it is situated, is not very suitable for canoes, and even today no significant towns are located downstream. A trail passed near Cachama leading to Cantaura and Aragua, but the former was a long day's journey, and the latter necessitated a trip of two or three days. Travel to the Orinoco for grain or to the coast for salt were not unknown, but they appear to have been infrequent and did not always involve visits to cities like Barcelona and Ciudad Bolívar.

Contact in Cachama was with rural criollos, but in the absence of local criollo towns or administrative centers they could hardly have exerted much influence on the Indians. Even today the subsistence patterns and standard of living of the rural criollo is hardly distinguishable from that of the Karinya. In many other respects Indian culture possesses something which is more or less lacking among the criollos. There was no reason to learn, there was little motivation for change.

Then, between 1935-40, the raw light of modern industrial civilization broke upon Cachama almost explosively. This was something entirely alien to the Indians (and rural criollos as well). They knew nothing about the oil industry. They did not understand. They neither desired its arrival, nor were they consulted or even informed at the time it appeared on the scene. It was just there for them to live with, if they could. Rejecting it did not mean that the petroleum industry and the myriad changes which followed in its wake would disappear from the conscious perceptions of the Cachaman. This is the condition which has continued to the present time. The Cachamans still have no active part. They have little choice in accepting or rejecting the traffic which daily passes them on the highway, or the urban centers which have grown up in El Tigre, "Tigrito" and Cantaura, the demands for goods and services in the urban centers which have brought the *mongueros* to Cachama to buy produce, etc., etc. Finding themselves passive participants in all these innovations, the Cachamans are not even sure whether they *could* have a decisive role in deciding whether or not the companies can search for oil on their property, on the disposition of right-of-way payments, or in controlling the movements and activities of outsiders on community lands. Having tacitly acquiesced in all these things thus far, it is quite unlikely that they could assume a decisive role concerning them now.

A second important factor is closely related to the degree of isolation, but it must be viewed as structurally distinct. The degree and kind of contact with the national political structure has been, I believe, significant in its effect on Mameño culture change. The fact that Mamo

(Arriba or Abajo) had been the *cabecera* of its *municipio* had kept it in direct contact with national and state government and the officials who represent it. This meant a continuing awareness of official policies and attitudes, and also kept the Mameños under the more or less continual surveillance of state officialdom. The combination of these probably served as one more pressure to change or adapt the traditional culture. So long as they continued to reside in *propio Mamo* the Indians could hardly avoid the local caudillo who maintained his control at the pleasure of state and national authorities. Likewise, they could hardly escape the restrictive regulations of the game and forest laws which were enforced by a local unit of the Guardia Nacional. The only choice was to acquiesce, or move to some more isolated settlement. Reports otbained from the Indians indicate that it was extremely difficult to avoid regulations, restrictions, and even outright discrimination on the part of such officials, for their unsympathetic criollo neighbors were not above informing on them as a means of harassment. Undoubtedly the consequence was not at all what the criollos expected. Rather than breaking down the Indian community, it only served to unite them and reinforce their sense of distinctiveness and cultural identity. As Lewis Coser has pointed out (1956:38), "Conflict with other groups contributes to the establishment and reaffirmation of the identity of the group and maintains its boundaries against the surrounding social world."

The Cachamans have always been rather distantly removed from their *cabecera* (which serves both the *municipio* and the district). Geographically it is a little more than twenty kilometers away, but a far greater social and political distance separates Cachama from Cantaura. Visits by municipal, district, or other governmental authorities are extremely rare. None came to our attention while we were in Cachama and the priest in Cantaura admitted he had never been there, though he has been resident in that parish for some years. The only formal contact occurs once each year during the Fiesta de Nuestra Señora de la Candelaria. The Indians are invited to the fiesta by the municipal authorities of Cantaura, presumably because they add color, and their simple music and dancing add to the entertainment. Clearly the official attitude continues to treat the Indians as second class citizens. At the fiesta we attended in 1962 a *separate* barbecue was to have been held for the Indians. From all reports, even this failed to come off as planned.

Finding thmselves thus, relatively free from official surveillance and harassment, the Cachamans have had no difficulty concealing many traditional activities from the authorities. They have been relatively successful in maintaining much of their culture away from official pressures to change. The use of fish poison is common in Cachama, yet it long since disappeared in Mamo. The Cachamans were little aware of federal prohibitions against unlicensed exploitation of timber, game, and other natural resources since there was little to be made use of in the first place, and since, in the second place, no official bothered to see that the regulations were enforced there. Cachama never suffered under a criollo caudillo. Such individuals preferred to set themselves up in municipal or district cabeceras. During the period when caudillismo was most rampant in Venezuela, Cachama remained fairly difficult of access.

However, it may very well be that isolation from the national political structure has contributed to present sociocultural disorganization in Cachama. Lacking any easily identified external enemy, without any need to unite as a community or as a distinctive cultural group, the Cachamans have instead turned to internal dissension and disputes, and the community has been torn apart by squabbling and factionalism.

A third important factor contributing to the difference between the two communities is the length of time they have been undergoing intensive change. Intensive change in Mamo began at least by 1912. The culture there has been in the process of change for at least two generations. This has given the Mameños sufficient time to develop a satisfactory adaptation to the different way of life which they were forced to adopt. The necessity of accomodating to Guayanese industry during the last decade was merely one more step in a process which had been under way for several decades. Therefore, industrial employment did not have any serious repercussions among the Mameños, rather they took it in stride. In part the present satisfactory adaptation was achieved because no truly radical changes were required at any particular point in time. Change proceeded slowly and was therefore easier to assimilate. In the early decades of this century the rural criollos differed from the Indians primarily in their lack of extensive kin ties, a sense of community, and in their religious concepts and traditions. They were hardly distinguishable in economy, amount of formal education, knowledge of the world beyond the immediate region, etc. The only town of any size was Ciudad Bolívar, which had attained no more than 20,000 inhabitants by 1941. Thus, many of the changes and accomodations which were made by the criollo were absorbed by the Mameño at the same time, as he was living among the criollos. There may very well have been some cultural distortion at first, during the period from 1912 until

1930 or 1940. But by the time the rate of change was accelerated following the second World War, the Mameño had the advantage, since he had already learned how to change in accomodating to criollo culture, while the bearers of the latter were only beginning to face strong pressures for rapid change. The three factors just discussed, and especially their effect in Mamo are very similar to the conditions of culture change among the Guayqueries of Margarita Island off the coast of Venezuela (Mc CORKLE 1965, especially p. 132), where "continuous, successful cultural adjustment was mainly responsible for the persistence of the Guayquerí community. . ."

One other factor may have been important as an acculturative medium in Mamo. COSER (1956: 125) further points out that conflict "revitalizes existent norms and creates a new framework of norms within which the contenders struggle." It would certainly seem that Indian-criollo conflict has had something to do with restructuring of the values system. The fact of ethnic discrimination may very well have been in the Indians' favor in the long run. Treated as inferiors, they have been motivated to accept new ideas readily, and to adopt many new ideas from the urban centers so as to prove that they too are civilized, and equal, or superior, to any carping criollo.

Current Mameño values, however, *approximate* those of the criollos. It is important to remember that *they are not exactly the same.* COSER (1956: 123-28) tends to argue that such shared norms are homologous in those groups which are party to the conflict. The evidence from Mamo indicates that conflict need not produce homology of norms. While such norms may approximate each other, they can remain merely equivalent, similar, equal in value, but need not be identical to each other.

A Dynamic Model of Culture Change[1]

THE IMPLICATIONS of what has been said about the processes of change and adaptation in Mamo are that they may differ from one point in time to another, i.e., change must be viewed as a dynamic

[1]The discussion which follows has been adapted from an earlier, unpublished paper (SCHWERIN ms).

process. BEALS (1953: 627) points out that many students of acculturation[2] emphasize this point of view. In practise, however, they have concentrated on types of contact (conquest, trade, missionization, etc.) and their results (addition, syncretism, nativism, etc.) and have ignored the actual process or processes which lead from one to the other (see e.g., REDFIELD, et al 1936; S.S.R.C. 1954). BEALS (1953: 636) also comes to this conclusion when he says:

> In very broad terms there are agreements among students of culture contact as to some of the possible results...
>
> Beyond these rather general terms, processual analysis does not seem adequately conceptualized. The majority of existing discussions of process are heavily psychological and essentially deal with the role of the individual in change or the impact of change upon the individual. Few explanations in sociological or cultural terms have been developed.

Numerous studies might be cited here which are essentially psychological in approach. Barnett's theoretical work on cultural change (1953) seems to fall into this category. While he certainly offers some stimulating insights, his orientation seems inadequate for our purposes. There is too much emphasis on the individual, and too little concern with the social system. I feel that the modification of social systems is far more basic in the process of culture change than is the change introduced by, or which takes place in, the individual.

This is not to deny that the individual's *position within the social system* may be important in encouraging change. Some missionaries have recognized this, and will seek to win persons in positions of leadership and authority before they concentrate on the common man. MC CORKLE (1965: 37) reports an analogous situation among the Guayqueries of Margarita Island. Of five Guayquerí communities still existing in 1900, only one survived the movement to distribute communal lands required by the Law of 1904. Among other important factors, the president of the surviving community had influence with the dictator who ruled the country. In such cases individual variability may affect a leader's decision, but it is always the *social* role of the person making the decision which determines its effect within the social system.

[2] "Acculturation" is the term commonly applied to the process being discussed here. At best this implies two cultures becoming more alike through contact. Where "acculturation" has been used by others, it will be employed here in references to their work. For reasons which will become obvious below, however, I prefer the more flexible term "culture change."

My approach is essentially sociological and evolutionary, rather than psychological and historical. The latter is not rejected, but rather considered to be of secondary importance. History may be valuable in shedding light on *what* sociological processes have been taking place, but cannot often explain how or why such changes have occurred. Again, psychological factors are not determinative of change. They function only to accelerate or retard it (one might call them the dependent variables). Systemic changes are frequently inevitable (and would thus represent independent variables). It was inevitable that the Spanish would eventually conquer Mexico; that *Cortes* succeeded in doing so depended on a number of psychological factors such as the burning of his ships and his insight into the current political situation.

When we look at culture change over time, I find it most instructive to view it as an adaptive process. Change comes about through the tendency for the various cultural systems to move towards equilibrium, that is to adapt to a given set of conditions. Any change in those conditions would of course change the point of equilibrium, and would probably necessitate more rapid systemic change than would ordinarily be found under *static conditions.* If we can consider the objective of change to be adaptation, I would define such change as an evolutionary process. A myriad of such microevolutionary changes would produce the broad patterns of development which are dealt with by such evolutionary theorists as Julian Steward, and, on a different level, Leslie White.

It should be stressed that I do not view cultural equilibrium as a static phenomenon. All cultures change through time, and I doubt that complete equilibrium is often achieved. Every culture tolerates a certain amount of chronic stress which probably serves as a constant motivation to change. (It may be that there is a threshold of stress beyond which the forces for change become more effective and the rate of change increases more rapidly.) To the extent that equilibrium is approached, however, I feel that it is most satisfactory to view it as a moving equilibrium. The very fact of change undoubtedly affects the culture in such a way that the point of equilibrium will also change.

It was pointed out above that acculturation theory has succesfully defined the relations which might obtain between two cultures that come into contact, and the end results of such contacts. The principal weakness to date has been the failure to come to grips with the *process* of acculturation or culture change.

Of all those who have dealt with acculturation theory, JOHN

GILLIN (1948: 557-69) appears to have come closest to developing a theory of cultural process. He visualizes acculturation moving through a) the changes introduced through contact, b) the development of new acquired drives, c) a period of cultural confusion, d) the remaking of foreign elements to make them consistent with the indigenous system, and e) a final terminative condition.

A model nearly identical to that of Gillin has been put forth by WALLACE (1956: 268-75), though he is concerned with change from a more limited point of view. He restricts himself to an analysis of revitalization movements, which are a frequent phenomenon in situations of acculturation or rapid cultural change. Nonetheless his scheme seems to me to have more general applicability. With only slight modifications it can be utilized as a dynamic model for various types of culture change. In a general way it delineates the forces which cause change, it describes the mechanism of such change, and it can also serve as a useful tool for prediction in specific instances of sociocultural change. Wallace's model, as I have modified it, can be briefly stated as follows:

I. Steady State. The culture or population is more or less in equilibrium. Some severe stress may occur without substantially disturbing the Steady State.

II. Period of Increased Individual Stress. Increasingly the culture fails to satisfy needs of the individual. The individual begins to have doubts. His picture of the culture begins to break down. Alternative ways of satisfying needs begin to be considered.

III. Period of Cultural Distortion. Individual and group behavior become disorganized and irresponsible. There are piecemeal attempts at cultural substitution, but rather than alleviating the situation most serve to multiply mutual conflict and misunderstanding. There is increasing disillusionment and apathy.

IV. Period of Restructuring (Wallace's "Period of Revitalization"). Individual, or group restructuring occurs which is at least moderately succesful, and provides a basis for further adaptations and modifications. Though essentially a process of trial and error, satisfactory modifications tend to be retained and reinforced through their success in reducing stress, whereas unsatisfactory modifications will be neglected or rejected because they do *not* reduce stress. Sometimes a visionary or charismatic leader will appear at this stage, and a revitalization movement is organized around his leadership.

V. New Steady State. Restructured elements are fully integrated into the total cultural system.

Stages II and III in Wallace's scheme seem to be the key points. Stress or tension is the mechanism which causes change, the motive force for the ongoing process, whether in individual behavior, or on the social and cultural levels.

Where tension or stress begin to appear in the functioning of any social system there will be a tendency to change, i.e. to avoid the stress and return to a smoothly functioning state, to an equilibrium. This tendency is what is described above as evolutionary adaptation (p. 234). As the cultural systems continue to break down, they are moving further and further from equilibrium. As each system moves from equilibrium the tendency for it to return will become greater. In all likelihood, however, the changes which have occurred make it impossible to return to the original Steady State. The only alternatives at this point are continued disintegration and total extinction, cultural extinction through assimilation into an intrusive culture, or movement ahead through uncharted territory to a point of new equilibrium (the New Steady State).

Under point IV Wallace emphasized the role of the prophet or other charismatic leader. No charismatic leaders emerged in either Cachama or Mamo, yet change, and in some cases profound change, occurred in both communities. On the basis of these observations it seems that change may just as well occur through piecemeal restructuring by many individuals, or what is more likely, through the joint action of the group. Faced with conflict and stress in their various cultural systems, they act together to reduce such stress through restructuring those systems. Such initial restructuring is probably far from a perfect solution to the problem of stress, but like the initial teachings of the prophet, it would tend to be further adapted and modified as it functioned within the system so as to reduce stress to a minimum.

As equilibrium is approached in one sphere of the system the forces tending to equilibrium will become stronger in those spheres which are still furthest removed from it. As each part approaches equilibrium the anxiety of the group will be further redirected to those which remain most out of line, and the likelihood of their succesful restructuring will increase. This phenomenon parallels that produced by the religious activity within a revitalization movement, which stimulates revitalization throughout the society. The major difference is that in most cases the rapidity of change and the degree of restructuring are rarely as spectacular as in the case of a religious revitalization movement.

It seems necessary, however, to enter one qualification on the universality of this model. While it seems highly useful in explaining the process of change in the majority of instances, I know of cases where it does not seem applicable. This is particularly true in circumstances where people adopt new crops or new techniques without outside pressures or conscious attempts to introduce them. In these cases the changes seem to provide increased gratification for the people and their society (by, for example, making industrial goods available through the sale of cash crops) which occurs in the absence of stress. Unless we want to take the somewhat ridiculous position that the society is moving from a level of zero stress to negative stress (!), such instances seem contradictory to the model presented above.

Applying the model to Mamo it is clear that the Indians of that community have achieved a New Steady State following a period of restructuring that must have been going on for from one to two generations. This is not to say that some restructuring is not continuing at the present time, but what we observe today is relatively unimportant and does not seriously disturb the present steady state.

It is equally clear that Cachama is far from occupying either an initial Steady State or a New Steady State following a period of restructuring. Where then does it best fit into the above model?

Pressures for rapid cultural change have been impinging on Cachama for a much shorter period of time (from about 1934 on) than was the case in Mamo. The impact of the oil industry and all that is associated with it, both directly and indirectly, was not really brought home to the Cachamans until 1947 when the first right-of-way contracts were concluded with the oil companies.

Undoubtedly there has been a slow process of acculturation taking place in all the Karinya communities for many years, but this appears to have created no profound or serious disturbances in most of them unless, like Mamo, they were subjected to direct criollo attack on their organization and institutions. Under these conditions Cachama can best be considered as having been in a Steady State prior to the discovery of oil in the vicinity during the mid-1930's.

The discovery of oil, the rapid and massive influx of workers, "by 1938, more than eight thousand were employed" in the east (LIEUWEN 1954: 87), the growth of satellite towns, and the sudden introduction of modern rapid communication produced a Period of Increased Individual Stress. The Cachamans are still attempting to develop a satisfactory adaptation to these new conditions which they must necessarily deal with almost every day.

The sale of part of the community lands in 1929 was something which affected the whole community and which might have initiated some cultural distortion, but this does not seem to have been the case. The loss was not considered to be particularly great since little or none of the land sold was under cultivation at the time. Perhaps, too, *cultural* distortion cannot occur until *individual* stress reaches a certain level. In any event cultural distortion does not seem to have been significant in Cachama until signing of the right-of-way contracts, which was followed by squabbles, factionalism, and break-down of contact and communication between neighborhoods, with consequent repercussions on kin organization and the values system. Were it not for certain centripetal economic factors, the community might have fallen apart completely.

At the present time Cachama provides a near classic example of the Period of Cultural Distortion. Individual and group behavior are irresponsible and disorganized. Group identification and group loyalties are weak. Attempts at cultural substitution have certainly been piecemeal and unsuccesful. Replacement of the hereditary cacique by an elected governor has produced weak and ineffectual leadership. Recourse to a strengthening of the compadrazgo has had little effect, and it is difficult to see how this could solve the present problems of community breakdown and lack of integration. There have been few values changes to date which can provide a strong base for extensive and adaptive restructuring. Present strengthening of kin groupings is more in the nature of reaction to a weakened superstructure even though it does represent a certain amount of restructuring. For the most part mutual conflict and misunderstanding are increasing in Cachama. There is no lack of apathy and even disillusionment. The present picture is a rather gloomy one, but the model for sociocultural change suggests that the future may not be as dark as present conditions make it seem.

How Might Change Have Been Effected More Easily?

IN ADDITION to analyzing the actual course of culture change in the communities under discussion here, I have given some thought to how the present might have been modified had certain key decisions been different in the past. The objective in doing so was to seek insights which might be generally useful in controlling and directing socio-cultural change. The results of this speculation are presented here, although the reader will undoubtedly find them disappointing. I have attempted to be realistic and keep speculation within the bounds of probable and likely conditions within the past. Consequently no radical alternatives are proposed. In fact, it will be seen that, in spite of the spontaneous nature of the processes which have been under consideration in this study, in spite of the inauspicious conditions which set off much of the change, the results have in many cases not turned out too badly. Nevertheless, there may be one or two places where a carefully formulated program of guided change might have produced better results.

In both communities economic changes have taken their own course. There have been no direct attempts on the part of outsiders to control, direct, or restrict economic activities in either case. As indicated in the section dealing with Cachama, payments received from the oil companies have had a minimal effect. The initial situation in Mamo came nearer to direct restriction of Indian economic activities through the threat of depredations by criollo livestock. Yet, beyond this threat in the home community there seems to have been little further concern with Indian economics on the part of non-Indians.

In principle we may deprecate inter-ethnic hostility. Official policies often enjoin such attitudes since they are usually considered deleterious and unjust. In the instance of Mamo, however, it seems to have been just these conditions of inter-ethnic conflict which have brought about the present highly satisfactory adaptation to contemporary conditions, including industrial employment and urban living.

This conflict forced them to face the criollo world. They had to familiarize themselves with it so as to know what to expect and be able to defend themselves from it. The exodus from *propio Mamo* reinforced the necessity of becoming familiar with criollo culture, in order that the emigrant Mameños might operate effectively within it. But at the same time that the community was becoming dispersed, the very fact of continuing hostility and conflict with the criollos served to increase group cohesion and integration.[3]

Would a clearly formulated plan of social change have been more satisfactory or more successful for the Mameño Indians? More successful —perhaps; more satisfactory—extremely doubtful. A policy of incorpora-

[3] See COSER (1956: 87-95) for a general discussion of this reaction to conflict with an outgroup.

tion might have been attempted. The Indians might have been allowed to participate in local politics. Intermarriage with criollos might have been encouraged. Either policy would have kept the Indians in *propio Mamo,* obviated the necessity of seeking fields elsewhere, and probably would have produced a rather different type of political adaptation.

But these are remote improbabilities. Given the political conditions of the Gómez era, none of the common people, Indian or criollo, were permitted meaningful participation at any level of politics. Given the colonial Spanish attitude of superiority toward the indigenous peoples of the New World and its survival among their neo-American descendents throughout Latin America, it seems hardly likely that inter-*marriage* would have been very frequent, though consensual matings between criollo males and Indian women would probably have varied little from their present incidence. Nonetheless such extralegal unions are expressive of a continuing attitude of superiority and dominance on the part of the criollo. If encouraged, they could lead, at the very best, only to biological and cultural extinction. Had this occurred in Mamo the present apathy, lack of unity, and lack of responsibility which are characteristic of the criollo group would doubtless be equally true of those with known Indian ancestry. This is not the case. The very necessity of learning to operate effectively in the criollo world has produced an energetic, forward-looking, progressive element in the Indian community, which is seeking gains that will benefit not only themselves, but the criollos as well. In this instance spontaneous change has been more successful than any program of guided change likely would have been.

In Cachama transition might have been eased somewhat had the oil companies had some orientation to an enlightened self-interest, something which is still markedly lacking in most company policies and activities. So far as I could determine no attempt was ever made to help the local people understand what oil exploitation was all about, or what the objectives of the oil companies are. Nor did the companies ever have any particular policy which encouraged employment of local people, as opposed to hiring immigrants who come from other parts of the country seeking work.

In my opinion the one policy which would have the greatest long-range value both for the oil companies and the local people would be one of more explicit standards in hiring of non-Venezuelan personnel. At the present time there are either no standards at all, or only very general ones. Foreign personnel are selected for their knowledge of some aspect of the petroleum industry, with no regard to how they will adapt to an unfamiliar environment. Many non-Venezuelan employees know nothing of the country, have no interest in learning about it, and only put up with their "unbearable" existence there because of the high salaries. There are even instances of personnel who "broke down" after a few weeks and had to be shipped home at company expense. There is a general resistance to learning Spanish which nearly amounts to outright refusal. I encountered several instances of supervisory personnel with years of experience in Venezuela who were still getting along with a few phrases of broken Spanish.

Such conditions manifestly do not contribute either to communication with the local people, or empathy with them on the part of company employees. Although Cachama is located on a major highway but twenty minutes from a major company town, we found the most appalling ignorance about the Indians among employees living there. Some didn't know they existed. Of those who did they had only the vaguest notions of how the Indians make their living. Beyond that they knew practically nothing.

The one bright spot is provided by the sportsmen, mostly fishermen, who have become familiar with the countryside and its inhabitants while in pursuit of their avocation.

A more satisfactory employment policy on the part of the companies would undoubtedly repay the additional effort both through a reduction of employee turnover and increased understanding of local problems. Indirectly, the benefit of improved public relations with local people would be invaluable. To achieve this it would be necessary to concentrate on hiring people who are interested in working in Venezuela as a place, over and above the generous salaries being offered. Supervisory personnel should be *required* to learn Spanish and all other employees strongly encouraged to do so. Furthermore, in-service programs designed to acquaint employees with local sociocultural patterns and areas of potential difficulty would go a long way toward improving the local image of the companies as well as avoiding many of the tensions and misunderstandings that have marked relations with local peoples.

The only real obstacle to this sort of approach is the companies themselves. To date they have not been much concerned with standards for hiring non-Venezuelans, assuming that such employment would be difficult and unattractive. I doubt whether such a program of diffuse self-interest would appeal to them, though it is probable that it would mean considerable savings, whether in terms of dollars and cents, or in terms of reduced conflict in local situations.

The fact that the Cachamans were not drawn into employment among the commercial enterprises in the towns leads one to question whether this might not have been encouraged or facilitated in some way. One point favoring Indian entrance into the national economy through this channel is that the transition in terms of income would not be so great as would employment in the petroleum industry, and would necessitate less drastic compensating changes in other parts of the Indian culture. However, such employment did not happen spontaneously, and it seems unlikely that criollo proprietors would actively seek Indian employees. Even so, a government program might be designed to encourage Indian employment in local business by providing the necessary training and seeking appropriate job placement. This is definitely within the realm of possibility, but the logical agency to coordinate such a program, the Comisión Indigenista, is sadly lacking in funds, staff, and authority to carry it out. What is more, it is likely that such a program would contribute little to strengthening the economy, family organization, or community unity in Cachama. In fact, the greatest danger would be the probability of cultural extinction and total assimilation of the Cachamans to the criollos.

The remaining alternative is to encourage extensive cash cropping among the Cachamans to supply more of the local demand for foodstuffs. This would seem most logical, since it is merely an extension of activities and techniques which are already familiar and would also help to satisfy urban demands for foodstuffs. Even the eventual introduction of mechanized agriculture would represent a less radical change than substituting a whole new field of employment. This, of course, still would not solve problems of community factionalism.

Turning to family and kinship organization, it appears that the changes which have taken place in Mamo have been wholly consistent with the other modifications of the culture. The present family and kindred organization are well adapted to meeting contemporary conditions, and at this point it is difficult to ascertain whether the transition might have been effected with less stress in some other way.

In Cachama family and ramage organization seem to be functional and adequate if one does not look beyond the neighborhood or the community. But because of the integration of these entities and the tendency to deny responsibility to all but the most mature individuals they do tend to inhibit economic activity outside the community. One rarely breaks his ties with the family or ramage to take advantage of some opportunity which offers itself. That is why most such employment is short-term—a few months at most. Because of the nature of his kin ties in the community the Cachaman is discouraged from seeking either advancement or career in El Tigre, Ciudad Bolívar, Caracas, or elsewhere. At the same time, continued employment outside the community (such as contract labor) or an extension of that pattern (in commerce or industry), would probably encourage development of the independent nuclear family, which would be more consistent with demands of the modern culture. Were this a desired objective, such modification of economic patterns would undoubtedly be more effective in attaining it than seeking to modify family structure directly.

The present political awareness and activity of the Mameños is largely the result of two factors, continuing conflict and competition with the criollos, and a reaction against the inadequacies of past caciques. The cacique appears to have been relatively weak ever since the establishment of a criollo caudillo in Mamo. One might have wished for a stronger cacique during that time to protect Indian interests and serve as a strong focus for integration of the Indian community. Such a situation was quite unlikely under the conditions of the Gómez era, though in all fairness the Indian cacique seems to have done what he could. Looking deeper, however, it becomes evident that a strong cacique would today prove disadvantageous. Such an individual would have protected his people from the necessity of learning to deal with criollos. He would have inhibited them from learning individual responsibility and self-reliance in the world at large. Certainly a strong cacique, by his very existence, would have effectively discouraged emergence of the kind of energetic public-spirited citizens which are found in Mamo today. All in all, it would appear that spontaneous political change has not come out too badly in that community in spite of the recency of the present structure.

In Cachama conflict and political factionalism within the community *might* have been avoided had the oil companies been more aware of the differences between Karinya culture and that of the criollos, and if they had engaged in an extensive program of public relations with the Indian community. I have already discussed why such an approach on the part of the companies would be extremely unlikely. They consider such matters to be of no concern to the conduct of their business. Even if such programs had been undertaken, there is no guarantee that conflict would have been avoided. In any event, conditions in Cachama seem to have been ripe for the development of factionalism. Arrival of the oil companies may have provided the necessary catalyst for the outbreak of internal conflict.

Such conflict has been further encouraged by the interference of criollo shysters and politicians. Probably what would best serve the interests of Cachama would be protection from such outside interference, leaving it free to work out its own difficulties. Admittedly, this is no guarantee that these people can or will resolve their disputes. It is difficult to see how one might consciously seek to dispel factionalism and bring new unity to the community. Any attempt to work directly in the political sphere would undoubtedly result in nothing but further conflict.

A religious revitalization movement might succeed in reuniting the community, but I am extremely dubious about the long-run value of such a development. Most revitalization movements are reactions born of frustration in attempting to deal with a dominant culture. They seek to circumvent the need to deal realistically with changed conditions, either by a return to the past (as e.g., in the Ghost Dance), or by attempts to bypass the processes of development and adaptation (as in the Cargo cults). Because of this unrealistic approach, revitalization movements tend to fail more often than they succeed.

The greatest probability of success in unifying the Cachamans would seem to lie in developing bonds of common economic interest. They need to work together for a common goal, but they need to do so in a situation which is completely divorced from political maneuvering and political loyalties. Everyone is interested in improving his economic condition, and they all share a more or less common inventory of techniques and skills in agriculture, wage labor, etc. The major difficulty in organizing any group with common economic interests, of course, would be to keep it free of political implications.

It is along such lines that an improved educational program might have a far-reaching effect. To date education has had minimal influence in Cachama. Only a fraction of those eligible are enrolled in the school, and even among these attendance is sporadic. Since the education offered in the local school appears to be wholly divorced from the mundane problems of making a living it is no wonder parents are lax in encouraging their children's attendance. A different sort of educational approach might be more successful.

The school in Cachama was built as a service project of the El Tigre Rotary Club. If some of the members of that organization were to have their way, a radically different "educational system" would be imposed on Cachama. To begin with, they have decided the root of the Indians' difficulties without the least investigation of actual conditions. "They are simply lazy. They need to be taught how to work." This conclusion is based on the fact that the Indians' fields are in the river bottoms away from the roads. Most work in the fields is accomplished during the morning hours before the heat of the day. The Indian houses, however, are conveniently located near the roads. Naturally the Indians that are seen by passing travelers are at home, and at rest. Hardly anyone ever sees them at work, since their fields are not visible from the roads.

One or two authoritarian members of the Rotary Club recommend harsh measures. "Build a fence around the community and force the Indians to work. I'd make a contract with them, 'We'll teach you to work. You work eight hours a day, and we'll build you a town with decent houses, lights, running water, and so on.' " It should be obvious from the start that this approach would be wholly unsuccessful. This Gestapo "discipline" assumes the Indians are incapable of accomplishing anything on their own, and would hardly permit them an opportunity to prove otherwise. At best it would create a dependent community of irresponsible, apathetic, unproductive social sponges.

On the other hand, a school which would *offer* instruction in not only reading and writing, but improved agricultural skills, simple carpentry, animal husbandry, and other useful trades, would undoubtedly be of much greater use for local Indian needs, and what is more, it would be much more attractive to local parents and their children. It is possible that a broader and more practical school program could go a long way in aiding Cachaman adjustment to the modern world. Naturally it will not solve all local difficulties. Better education can be of little direct value in solving such thorny problems as are posed by continuing political factionalism. But the greater sophistication and self-assurance which may come with better education might help to build a climate that would encourage the settling of such problems.

As a matter of fact, continued education of even the usual type will probably contribute something toward such ends. The standard education which has been available to the Mameños has certainly been an important factor in their adjustment to contemporary conditions. The major problem with the standard educational program is that without strong family and group commitment it will be difficult to attract a sufficient number of students for a long enough period of time that some lasting influence can actually result from their exposure to formal education.

When we look at the values system in Mamo we find that the old values have been restructured in such a way as to produce a superior system which is well adapted to contemporary conditions. It would be hard to conceive any way in which the present system could have been developed more effectively, with less tension, or with better results.

The Cachamans are still groping for ways to modify their values so as to be more appropriate to their present condition. To begin with, non-Indians—company employees, government officials, missionaries, and others—should avoid trying to impose *their own* values on the Cachamans. They may not serve the needs of these people, and this sort of approach will only lead to greater confusion and loss of direction on the part of the Indians.

On the other hand, there may actually be some utility in permitting outsiders to openly express criticism of certain Cachaman values, for this will create tension and should facilitate change. It would be even more valuable, of course, if certain values which are thought to be useful could be encouraged. Thus one might attempt to reinforce values relating to the utility of formal education, continued responsibility to the family, extension of reciprocal economic exchange within it, etc.

In summary, it would appear that guided social change would not have been particularly advantageous for the Mameños. Most of the programs which are conceivable and likely would probably have proven disadvantageous in the long run, though there may have been some short-term benefits. As it works out, the Mameños found their own way quite succesfully without outside help. This is not to say that they could not have been assisted in reaching their present Steady State. *Judicious* guidance *might* have enabled them to find their way much more rapidly than they did on their own.

In Cachama the best possibilities for success in guiding change lie in the economic sphere. One might also be sucessful in encouraging transition to the independent nuclear family, or in promoting modification of certain values, but there is little assurance that one could be effective in diminishing factionalism and creating new group unity. Looking at the total picture, it appears that most attempts to introduce any radically new trends would not be to the Cachamans' advantage in the long run. Employment by the companies or in local commerce would undoubtedly bring about the demise of the community. Imposition of alien values will only bring confusion and disorientation. On the other hand, several trends have already begun in Cachama which might be encouraged. To date they represent nothing more than tentative attempts at restructuring. Development of cash cropping, encouraging formal education, etc., would exploit some of these trends. Those new ideas which one might introduce are mostly consistent with established practise in traditional contexts, such as extension of reciprocal economic exchange, reinforcing values relating to pride in the Indian heritage, responsibility to one's kinsmen, etc. The only really new objective which is suggested is to work for the independent nuclear family. Essentially, the best approach would be to encourage those *existent* trends which give greatest promise of providing a satisfactory adaptation within a new Steady State, in order to speed up the present process of change. This approach should be far more effective than any attempt to introduce wholly new patterns.

One word of caution, however. In any attempt to guide and control social change great care should be exercised to prevent its degenerating into a simple program of "social eugenics." Whose definition of what constitutes "desirable improvement" is going to be employed? The proposals of the Rotary Club members were highly desirable in their minds. They did not understand why anyone should disagree with them. A government agency might have quite different ideas about directing sociocultural change, but again one might ask whether *their* long term objectives are formulated in terms of the best interests of the Indians, or the Venezuelan nation, . . .or perhaps neither (see e.g. McCorkle 1965: 33-38, 129-30, and *passim*).

It seems to me that, at the present state of our knowledge, the best, and perhaps the only, policy which one can follow in attempting to control sociocultural change is one which will aid the group in question in working out an adaptation that will enable them to function effectively within and contribute materially to the larger society that is the modern world, *while at the same time retaining as much cultural distinctiveness as possible.* This may sound like a radical proposal in view of the attitudes expressed at the El Tigre Rotary Club (or of both the society and government of the United States, for that matter). It is premised, however, on my view of the nature of sociocultural evolution, which is that *natural selection* is an important force on the superorganic level of phenomena as well as the organic. This being the case, the greatest possible variety of cultural adaptations will prove most advantageous to man as he faces continuing change in the future. While considerable variability still exists among human cultures, the current trend is toward greater uniformity, which may in the long run be a mistake for survival of the human species. So long as a culture can take its place in the larger national or international society, there is no logical reason why it should become identical to other similar groups, and *no* governmental policy is justified in attempting to make it so. Nor does this necessarily mean that race riots, interethnic conflict, or caste distinctions are the unavoidable consequences, though they certainly may represent a danger which needs to be guarded against.

One further justification for guided sociocultural change is not to eliminate tension and conflict, but merely to reduce it in situations which have gotten out of hand, where tension has built up to an excessive degree and where it threatens to become wholly destructive rather than forcing constructive modification of existent culture patterns. It seems to me that in some cases tension could be encouraged in order to facilitate change without too much concern for any *particular* objective. The objectives could still be achieved more or less spontaneously and, once achieved, would result in a reduction in tension which would probably facilitate the emergence of a satisfactory adaptation.

PROGNOSIS FOR THE FUTURE

LOOKING TO THE FUTURE, what can be expected as the final outcome of the present processes of change in these two communities? Whatever predictions are made, they must necessarily rest on the assumption that no new factors will be introduced, and that change will continue in the same general direction in which it is proceeding at the present time.

The Mameños give the impression of being quite fully acculturated. In a certain sense this is an accurate representation, but they have maintained certain distinctive characteristics which set them off from their criollo neighbors. What is even more important, *they* consider themselves to be different and consciously contrast themselves to the criollos. It can be expected that they will continue to acculturate in all matters which are not critical to maintaining this difference. In the latter regard however, I expect that the process will continue to be one of restructuring in order to maintain the sense of "Indian superiority" rather than direct assumption of criollo patterns. Barring the loss of community lands, or a complete dispersal from *propio Mamo,* the community will most likely persist as a distinctive entity. Cultural differences will continue to be leveled, although it is to be expected that a distinctive system of values will be maintained for a long time. The direction of change in Mamo then is much like that which was followed by the "Guayqueri" community of El Poblado which has survived on the island of Margarita (McCorkle

1954, 1965: 131). It is interesting that similar trends have emerged in these two neighboring areas of Venezuela, but it is almost certainly fortuitous, rather than representing any kind of common cultural heritage or a similar history of contact (compare pp. 23-27, 32-38, above; with McCorkle 1965: 15-38).

Considering the present situation in Cachama, the future looks rather bleak; one could hardly expect anything other than complete disintegration and eventual extinction of the community and the culture. Nonetheless, the dynamic model for culture change suggests that the present period of cultural distortion may be succeeded by one of cultural revitalization, a restructuring of old patterns to attain a New Steady State. This remains in the future, however, and it is extremely difficult to attempt to characterize what that Steady State will be like.

The probability that a New Steady State will occur in any given instance of culture change or acculturation may explain why it is that groups which were expected to become extinct within a few years have survived long after such predictions were made. I have encountered innumerable cases where the dismal prediction was made two or three generations ago that such and such group had no more than ten, twenty, or twenty-five years left. Yet many of them are still viable, and sometimes even stronger today than when they were given up as lost. Might not the original description have been written at a time of cultural distortion, whereas the surviving group is today at or near a New Steady State? Just so, Cachama can be expected to reach a New Steady State *unless* criollo exploitation leads to a loss of their lands and complete destruction of the community.

Conclusion

THE OBSERVATIONS which have been made in this study suggest certain generalizations which can now be brought together in a summary statement. It would appear that change inevitably produces tension and conflict. This is not to be avoided, since it is through such tension that forces promoting adaptation are generated. The more rapidly change occurs, or the more extensive change is, the greater will be the tensions and the harder it will be to accept change. This being the case, it would seem desirable to proceed slowly in the introduction of new techniques or ideas. Yet, since human beings are impatient, other considerations often require change to be as rapid as possible.

Even so, man is a flexible creature, and often can adapt to quite radical innovations even though the process may be extremely disruptive and discouraging. The easiest sort of adaptation is through assimilation into the dominant culture, a process that has occurred all too frequently. More difficult is the redefinition or restructuring of the indigenous culture to meet the new conditions which have been imposed on it. In spite of the initial difficulties involved in this course, it is highly preferable to direct assimilation, since the former is more likely to result in continued cultural variety. Variety is desirable since it increases the probability that some human group (or several) will always be able to adapt successfully to the increasingly diverse conditions man may face, now or in the future.

There seems to be little gain in arbitrarily setting out to change a particular culture in some predetermined direction. It would seem best to provide the opportunities for change, then allow the culture to take its own course. Nonetheless, if we recognize the patterns which are followed by sociocultural change it may be possible to exploit them to facilite change. If we can identify trends which might lead to subsequent stages in the process it is possible that by encouraging such trends the process of change could be speeded up while at the same time reducing tension. When and if this proves to be a valid approach it will be a powerful tool for seeking human betterment in a world which is constantly seeking ever more progress.

APPENDICES

Appendix A

NOTE ON KARINYA ORTHOGRAPHY

THE CONVENTION that has been used in the transcription of Karinya vocabulary is based on the phonemic system which was tentatively established by Swadesh (Ms) for that language in 1959. No pretense is made that my version represents an exact *phonemic* system, however. My transcriptions more nearly represent the commonest *phonetic* sounds, as it proved to be much easier to record vocabulary on this basis. There is some indication, for example, that *w* should be included with *b, v* as a single phoneme, *sh* and *ch* may represent nothing more than phonetic variations of the phoneme *s*, etc. Symbols marked with * are different from, or additions to Swadesh's list (*x* is equivalent to his *j*, and *?* to his ').

p	as in Spanish *p*ez	t	as in Spanish *t*u
b, v	as in Spanish *b*anco	d	as in Spanish *d*ar
w	as in English *w*ill	*th	voiced alveolar fricative, resembling English there
m	as in Spanish *m*isa	s	as in Spanish *s*ei*s*
n	as in Spanish *n*ada	*sh	as in English *sh*ine
*n	as in English si*ng*	*ch	as in Spanish *ch*i*ch*arro
l, r	covers the range between Spanish *l* and *r* as in fami*l*ia*r*	k	as in English *k*ing
y	as in English *y*ellow	*x	voiceless guttural fricative, resembling that in German zwanzig

*?	the glottal stop	u	as in Spanish *u*ndecimo
i	as in Spanish p*i*co	ü	very broad, open vowel as in French f*eu*
e	as in Spanish m*e*r*e*c*e*r	o	as in Spanish n*o*che
a	as in Spanish *a*p*a*rt*a*r	.	preceding phone is terminated sharply
*ï	a middle high vowel		

DATE ______________ COMMUNITY ______________

DATA PER HOUSEHOLD

ADULTS: Name and spouse	Age	Sex	Where born	Names of parents	Marriages	Number birth (women) Occupation (men)
a.						
b.						
c.						
d.						
e.						
f.						
g.						

CHILDREN: Name (living)	Age	Sex	Where born	
1.				
2.				
3.				
4.				
5.				
6.				
7.				
8.				
9.				
10. (deceased)			Cause of death	
11.				
12.				
13.				
14.				
15.				
16.				
17.				
18.				
19.				
20.				

Comments:

I. Relatives elsewhere?

II. Church or civil ceremony?

III. Ownership?

IV. Racial mixing?

V. Consider selves indian?

VI. Education?

VII. Previous marriages?

Appendix C

DOCUMENTS

SINCE THE READER would have difficulty consulting most of the documents cited above from the Registro Subalterno, Cantaura, Venezuela, their text is reproduced here in whole or in part:

EJIDOS DE CANTAURA y Tierras de Cachama. Registrado bajo el Nº 8, folio 1º, octubre de 1,904.

This is an official copy of an original document, preserved either in Cumaná or Caracas, which records the royal survey and grant of lands in 1783 (the text may be found in PEREZ RAMIREZ 1946) and placed on record here in compliance with the *Ley sobre Resguardos de indígenas* of 1904 (see ARMELLADA 1954: 261-62). The following marginal notes may, however, be of interest:

1. Nota marginal. Por documento registrado en esta oficina hoy 8 de enero de 1947, bajo el Nº 2, folios 5 al 10, Protocolo Primero, Tomo Primero. Miguel Tamanaico y Francisco Martínez por sí y en representación de la Comunidad de Yndígenas de Cachama conceden servidumbre a favor de la Mene Grande Oil Company, C. A. sobre 1,952 hectáreas de terreno a que se refiere esta inserción. Nº 8 — El Registrador Antonio Ovalles.

2. Nota marginal. Por documento registrado en esta oficina hoy 11 de febrero de 1,947, bajo el Nº 19, folios desde el 33 ato hasta el 39, Protocolo Primero, Tomo Primero, Miguel Tamanaico y Francisco Martínez, por si y en representación de la Comunidad de Yndígenas de Cachama, conceden servidumbre a favor de la Socony Vacuum Oil Company of Venezuela sobre 3825 hectáreas del terreno a que se refiere esta inserción. Nº 8 — El Registrador, Antonio Ovalles.

* * *

DOCUMENTO DE VENTA que hace por la Tribu Caribe de Cantaura al señor Antonio Boccalandro, su cacique Leonardo Tamanaico. Registrado bajo el Nº 9, 18 de julio de 1,934.

Nº 9. — Nosotros, Leonardo Tamanaico, Cacique, Gobernador y representante de los indígenas de este Municipio, Simón Abaduca, Miguel Tamanaico, Francisco Martínez, José Antonio Tamanaico, Francisco Tamanaico, Francisco Antonio Tamanaico, José Francisco Machuca, Francisco Machuca, Antonio Abaduca, Pedro Abaduca, Pedro Ramón Arai, José Eusebio Arai, Florencio Tempo, Francisco Tempo, Julio Tamanaico, Alejandro Tamanaico, Francisco José Tamanaico, Guillermo Tamanaico, Domingo Tamanaico, Domingo Antonio Tamanaico, Obdulio Tamanaico, Candelario Tamanaico, Simón Tempo, Pedro Tempo, Antonio Tempo, Francisco Martínez, José Martínez, Alejandro Martínez, Antonio Acare, Nicoro Acare, Francisco Acare, Caldaba Abaduca, Pedro Tamanaico, Juan Acare, Pedro Machuca, Alejandro Machuca, José María Guare, Vicente Abaduca, Pedro Pablo Tamanaico, Ramón Maita, José Guaimarata, Pedro Antonio Guaimarata, Pedro Maduraba, Tereso Abaduca, Margarito Abaduca, Bernardino Abaduca, José María Tamanaico, Hilario Abaduca, y Pedro Machuca, de la Comunidad, mayores de edad, de este domicilio y habiles para contratar, por la presente escritura declaramos: que hemos dado en venta real, pura, perfecta e irrevocable al señor Antonio Boccalandro, también mayor y del mismo domicilio, en capacidad para contratar, una legua de terreno del sitio denominado "Cachama" de esta jurisdicción, cuyo sitio se compone de cuatro leguas superficiales, y el cual hubimos por donación que nos hizo Su Majestad Real el Rey de España, con fecha 21 de octubre de 1.783, según los documentos auténticos y legales que reposan en nuestro poder; la mencionada legua de terreno se encuentra alinderada así: Norte; río Guanipa; Sur; terrenos de los vendedores; Este; Río Cachama; y Oeste; terrenos de los mismos vendedores.—También declaramos: que con el producto de esta venta se pagarán los gastos ocasionados en mensuras, arreglos de Títulos, Tribunales y los demás que se hayan hecho necesarios, todo ésto, de acuerdo con la cantidad del valor de la legua, y con el remanente, comprar alambre que en proporción se pueda, para cercar nuestros conucos.—Además nos comprometamos, que si por alguna necesidad urgente nos vierémos en el caso de vender otro lote de terreno, preferir en la venta al comprador Boccalandro, en igualdad de circunstancias, antes que a otra persona.—Esta venta la hemos pactado por la suma de 2.200 bolívares, que hemos recibido del comprador en dinero efectivo y a nuestra entera y cabal satisfacción.—Al saneamiento de la referida venta caso de evicción, nos comprometemos en todo lo que esté sujeto a las leyes que rigen en la República.—Así lo decimos, otorgamos, autorizando para que firmen a nuestro ruego, por nosotros no saberlo hacer a los ciudadanos General Desiderio Centeno, Miguel Angel Tovar, Francisco Antonio Ovalles, Modesto R. García, Ramón Rafael Pérez, Rafael Fernández, Arístides Pérez Rojas, David Betancourt y Luis Fermín Medina.—

Cantaura: 31 de julio de 1929...

Juzgado del Distrito Freites.—Cantaura: 31 de julio de 1.929.—120º y 71º.—

* * *

CONTRATO DE SERVIDUMBRE entre los representantes de los indígenas de Cachama y la Mene Grande Oil Company, C. A., respecto a los terrenos de aquellos. Registrado bajo el Nº 2, folios 5 al 10, Protocolo Primero, Tomo Primero, 8 de enero de 1947.

Entre nosotros, Miguel Tamanaico y Francisco Martínez, mayores de edad y vecinos de Cachama, en el Municipio Cantaura, Dist. Freites del edo. Anzoátegui, obrando por nuestros propios derechos y en representación de los demás miembros de la "Communidad de Yndígenas de Cachama", quienes en éste documento en lo sucesivo se denominarán "Los Propietarios", por una parte, y por la otra, la Mene Grande Oil Company, compañía anónima venezolana, domiciliada en la ciudad de Caracas, representada en este acto por su apoderado, Pedro Elías Chacín, también mayor de edad, comerciante y vecino del Municipio Cantaura, según poder registrado en la Oficina Subalterna de Registro del Dist. Freites en fecha 5 de septiembre de 1.945, bajo el Nº 11 a los folios 12 vuelto al 15 del protocolo Tercero, sus sucesores designarios y causahabientes, quienes en este documento se denominarán en lo sucesivo "La Compañía", se ha convenido en celebrar el contrato de servidumbre que se consigna en las cláusulas siguientes:

Primera: "Los Propietarios" declaran que son dueños únicos y exclusivos de una porción del terreno general denominada "Cachama", de acuerdo del plano levantado en noviembre de 1.939 y revisado en fecha 10 de agosto de 1940, por el Agrimensor Público P. López Bompart, ubicada en la misma juridicción de nuestro domicilio, bajo los siguientes linderos generales: Norte, el Río Guanipa; Este, terrenos del sitio "Güico" de la sucesión Sthory: Sur, terrenos baldíos; y Oeste, sitio de "Tascabaña" de la sucesión Bruces. La porción de terreno que nos pertenece es parte de los terrenos que nos fueron adjudicados por el Gobierno Colonial de España en fecha 21 de octubre de 1.783, de acuerdo con el documento registrado en la Oficina Subalterna de Registro del Dist. Freites del Edo. Anzoátegui, bajo el N° 8 del Protocolo Primero, en fecha 16 de diciembre de 1904.

Segunda: "Los Propietarios" constituyen sobre los citados terrenos de su propiedad, en beneficio de "La compañía", de sus concesiones de hidrocarburos denominadas "V-67-8", "V-67-9", "V-67-10", "V-349.5", "V-349.8", y "V-349.9" y de cualesquiera otras que tenga actualmente o que adquiera en el futuro, y de las concesiones que tengan o adquieran las personas o compañías a quienes les sea traspasado el todo o parte de los derechos aquí constituidos, de acuerdo con la Cláusula Sexta del presente contrato todas las servidumbres que fueren necesarias o convenientes para la exploración, explotación, producción, almacenaje, manufactura, refinación, y transporte de petróleo, gas, asfalto y demás hidrocarburos y sustancias similares. Ygualmente tendrá "La Compañía" el derecho de hacer y llevar a cabo en dicho terreno mensuras, trabajos de exploración, estudios geológicos y geofísicos, aperturas de picas y de caminos, limpias y excabaciones, trabajos de construcción y de transporte, la instalación conservación, reparación, y uso de oleoductos, y líneas de tubería de toda clase, construcción de edificios, campamentos, habitaciones, hospitales, estaciones de bombas, almacenes, talleres, depósitos de materiales y de petróleo; perforación de pozos de cualquier especie, extracción de hidrocarburos, gas y agua; así como el derecho de tomar y usar el agua, leña, granzón, arena y piedras de construcción que que se encuentren en los citados terrenos y en general todos los derechos que fueren necesarios o convenientes para el debido y amplio ejercicio de las servidumbres que, por la presente cláusula se reconocen y constituyen, quedando entendido que "La Compañía" podrá ejercer dichas servidumbres y demás derechos en cualquier momento dentro del término de duración del presente contrato, y tendrá siempre y en cualquier tiempo el derecho de suspender en todo o en parte los referidos trabajos y de remover las construcciones e instalaciones sin limitación alguna. Estas servidumbres se establecen convencionalmente y en virtud de los derechos que la Ley de Hidrocarburos acuerda a los concesionarios para constituir servidumbres a su favor a los fines de sus exploraciones y explotaciones petrolíferas por lo tanto, se declara que tales servidumbres pesan sobre el fundo a que se contrae, cualesquiera que sean las manos a que pase dicho fundo.

Tercera: Este convenio quedará efectivo por la duración de las concesiones que actualmente pertenecen a "La Compañía", y de las que adquieran en el futuro, incluyendo las parcelas de explotación que provengan de estas concesiones, así como de las concesiones de las personas o compañías a quienes se trasmita el todo o parte de los derechos que por este contrato se constituye a favor de "La Compañía", de acuerdo con la Cláusula Sexta, existente para el momento del traspaso, y el de las que dichas personas o Compañías adquieran en el futuro, incluyendo en todos estos casos las prórrogas que la autoridad competente otorgue sobre dichas concesiones; pero "La Compañía" podrá en cualquier tiempo dar por terminado el presente contrato o limitarlo a una parte o partes de los referidos terrenos, con la única condición de expresar su voluntad por documento registrado en la Oficina Subalterna de Registro en cuya jurisdicción se encuentra el terreno objeto de este contrato.

Cuarta: "La Compañía" pagará como compensación única y plena por las servidumbres y demás derechos que por el presente contrato se le constituyen y conceden, las pensiones o cánones siguientes: a) Un canon o pensión anual de setenta y cinco céntimos de bolívar por hectárea, calculado sobre el área de las concesiones de "La Compañía" en estos terrenos o sean mil ciento cincuenta y dos hectáreas (Hs. 1.152) aproximadamente, pagadero por trimestres anticipados, dentro de los cinco primeros días de cada trimestre. b) Al comenzar "La Compañía" la perforación de un pozo en busca de petróleo en los referidos terrenos, y desde el día en que se comience a taladrar (no contándose el tiempo empleado en la instalación del equipo del taladro y en las demás obras y trabajos preparatorios), la referida pensión o canon anual se pagará a razón de cuatro bolívares (Bs. 4) por hectárea sobre el área de las concesiones de "La Compañía" en los terrenos de "Los Propietarios". El aumento de la pensión o canon el cual es a razón de tres bolívares, veinticinco céntimos por hectárea por año, será pagado durante todo el tiempo que continue la perforación del pozo referido o de otros en dichas concesiones, así como durante las épocas en que se esté transportando fuera de los terrenos objeto del presente contrato el petróleo allí producido; quedando expresamente convenido que, al ser paralizado por cualquier motivo o causa los referidos trabajos de perforación y transporte de petróleo, volverá a regir la pensión anual expresada en el inciso (a) de ésta Cláusula. Las liquidaciones de la pensión o canon a que se refiere este inciso (b) se harán por trimestres vencidos y dentro de los primeros cinco días del siguiente trimestre, y por el número de días en que dicho aumento haya sido aplicable. Por el corte de maderas en los terrenos objeto de éste contrato "La Compañía" pagará a "Los Propietarios" la suma de un bolívar por cada árbol de madera de corazón que élla destruya, cuyo diámetro al punto de corte sea de quince centímetros o más, pero nada por lo demás árboles, arbustos y malezas. Por el presente acto "Los Propietarios" autorizan a "La Compañía" para que formule ante la autoridad competente las notificaciones y solicitudes respecto a la tala de maderas y limpias de terrenos que sean necesarias a los efectos de este contrato, así como para cualquiera otra diligencia por ante las autoridades administrativas, siempre que se limiten a las necesidades que por sus trabajos de exploración y explotación tenga "La Compañía".

Quinta: Todos los pagos que "La Compañía" tenga que hacer a "Los Propietarios" se harán en la Oficina de "La Compañía" en San Tomé, y a un solo representante de "Los Propietarios", quién tendrá facultades amplias para el desempeño del cargo, para recibir los referidos pagos en nombre y representación de "Los Propietarios", otorgar los recibos y contestar los avisos que "La Compañía" haga a "Los Propietarios" en relación con el presente contrato. Para estos efectos "Los Propietarios" han designado al otorgante, Francisco Martínez. Los pagos que se hicieren al referido representante de acuerdo con lo aquí estipulado obligarán a "Los Propietarios", sus sucesores y causahabientes, mientras no reciba "La Compañía" aviso por escrito informándola con un mes de anticipación a lo menos, del nombramiento del nuevo representante con facultades amplias.—Asimismo "La Compañía" podrá a su obción, hacer los pagos aquí referidos mediante depósito en el Banco de Venezuela en Barcelona, el cual Banco queda también apliamente facultado para recibir dichos pagos en nombre y representación de "Los Propietarios", otorgar los recibos y contestar los avisos que "La Compañía" haga a estos en relación con el presente contrato.

Sexta: "La Compañía" queda ampliamente facultada para traspasar a quienes tengan o adquieran concesiones de hidrocarburos, las servidumbres y demás derechos aquí concedidos, con respecto a porciones o a la totalidad de dichos terrenos, con la única condición de notificar a "Los Propietarios" de cualquier cesión que se haga, y el cesionario o causahabiente quedará subrogado en los derechos y obligaciones de "La Compañía" en cuanto a lo que haya sido materia de la cesión y libre élla, en consecuencia, de toda obligación para con "Los Propietarios" en lo concerniente a la porción o porciones objeto de tales cesiones o traspasos; siendo expresamente sobreentendido que mientras subsista esta servidumbre sobre porciones o la totalidad de los terrenos objeto de este contrato, tanto "La Compañía" como sus cesionarios tendrán el derecho de pasar sobre toda la extensión del terreno objeto del contrato, derecho de paso que comprende la apertura de picas y caminos, de construir, mantener, y usar vías de comunicación, y transporte y oleoductos, así como también líneas telefónicas, telegráficas y de fuerza eléctrica.

Séptima: Es condición expresa del presente convenio que "Los Propietarios" no podrán permitir a terceros que hagan construcciones ni mejoras de cualquier especie, ni que introduzcan cualquiera clase de comercio, en las porciones de su terreno cubiertas por las mencionadas concesiones de "La Compañía", sin el previo concentimiento, por escrito, de ésta. Asimismo, "Los Propietarios" convienen en no hacer nuevas construcciones en dichas porciones de sus terrenos, sino en los lugares escojidos de acuerdo con "La Compañía", la cual podrá remover a su propio costo las construcciones que existen o que en el futuro se fabriquen en tales porciones de sus terrenos cuando el desarrollo de sus concesiones así lo exija, indemnizando a "Los Propietarios" su justo valor y estableciéndolas en otra parte no requerida para los trabajos de "La Compañía".

Octava: "Los Propietarios" manifiestan que los terrenos objeto del presente contrato se hallan libres de todo gravamen y se obligan a mantener a "La Compañía" en pacífica posesión y pleno goce de las servidumbres y demás derechos aquí constituidos y concedidos, así como el saneamiento de Ley. Asimismo, todo cesionario o causahabiente de "Los Propietarios" tendrá la obligación de respetar en un todo las referidas servidumbres y demás derechos.

Novena: Para todos los efectos de este contrato, "Los Propietarios" designan a la residencia del señor Luis Gimón, cerca al Río Guanipa donde lo cruza la carretera El Tigre-Puerto La Cruz, como la dirección a la cual debe mandarse cualquier aviso o communicación que "La Compañía" les dirija en conexión con el mismo, quedando a salvo la obción de ésta de enviar dichos avisos y comunicaciones al Banco de Venezuela en Barcelona, de acuerdo con la Cláusula Quinta.—

Firma a ruego de Francisco Martínez quien dijo no saberlo hacer, el señor Luis Gimón Requena. Cachama: veintitrés de diciembre de mil novecientos cuarenta y seis. Miguel Tamanaico.—P. E. Chacín.—Luis Gimón Rodríguez.—

Juzgado del Municipio Simón Rodríguez. El Tigre: 23 de diciembre de 1.946.—137º y 88º.

En la audiencia de hoy el anterior documento fue presentado para su reconocimiento y devolución por sus otorgantes Miguel Tamanaico, Francisco Martínez y Pedro Elías Chacín, mayores de edad y vecinos del Municipio Cantaura y aquí de tránsito. Leídoles y puéstoles de manifiesto dicho documento expusieron: el contenido es cierto en todas sus partes, y nuestras de puño y letras las firmas que lo autorizan menos la de Francisco Martínez quien dijo no saberlo hacer, habiéndola puesto a su ruego el señor

Luis Gimón Requena. El Tribunal en vista de la anterior manifestación lo declaró reconocido en todas sus partes, tanto en las firmas como en el contenido. Se hace constar que los otorgantes prestaron juramento legal. Terminó, se leyó y conformes firman.—El Juez.—P. Elías Armas.—Los Otorgantes.—Miguel Tamanaico.—P. E. Chacín.—Rogado: Luis Gimón Requena.—El Secretario M. Guevara.—Oficina Subalterna de Registro del Distrito Freites del Estado Anzoátegui.—Cantaura: ocho de enero de mil novecientos cuarenta y siete. 137º y 88º. . .

* * *

CONTRATO DE SERVIDUMBRE entre los representantes de los yndígenas de Cachama y la Socony-Vacuum Oil Company of Venezuela, C. A. respecto a los terrenos de aquellos. Registrado bajo el Nº 19 folios 33 al 39, Protocolo Primero, Primer Trimestre, Tomo Nº 1, 9 de febrero de 1947.

(The greater part of the text is comparable to that of the preceding document, with the following exceptions):

. . . *Quinta:* "La Compañía" pagará como compensación única, y plena por las servidumbres y demás derechos que por el presente contrato se le constituyen y conceden, las pensiones o cánones siguientes: (a) un canon o pensión anual de setenta y cinco céntimos de bolívar por hectárea, calculado sobre el área o superficie de las concesiones de "La Compañía" en estos terrenos o sean tres mil ochocientas veinte y cinco hectáreas (Hets. 3.825) aproximadamente, pagadero por anualidades anticipadas; b) Para llevar a cabo los trabajos de perforación "La Compañía" tendrá el derecho de seleccionar dentro de los referidos terrenos uno o más bloques de quinientas hectáreas (Hts. 500) cada uno, de perímetros irregulares, contiguos o no, y desde el día en que se comience el taladro del primer pozo en algunos de dichos bloques (no contándose el tiempo empleado en la instalación del equipo de perforación) comenzará a pagar a razón de cuatro bolívares (Bs. 4.00) por hectárea y por año sobre las quinientas hectáreas (Hts. 500) cubiertas por el bloque respectivo.—Este pago se hará por trimestres anticipados; c) a medida que "La Compañía" lo vaya requiriendo para el desarrollo de sus trabajos de perforación, podrá seleccionar nuevos bloques, contiguos o no, de perímetros irregulares de quinientos hectáreas (Hts. 500) cada uno, pagando a razón de cuatro bolívares (Bs. 4.00), por hectárea y por año, desde el día en que se comience el taladro del primer pozo en cada nuevo bloque; d) Es entendido que sobre el remanente de la superficie que vaya quedando después de cada selección que "La Compañía" vaya haciendo de bloques de quinientas hectáreas (Hts. 500), se continuará pagando a razón de setenta y cinco céntimos de bolívar (Bs. 0,75) por hectárea y por año; e) Cuando se aumenta el canon o pensión anual a *cuatro bolívares* (Bs. 4.00) por hectárea y por año sobre cada bloque de quinientas hectáreas (Hts. 500) que "La Compañía" elija, cesará el pago de setenta y cinco céntimos de bolívar (Bs. 0,75) por hectárea y por año sobre dicho bloque, y en consecuencia se deducirá proporcionalmente del total a pagar por el trimestre correspondiente la cantidad entregada como anticipo conforme al aparte *a* de esta cláusula si hubiere lugar; f) Es expresamente entendido que en caso de ser paralizados por cualquier motivo los trabajos de taladro o de explotación en cualquiera de los bloques de quinientas hectáreas (Hts. 500) elegidos por "La Compañía", el canon o pensión anual de *cuatro bolívares* (Bs. 4.00) sobre este bloque se rebajará nuevamente a setenta y cinco céntimos de bolívar (Bs. 0,75) por hectárea y por año mientras dure la paralización de los trabajos.—Esta deducción se hará en el próximo pago que tenga que hacer "La Compañía" a "Los Propietarios" por cualquier concepto; g) Es entendido que "La Compañía" podrá en cualquier tiempo abandonar cualquiera de los bloques de quinientas hectáreas (Hts. 500) que haya escogido para los trabajos de perforación. En este caso "Los Propietarios" no estarán obligados a reembolsar a "La Compañía" ninguna parte de la suma que hayan recibido como pago anticipado del trimestre correspondiente, continuando "La Compañía" pagando el canon anual de setenta y cinco céntimos de bolívar (Bs. 0.75) por hectárea sobre el bloque abandonado; h) En los casos de rescisión, término o limitación de este contrato, "Los Propietarios" no estarán obligados a reembolsar las pensiones anticipadas que hayan percibido; y en caso de limitación, "La Compañía" solo continuará pagando las sumas estipuladas en este contrato sobre la superficie a que queda limitada la servidumbre; i) Es entendido que para la selección de algunos de los bloques de quinientas hectáreas (Hts. 500), prevista en el presente Contrato, o para el abandono de uno de esos mismos bloques, bastará que "La Compañía" haga una manifestación por escrito al respecto, a "Los Propietarios" identificando el bloque respectivo de la mejor manera posible; j) Por el corte de maderas en los terrenos mencionados en la Cláusula Primera, "La Compañía" pagará a "Los Propietarios" la suma de un bolívar (Bs. 1.00) por cada árbol de madera de corazón, cuyo diámetro medido a la altura de un metro del suelo, sea de quince centímetros o más, —utilícelo o no,— pero nada pagará por los demás árboles, arbustos y malezas...

* * *

DOCUMENTO QUE CONFIERE poder especial al señor Roberto Noroño Camacaro en representar a la Comunidad Indígena de Cachama. Registrado bajo el Nº 1, folios 1 y 2, Protocolo Tercero, 12 de agosto de 1958.

Número uno. Yo, Ysidro Guare, mayor de edad, soltero, venezolano, agricultor, titular de la Cédula de Identidad Nº 1981260, domiciliado en Cachama, jurisdicción del Municipio Cantaura, Distrito Freites del Estado Anzoátegui y aquí de tránsito, obrando por mis propios derechos y en representación de los demás miembros de la Comunidad Yndígena de Cachama, procediendo en mi carácter de Gobernador de la Tribu de Cachama, según nombramiento conferido por el ciudadano Prefecto del Distrito Freites de este Estado Anzoátegui, mediante oficio de fecha trece de marzo del presente año de mil novecientos cincuenta y ocho, por el presente instrumento declaro: Que confiero poder especial pero amplio y bastante cuanto en derecho se requiere al señor Roberto Noroño Camacaro, quien es mayor de edad, casado, oficinista, venezolano, portador de la Cédula de Identidad Nº 232673 y de este domicilio para que nos represente y sostenga nuestros derechos en todos los asuntos que nos concernan. En tal virtud, queda facultado nuestro expresado apoderado para reclamar de las Compañías Petroleras Socony Mobil Oil Company y Mene Grande Oil Company, ambas domiciliadas en Venezuela, los pagos correspondientes a los daños y perjuicios ocacionados por las aludidas Compañías en los terrenos de la referida Comunidad Yndígena de Cachama, de los cuales somos copropietarios.—En consecuencia, facultamos a nuestro expresado apoderado para recibir en nuestro nombre y representación cantidades de dinero otorgando los recibos correspondientes, recibir asimismo los pagos que por daños y perjuicios nos hagan a nuestra propiedad durante la vigencia de los contratos de servidumbre que tenemos celebrados con las aludidas Compañías Petroleras, concurriendo al avalúo de los mismos o impugnarlo.—En una palabra, queda facultado para convenir, transigir desistir sobre cualquier punto relacionado con los mencionados contratos, o otorgar finiquitos, recibos y en general, realizar todos aquellos actos destinados a la mayor defensa de nuestros derechos e intereses.—Cantaura: doce de agosto de mil novecientos cincuenta y ocho.—Ysidro Guare.—Oficina Subalterna de Registro del Distrito Freites del Estado Anzoátegui:

Cantaura: veinte de agosto de mil novecientos cincuenta y ocho. 149º y 100º.

El documento anterior, redactado por el Doctor José Urbáez Hernández, abogado; me fue presentado para su protocolización por su otorgante, ciudadano Ysidro Guare, mayor de edad, soltero, agricultor, venezolano, con Cédula de Identidad Nº 1981260, domiciliado en Cachama de esta jurisdicción y aquí de tránsito; quien lo leyó y verificó junto con el suscrito Registrador y los testigos instrumentales, ciudadanos Víctor Velásquez y Juan V. Maita, mayores y vecinos, con Cédulas de Identidad Nos. 487255 y 2426877, respectivamente; la exactitud de las copias en los Protocolos firmando en estos últimos y en el original, ante mi y los expresados testigos instrumentales, que conmigo dan fe del acto, de la exactitud de las copias y del conocimiento personal del otorgante, quien queda así identificado. . .

El Registrador Subalterno. Antonio F. Ovalles.

* * *

DOCUMENTO QUE CONFIERE poder general a los Doctores Francisco Zapata Luigi, y Henrique Sánchez Risso en representar a Pedro Angel Medina, et al (de la Comunidad Indígena de Cachama). Registrado bajo el Nº 1, folios 1 al 19, Protocolo Tercero, 16 de enero de 1962.

Número uno. Nosotros Pedro Angel Medina, *et al* (the next eleven folios list the names of most, if not all, members of the Indigenous Community of Cachama) . . .

Folio 12) por el presente documento declaramos: que conferimos poder general pero amplio y bastante cuanto en dercho se requiere a los Doctores Francisco Zapata Luigi, José Rafael Zapata Luigi, y Henrique Sánchez Risso, abogados en ejercicio domiciliados en la ciudad de Caracas y con Cédulas de Identidad Nos. . . . . . . , respectivamente, para que actuando ya sea conjunta o separadamente, nos representen, sostengan nuestros derechos y defiendan nuestros intereses por ante cualesquiera autoridades Civilies, Mercantiles, Administrativas o Judiciales, o entidades públicas o privadas, personas naturales o jurídicas y en especial, para que sostengan nuestros derechos y ejerzan nuestra representación por ante las Compañías petroleras "Mene Grande Oil Company" y "Mobil Oil Company de Venezuela", antes "Socony Vacuum Oil Company", ambas con domicilio en la República de Venezuela, Ciudad de Caracas, o ante cualesquiera otras empresas petroleras domiciliadas en Venezuela. En virtud de este mandato podrán nuestros apoderados, sostener judicial o extradjudicialmente la reclamación que tenemos intentada, o cualesquiera que intentemos contra las mencionadas Compañías petroleras, ejerciendo las acciones correspondientes así mismo están facultados nuestros apoderados para tramitar cualquier reclamación indemnizatoria que se refiera a las tierras que son de nuestra propiedad o poseemos en el sitio denominado "Tascabaña", Mesa de Guanipa, Distrito Freites del Estado Anzoátegui, firmando por nosotros toda clase de trasacciones judiciales o extrajudiciales, celebrando convenios y contratos de cualquier naturaleza o clase, firmando solicitudes, actas o documentos, efectuando cesiones, permutando, firmando Protocolos en los Registros Públicos, o Notarías; podrán efectuar avalúos, designando las personas capacitadas para ello; podrán hacer pagos y recibidos, ya sea en dinero o en especies, aceptar cualquier cantidad de dinero proveniente de transacciones, arreglos, convenios o contratos, otorgando los recibos y finiquitos correspondientes, pueden comprometer en árbitros arbitradores o de derecho; consecuencialmente podrán nuestros referidos apoderados ejercer plenamente nuestra representación por ante los Tribunales de Justicia competentes, intentando y contestando toda clase de demandas, oponiendo y contestando excepciones y reconvenciones, seguir los juicios en todos sus grados, incidencias e instancias; desistir, convenir, transigir, promover y evacuar toda clase de pruebas, incluso la de posiciones juradas, hacer uso de toda clase de recursos ordinarios y extraordinarios; hacer posturas en remate; recibir cantidades de dinero o pagos en especie, otorgando los correspondientes recibos y finiquitos, darse por citados en juicios, sustituir este poder total o parcialmente en persona o abogados de la entera confianza de nuestros apoderados, reservándose su ejercicio. Conferirnos expresamente a nuestros apoderados, la facultad de abrir y movilizar cuentas bancarias; aceptar, endorsar y emitir efectos de comercio; y en fin, hacer todo lo que crean conveniente y esté ajustado a derecho, sin limitación alguna, en defensa de nuestros intereses y derechos, como si fueran nosotros mismos, ya que las facultades enumeradas son simplemente enunciativos. Así lo decimos, otorgamos y firmamos, menos. . . (varios que no saben firmar, firmando a ruego de ellos José de la Cruz Rojas y Luis Víctor Campo, y también varios quienes saben firmar).

Cantaura: dieciseis de enero de mil novecientos sesenta y dos.

BIBLIOGRAPHY

Manuscript Sources

CANTAURA. REGISTRO SUBALTERNO

1904 Ejidos de Cantaura y Tierras de Cachama. Registrado bajo el N° 8, folio 1°, octubre de 1904.

1934 Documento de venta que hace por la Tribu Caribe de Cantaura al señor Antonio Boccalandro, su cacique Leonardo Tamanaico. Registrado bajo el N° 9, 18 de julio de 1934.

1947a Contrato de servidumbre entre los representantes de los indígenas de Cachama y la Mene Grande Oil Company, C. A. respecto a los terrenos de aquellos. Registrado bajo el N° 2, folios 5 al 10, Protocolo Primero, Tomo Primero, 8 de enero de 1947.

1947b Contrato de servidumbre entre los representantes de los yndígenas de Cachama y la Socony-Vacuum Oil Company of Venezuela, C. A. respecto a los terrenos de aquellos. Registrado bajo el N° 19, folios 33 al 39, Protocolo Primero, Primer Trimestre, Tomo N° 1, 9 de febrero de 1947.

1958 Documento que confiere poder especial al señor Roberto Noroño Camacaro en representar a la Comunidad Indígena de Cachama. Registrado bajo el N° 1, folios 1 y 2, Protocolo Tercero, 12 de agosto de 1958.

1962 Documento que confiere poder general a los Doctores Francisco Zapata Luigi, y Henrique Sánchez Risso en representar a Pedro Angel Medina, et al (de la Comunidad Indígena de Cachama). Registrado bajo el N° 1, folios 1 al 19, Protocolo Tercero, 16 de enero de 1962.

SOLEDAD. REGISTRO SUBALTERNO

1911a Documento de venta de una porción de los Resguardos de Yndígenas del extinto Municipio Tabaro por su apoderado especial Juan Perdomo Rendón al Sr. Andrés Orsoni; acompañado con una copia certificada del poder de mandatario conferido al dicho Juan Perdomo Rendón por los miembros principales de la Comunidad de Yndígenas de Tabaro en representación de las demás co-partícipes de dicha comunidad. Registrado bajo el N° 1, Protocolo I, 4° Trimestre, folio 1, 25 de octubre de 1911.

1911b Documento de cesión de una porción de los Resguardos de Yndígenas por la Comunidad de Yndígenas de Tabaro a Juan Perdomo Rendón en pago de sus honorarios y su venta subsiguiente al señor General Cruz Mirabal Núñez. Registrado bajo el N° 2, Protocolo I, 4° Trimestre, folio 4, 27 de octubre de 1911.

1911c Documento de venta de una porción de tierra, la cual hubo por pago de la Comunidad de Indígenas del extinto Municipio Tabaro, por Juan Perdomo Rendón al señor Andrés Orsoni. Registrado bajo el N° 9, Protocolo I, 4° Trimestre, folio 11, 12 de diciembre de 1911.

Published Sources

ALVARADO, Lisandro

1919 Observaciones sobre el caribe hablado en los llanos de Barcelona. Caracas.

1956 Noticia sobre los Caribes de los Llanos de Barcelona. *in* Datos Etnográficos de Venezuela, pp. 395-423, Caracas. Ministerio de Educación.

"ANTORCHA"

1962 Continúa la Disputa Grupal en Comunidad de Cachama. Un grupo acusa de estafa al cacique Francisco Tempo. "Antorcha", jueves, 7 de junio de 1962, pág 7. El Tigre, Venezuela.

ARMELLADA, Cesareo de

1954 Fuero Indígena Venezolano. Parte II: Período de la República (1811 a 1954). Caracas. Ministerio de Justicia.

BARNETT, Homer G.

1953 Innovation: The basis of cultural change. New York.

BEALS, Ralph L.

1953 Acculturation. *in* A. L. Kroeber, Anthropology Today, pp. 621-41. Chicago.

BEFU, Harumi

1963 Classification of Unilineal-Bilateral Societies. Southwestern Journal of Anthropology 19: 335-55.

CARNEIRO, Robert L.

1961 Slash-and-Burn Cultivation Among the Kuikuru and its Implications for Cultural Development in the Amazon Basin. *in* The Evolution of Horticultural Systems in Native South America: Causes and Consequences, ed. by Johannes Wilbert, pp. 47-67. Caracas.

CARRASCO, Pedro

1963 The Locality Referent in Residence Terms. American Anthropologist 65: 133-34.

CAULIN, ANTONIO
1958 Historia Corográfica, Natural y Evangélica de la Nueva Andalucía. Biblioteca de Autores Españoles, Tomo 107, pp. 243-567. Madrid. (First publ. 1779).

COSER, LEWIS A.
1956 The Functions of Social Conflict. Glencoe, Ill.

CRUXENT, JOSE M.
1951 Un grupo de Indios de los Llanos del Estado Anzoátegui, Venezuela. América Indígena 11: 115-29.

DUPOUY, WALTER
1953 Noticias preliminares sobre la comunidad indígena de San Joaquín de Pariri, Estado Anzoátegui. Boletín Indigenista Venezolano 1(1): 91-126.

FEBRES CORDERO, JULIO
1946 Un vocabulario Caribe del Oriente Venezolano. Revista Nacional de Cultura, Nº 57: 117-32. Caracas.

FIRTH, RAYMOND
1947 A Note on Descent Groups in Polynesia. Man 57: 2.

FISCHER, JOHN L.
1958 The Classification of Residence in Censuses. American Anthropologist 60: 508-17.

FLEURY CUELLO, EDUARDO
1953 Indios Petroleros. Boletín Indigenista Venezolano 1(1): 67-90.

GILLIN, JOHN P.
1936 The Barama River Caribs of British Guiana. Peabody Museum of American Archaeology and Ethnology, Harvard University, Papers, vol. 14, Nº 2. Cambridge.

1948 The Ways of Men. New York.

GOEJE, C. H. DE
1909 Etudes Linguistiques Caraïbes. Amsterdam.

LEEDS, ANTHONY
1961 Yaruro Incipient Tropical Forest Horticulture: Possibilites and Limits. *in* The Evolution of Horticultural Systems in Native South America: Causes and Consequences, ed. by Johannes Wilbert, pp. 13-46. Caracas.

LEVINE, ROBERT A.
1966 Sex roles and economic change in Africa. Ethnology 5: 186-93.

LIEUWEN, EDWIN
1954 Petroleum in Venezuela. Berkeley.

McCORKLE, THOMAS

1954 La persistencia comunera y los Guayqueríes. Boletín Indigenista Venezolano, Año II, Tomo 2(1-4): 85-95.

1965 Fajardo's People: Cultural adjustment in Venezuela; and the Little Community in Latin American and North American contexts. Los Angeles.

MURDOCK, GEORGE P.

1949 Social Structure. New York.

1960 Cognatic Forms of Social Organization. *in* Social Structure in Southeast Asia, pp. 1-14. Viking Fund Publications in Anthropology, Nº 29. New York.

MURPHY, ROBERT

1960 Headhunter's Heritage. Berkeley.

"EL NACIONAL"

1962 Desapareció el Cacique de los Indios Cachama. En su poder se encontraban diez mil bolívares pertenecientes a la tribu. "El Nacional", lunes, 11 de junio de 1962, pág. 17. Caracas.

NASH, MANNING

1958 Machine Age Maya. The Industrialization of a Guatemalan Community. Memoir Nº 87, American Antropological Assn.

ORAMAS, LUIS R.

1949 Ceremonias Fúnebres de los Caribes del Estado Anzoátegui. Memoria de la Sociedad de Ciencias Naturales La Salle, Nº 25: 319-23. Caracas.

PEREZ RAMIREZ, CESAR

1946 Documentos para la Historia Colonial de Venezuela. Caracas.

RALEIGH, WALTER

1928 The Discoverie of the large and bewtiful Empire of Guiana. Introduction, notes and Appendixes of hitherto unpublished documents by V. T. Harlow. London.

REDFIELD, ROBERT; LINTON, RALPH; & HERSKOVITS, MELVILLE J.

1936 Memorandum for the Study of Acculturation. American Anthropologist 38: 149-52.

RUIZ BLANCO, MATIAS

1892 Conversión en Píritu de indios Cumanagotos y Palenques. Madrid. (First publ. 1690).

SCHWERIN, KARL H.

1963 Family Among the Karinya of Eastern Venezuela. América Indígena 23: 201-09.

1964 Family Among the Karinya of Eastern Venezuela. (Summary). Actas y Memorias, XXXV Congreso Internacional de Americanistas, Vol. 2, pp. 143-45. México.

ms Some Cases of Contemporary Indian Acculturation in Latin America. Unpublished ms, submitted in partial fulfillment of the requirements for the Ph. D. in Anthropology, U.C.L.A., May 15, 1963.

S.S.R.C. (SOCIAL SCIENCE RESEARCH COUNCIL)
1954 Acculturation: An Exploratory Formulation. Social Science Research Council Summer Seminar on Acculturation, 1953. American Anthropologist 56: 973-96.

TAYLOR, DOUGLAS
1946 Kinship and Social Structure of the Island Carib. Southwestern Journal of Antropology 2: 180-212.

VENEZUELA. OFICINA CENTRAL DEL CENSO NACIONAL
1955 Octavo Censo General de Población, 26 de noviembre de 1950. Vol. 1, Distrito Federal y Estado Anzoátegui. Caracas.

VILA, MARCO-ANTONIO
1953 Aspectos Geográficos del Estado Anzoátegui. Caracas.

WALLACE, ANTHONY F. C.
1956 Revitalization Movements. American Anthropologist 58: 264-80.

WILBERT, JOHANNES
1957 El sistema de parentesco de los Cariña. Antropológica, Nº 3: 53-61. Caracas.

PLATE 1.—Main Street, Mamo, looking west. A typical nucleated village cluster.

PLATE 2.—Juan Guevara (Mamo) planting a stem of manioc with the machete.

Plate 3.—Juan Guevara (Mamo) chopping weeds from the conuco with machete and *garrabato*.

PLATE 4.—Delia, Teresa and Luis Tamanaico (Cachama) harvest manioc tubers and load them into the *caramiche* to be carried home.

PLATE 5.—Juana Ñávarez (Mamo) uses the *sebucán* or manioc press to extract the moisture from grated manioc.

PLATE 6.—Pedro Poito (Mamo) fishing with the *chuso* or barbless spear in Caño Mamo.

PLATE 7.—Weaving an *aguja* hammock. Carmen Elena Maita (Cachama) pulls the "aguja" through a loop of the partially woven hammock.

PLATE 8.—Lorenzo Tempo (Cachama) in traditional kilt and ıandwoven *alpargatas* or sandals collects red clay for his wife's use in making pottery. The clay was loosened with the *chícor* or metal-bladed *coa*, which is leaning against the bank behind him. The handle for the *chícora* was prepared on the spot rom an appropriate sapling.

PLATE 9.—Mariquita Tamanaico (Cachama) builds up a jar by coiling and modeling.

PLATE 10.—House Building. Emilio Ñávarez (Mamo) prepares mud plaster for the house frame (background) by mixing in water and grass straw.

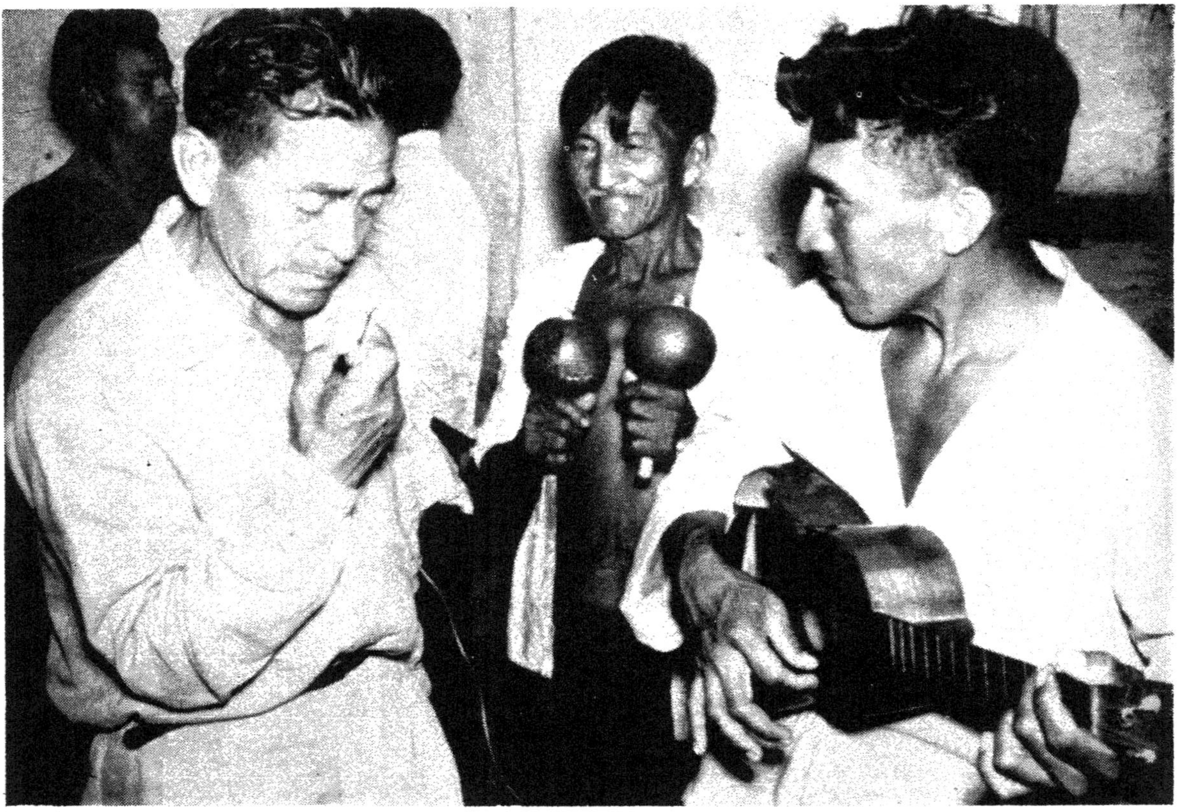

PLATE 11.—Saturday night in Mamo. Pedro Poito records a woeful *maremare*, accompanied by José Manuel Rodríguez with the maracas and Vicente Chiroco on the *cuatro*.

PLATE 12.—Preparing the *carrizos* or panpipes. Simón Tempo (Cachama) checks the tone on the *varón* (l.) and the *hembra* (r.). The making and playing of *carrizos* is a dying art, remembered only by a handful of men, and made but once a year, for the annual Fiesta de la Candelaria in Cantaura.

PLATE 13.—Change comes to Mamo. Three Mameño men (r.) help two Fomento workers (l.) to install poles for electric lights.

www.ingramcontent.com/pod-product-compliance
Lightning Source LLC
LaVergne TN
LVHW020540100826
845148LV00010B/1549

* 9 7 8 1 5 9 7 4 0 6 5 9 8 *